CEDAR WHACKER

Stories of the
Texas Hill Country

by
C.W. Wimberley

Compiled and Edited By
Dorothy W. Kerbow

EAKIN PRESS ☆ **Austin, Texas**

SECOND PRINTING

Published in the United States of America
By Eakin Press
A Division of Sunbelt Media, Inc.
P.O. Box 90159
Austin, TX 78709
email: eakinpub@sig.net

ISBN 0-89015-664-6

Library of Congress Cataloging-in-Publication Data

Wimberley, Charles W. (Charles Weldon), 1913-
    Cedar Whacker: Stories of the Texas Hill Country / by C. W. Wimberley: com-
piled and edited by Dorothy W. Kerbow.
        p.   cm.
    ISBN 0-89015-664-6
    1. Texas Hill Country (Tex.)—Social life and customs. 2. Folklore—Texas—Texas
Hill Country. I. Kerbow, Dorothy W. II. Title.
F392.T47W56   1988
976.4'06--dc19   88-16416
                                                                              CIP

Cover art and Illustrations
By Bernice Brown

To

Iolene Rogers Wimberley

Charles Weldon Wimberley and Iolene Rogers Wimberley—Craftsmen (sonte mill-ing) participating in the Smithsonian Institution Summer Festival of American Folklife held on the Mall in Washington, D.C. July 3-7, 1968.

Contents

Part II: San Marcos

Part III: Wimberley

Part I:

Llano

Hill Country History

These hills are mine. From the Cap Rock to the coastal prairies and beyond, these Texas hills are mine. Only as a Comanche could own the land—I own them. Unencumbered by deeds, abstracts, titles, liens or lease, I own these hills through all I have seen, from the paths I have walked, the trails I have ridden and the roads I have traveled; by what I have heard from the old ones' talk and by what I have learned of those who made their way before me. My humble effort here will be to preserve, in the true vernacular of the period, some facets of a way of life that is soon to be past and gone forever from these hills—a part of our heritage, yours and mine, for those who might give a damn.

— C.W.W.

The Land

It's cow country. Before man attacked this land with ax and plow and confined his wandering herds with barbed wire, the post oak flats and rolling hills on the granite uplift of Llano County were the finest natural grazing range in all Texas. Trace minerals in these soils produced nutritious grasses that matured as a strong dry forage.

According to twice-told tales of those who rode here first, the tall grasses dragged at their horse's bellies and the creeks ran clear. So long as these grasses blanketed the soil, there was no invasion of South Texas mesquite and bee weed (white brush) into the area, and the cedars grew only in dense brakes along the Colorado River and the hilltops of Riley and Cedar mountains with minor coverage on Packsaddle.

And I have seen matured steers come out of the Click Country with tallow on their backs after wintering on a native bristle-topped grass that grew in knee-high matted masses to cover the ground beneath the cedars on the southern slopes of Riley Mountain—at that time, a cedar brake country as rough as they come. Reliable old-timers claimed this species of grass to be common to the virgin cedar brakes of yesteryear.

My Corner

Extending southward from the Fall Creek bluffs on Lake Buchanan, a ragged escarpment of cedar-covered hills skirts Tow Valley to arc its way across the northeastern corner of Llano County to Jess Carter's place on the Little Llano River; thence northward past Wilbern's Glen into San Saba County.

Forty-odd years ago these cedar-covered hills and adjacent post oak flats were inhabited by some real characters and true descendants of the pioneering stock. These old ones were my touchstones — they belonged. And the old landmarks were more easily read in those days.

Fox Smith kept bees and farmed about forty acres of hickory red sand with a big sorrel mare and a fence-jumping mule. Though Will P. Miller no longer walked round-trips from his Bluffton home to teach in Baby Head school, shank's mare remained his favorite mode of travel. Master craftsman of cedar post and barbed wire Buck Nobles was busy at building fences, many of which still stand today in Llano and adjoining counties. Turkey and Little Jimmie Johnson let things slide at their own ranches for a week or more in order to cowboy for Slator Brothers Ranch during fall roundups. Confined to a room filled with his rock and ore samples, Kellus Carter sat in a wheelchair clinging to an unwaning, unyielding faith that his collection held the keys to fortunes untold.

Cedars were Christmas trees or kindling wood before I delivered my first load of posts to Forrest Ross's cedar yard and grocery store in Lone Grove. I would return home with that cedarcutter's wax in my hair. Logan Templeton ran the old store and post office. Grover Cook was our shade tree mechanic. Took a gunny sack to tote the squirrels when Leroy and Elmer Birk scoured the countryside with their cur dogs. An observation: A good fat doe carried more meat than a sack of squirrels; one .22 shell, no dogs, and less time.

The Tow log cabin stood by the springs; the old Salt Works evaporating pot used by Hodge Nobles to scald hogs in at butchering time; the lone grave of an unknown cowboy in the Behrns pasture, a piece of white quartz as its only marker; fences of barbed wire destined to become collectors' items standing with prescribed one-by-two lumber stays hanging in place with ends rotted away a foot from the ground; deep ruts worn into rock ledges where ox carts and wagons had traveled forgotten roads; bits and pieces of heart cedar imbedded about a hillside spring; the last remains of a picket pen erected to protect his water supply during a squatter's stay upon the land when no deed or claim need explain his presence; shards of glass and square nails scattered about an old chimney site where a family had lived, loved, and lost their grip upon the land. And bulldozers have played hell with most of these.

Cedarcutter Dance Grounds

Near the springs at the head of Cedar Holler, there is a little level flat of black soil which the cedarcutter clan used as their dance grounds. Jess Carter was a young man when he fiddled here as the cedarcutter families danced barefoot on the raw earth.

Traces of older dance grounds can be found on the hillside above Boiling Springs on Falls Creek. While Pfieffer ran the cedar yard at Tow Valley, a jealous cedarcutter waylaid a couple returning from a dance and, in the dark, murdered his rival by bashing in his skull with a rock.

Old-timers from Tow Valley claim they have heard strains of fiddle music and strange sounds while coon hunting in the area during the dark of the moon.

Points Peak

About four miles northeast of Lone Grove, Points Peak juts out into the post oaks as the southernmost sentinel of this cedar-covered escarpment. It's a good benchmark from which to gain a feel for the land and put a handle, of sorts, on things thereabouts.

From the heights of Points Peak, you can see most of Lake Buchanan; the dam, and beyond the bend in the Colorado River past Packsaddle, into the area where the hills of Burnet, Llano, and Blanco counties meet. Southward across the Llano River valley, Riley and Cedar mountains loom; dark at the horizon. A bit farther west, past Llano town, the Bull Head country and Mason County are lost in the haze.

Across the Little Llano to the west, the barren granite spires of Lockhart Mountain stand clothed only with scattered motts of stunted oaks.

Weather Indicators

With these hills in view, you could take a good reading on the weather without checking the rain gauge or thermometer, without running to see how much water was in the creek, or listening to Henry Howell's report on WOAI radio station. The hills told the whole story.

During drought seasons, Lockhart Mountain stood drab in lackluster hues. After a good rain the sparse vegetation among the red granite crags presented a scene worthy of a western calendar picture in living color. Days after a prolonged rainy spell or real chunk floater, seeps along the slopes send streamers of water glistening in the morning's sun as they run down granite walls through the maze of rocky ledges, creating a myriad of tiny waterfalls along the way. It's a sight to see and a time for good neighbors to meet beside creeks to fix the flood-torn watergaps or go to town and hang around the Corner Drug Store until the other fellow has done it.

When winter gets around to one of those rare occasions of covering these hills with a blanket of snow, the patches of white on ole Lockhart leave more exposed territory than a Dallas Cowboy cheerleader's suit.

Then, after an ice storm has roared through the hills during the night, leaving everything sheathed in ice, the morning might reveal the most disconcerted sight. The upper half of Points Peak has been turned into a fairy land of sparkling ice without so much as a trace of frost on the lower slopes, and birds twitter about in the underbrush on the lowlands.

About halfway up the northwest slope of Points Peak, an elm stands on the lee side of an oak and cedar mott. Each year this elm is the peak's first green harbinger of spring. While other elms in the area bear only the heavy, brown leafbuds, this elm is completely canopied with fully developed tender young leaves.

More Peaks

Scattered across Llano County and the Texas Hill Country are many of these little peaks and rounded hills bearing local identities, legends, and lore which should be preserved as a part of our heritage.

Baby Head Mountain, north of Llano, gained its name when

5

a band of settlers in pursuit of marauding Indians made the grisly discovery of a severed infant's head atop this hill.

Out in Moss country you don't have to tax your imagination to see that Bull Head has been properly monikered. The cone peaks of Sandstone and Sharp mountains stand in close proximity southeast of Llano. There is one route by which someone like the Fowler boys can get their horse to the granite summit of Sharp. Also, there is a box canyon where you may have a deer trapped by merely standing in the narrow entrance; that is, if the deer happens not to be an old moss head buck. In lieu of floundering among granite boulders, he is apt to bristle the hair on his back and charge, giving you the choice of clearing the track or getting run over.

In the early days of the railroad, a promoter, more visionary than mathematically inclined, attempted to operate a quarry from atop Sandstone. To eliminate dray cost he planned to trolley the sandstone down a four-inch cable strung from the top of the peak, across the river to a site beside the railroad track. The laws of gravity overtook him on the maiden trip. The first slab of sandstone did not get to the river. Gray Fowler told me that it was a rather distracting sight to be headed home and see a slab of sandstone hanging in the sky past Barler Flats. The four-inch cable now serves as reinforcing material in the old dam at Llano.

On the Burnet side of Lake Buchanan, there is a red granite knob quilted with broken slabs, boulders, and scrub live oaks. This old landmark has been renamed 'Tater Head.

Down the old Birdtown road, to the east, stands a little hill known as Round Mountain. This caliche peak has usurped the Reverend Bird of his namesake, Birdtown. Today, he and the old road have been abandoned to the past.

In her time, Granny Stribling was the frugal grande dame of the Birdtown road with holdings along this road which, at the north end, included a large portion of Riley and the area about Sandstone and Sharp mountains. Headquartered in Round Mountain (then Birdtown), she managed these holdings by traveling this road in a one-horse buggy, checking the outposts along the way.

In addition to his usual chores, each cowhand was required to save all cobs from the corn he had used. By counting these corncobs, Mrs. Stribling could determine whether or not the hand had been feeding his horse properly. After the count, the cobs were put in the buggy to be used to fire her cookstove.

On Down the Road

Among the hills of Wimberley, Texas, there are caliche peaks galore.

Mt. Gaynor and Mt. Sharp lend their names to communities of the past. When seen from the old wagon road the Twin Sisters were lookalikes, but the automobile highway brought a new perspective so that we now have Old Baldy and "the other one."

Parks Johnson helped perpetuate Joe Wimberley Hill as Great Uncle Joe's namesake. Descendants of unreconstructed Confederate, maternal great-grandpa Bill Adare have their say about Moon Peak on the Blanco River. After all, Uncle Billy Moon was among the first to come to these parts.

Joe Cruze's legend of Lone Man and Lone Woman mountains is a plausible epilogue to historic Comanche raids on Linnville and the Battle of Plum Creek. And Joe held a store of vintage folktales about Indians, outlaws, and wild mustangs of Pilot Knob near Creedmoor.

Unique Peak

Unlike most of these little hills, Points Peak's name is not in jeopardy of being forgotten or changed according to the whim of future generations. Like many of the cedar-covered hills of the Llano area, it is capped by layers of Ellenberger limestone, exposed in many places by a thin cover of black topsoil. But at this site, there is embedded in the Ellenberger a tiny fossil, a geological find known as the Points Peak bug. And nobody is going to change that.

Below the Ellenberger the slope is a changing strata of sandstones of various textures and hues of color ranging from hickory red to brown, greens to blue-greens, and adobe grays to sugar white sands. Vaughn Taylor, Frank Beal, and I built a fence on this slope. While strung out along this fenceline digging eighteen-inch postholes at ten-foot intervals, much of the time each of us was removing a different colored soil from his posthole.

The whole escarpment was skirted with a band of a similar assortment of soils and sands, some areas suitable for cultivation. Just find a good plot of hickory red sand with a clay sub-soil and anybody could have a green thumb — fist-size tomatoes, Bermuda onions big as saucers, and watermelons ripe by the Fourth of July if it rained.

Fences

The original survey lines crossed Points Peak to corner amid rock ledges a short distance southeast of the apex of the peak — a hell of a place to build a fence and a prime factor in the creation of a bone of contention for later landholders to gnaw on over the years.

From the looks of things to the south, the old codger who built the rock fence there was pretty well on the line as he approached Points Peak. But, far short of the survey corner, he angled across the slope, following the course of least resistance to join a hodge-podge of rock fences on the west, built with more concern toward enclosing tillable acreage than following survey lines.

To the north, John Scott strung the first mile of barbed wire fencing in the area. When he got into the big cedars, using living trees as line posts, he too established another corner of Points Peak. And he thereby added more broth to the pot of confused claims about whose pieces of land lay in the other feller's pasture. This pot did not get to boiling point until Angora goats were introduced to the area. Taking to the hills, crawling through barbed wire, and playing hell with rock fences, it didn't take long for the Angora to stir up a head of steam among neighbors.

In-laws and Kinfolks

Somewhere along the line, my wife's folks lost a generation or mine gained one. My wife and I are near the same age, but her older half brother and my mother were about the same age; her mother and a grandma of mine were near the same age; and her Grandpa John Scott and my Great-grandpa Pleasant Wimberley came to Texas about the same time, bounced once to settle in Llano County.

Both were pioneers when the county was young and the days of the Old West came to pass.

John Scott

John Scott moved from Arkansas to Georgetown, Texas, in 1850. According to a letter he received November 8 of that year, crops were tolerable good back at Cove Creek, but in some places they had barely enough for making bread. Corn was worth 50 cents a bushel; wheat, 75 cents; oats, two bits; apples, a dollar. At Ft.

Smith a good farm horse cost $50 to $60, while oxen were $25 to $40, and second-rate milch cows, $8. Mules brought $50 to $100; a good saddle horse, $100 – $125. Due to the dry summer, pork was expected to go as high as five cents a pound.

In 1852, John Scott moved to Hoover's Valley above Kingsland. During the 1880s, he moved to build his final home near the base of Points Peak. Family man, farmer, and stockman, he led a fruitful life.

Through the memoirs of his daughters Dollie and Annie, I recall the years. Dollie (Mrs. W. T. Rogers), my mother-in-law, and Aunt Annie (Mrs. G. B. Spivey) were the most kindly and gentle older ladies I have known. Mrs. Rogers never lost her way with horses and remained a fair judge of horse flesh all her days.

Home

John Scott farmed primarily for his own use. With an orchard, gardening and row crops, he met the needs of his table and livestock. And he had chores for all the children.

The girls milked about twenty cows each day. In those days any old range cow was a milch cow if you could get as much as a quart of blue John from her without getting your teeth kicked out or starving the calf, and dandy if she gave as much as a gallon a day.

The boys plowed, rode the range, chopped wood, and looked forward to Saturday.

It was a place where circuit-riding preachers came for Sunday dinner and stayed a month or more.

Cattle buyers left their saddlebags heavy with gold and silver on the porch while they rode the range buying cattle and rounding up herds to be trailed to market. Little Dollie and Annie played with the gold and silver coins while no one was looking.

Then there was the time when big brother George brought in his string of would-be racehorses and warned the girls to stay away from the pen for they were a wild, dangerous lot. In less than a week the girls were sneaking horses from this pen to ride in the woods — bareback with rope hackamores. The only mishap took place when Dollie ran her horse to the river to water him. With a sudden stop at the brink, the horse lowered its head and Dollie came scooting down his back into the Colorado River.

9

Indians

According to the headstones in the Hoover's Valley Cemetery, the Indians murdered the Whitlock family at Long Mountain on December 7, 1870. John Scott was living in the area at the time, saw the blaze of the burning home, and visited the site. But, for the remainder of his days, he entertained grave doubts as to who the murderers really were.

All the horses the band rode were shod. From unrevealed logic Scott believed they were wearing boots and white man's clothing beneath their Indian garb. And the scene about the smokehouse stirred more serious doubts.

Each of the buckets and containers of honey and molasses had been carried out into the sunlight, where it was quite evident that each container had been opened and probed by a hand plunging to the bottom — searching for what? Strange behavior for an Indian at a massacre site, and hidden treasure would have been their least likely booty.

F. M. Whitlock had created quite a stir when he paid for his land with gold coins, and rumor spread that this purchase represented but a small portion of his hoard of gold.

In any event, no other gold was found. And gold fever affects the white man in ways foreign to the red man.

Slavery

During the late 1850s, a demeaning cloud cast its shadow upon the homes of the settlers in the Lone Grove area. Hardships, drought, and dangers they could endure, but they did not care to talk about this matter and evaded the questioning eyes of their children.

On the lower reaches of Board Branch, there lived a meager landholder who owned a slave, an old Negro woman. Each night, or so it seemed, he would beat this poor old woman until her cries of anguish echoed down the creek bottoms and up to the hills. How long this state of affairs existed, no one cared to say.

One dark night after one of these beatings, a loud rapping brought him to his door. While standing in the doorway of his cabin, this man was shot dead in his tracks by a person or persons unknown.

Next day the county sheriff rode out to see into the matter. After looking over the site and talking among the neighbors, he drew his conclusions that the feller was dead, all right, and somebody ought to see to the burying. Then the good sheriff rode back to town.

A hundred years later, most people claim they never heard of such a tale and some just don't want to talk.

The War

While Mrs. Carter's husband was away fighting the Yankees, she kept his brand and earmark alive with a branding iron and her sewing scissors. Taking to the saddle, she rode the range, roping and branding their fair share of cows and calves and cutting her husband's mark into the ears with her scissors.

No one questioned the legal aspects of her activities, but many expressed the opinion that it was very unladylike to ride astride a horse as a man would. And then scissors! Must have frosted many a beard when the best all-around cowhand in these parts was a woman.

Some of the worthies who chose to stay on the home front became night riders who marauded families and war widows left behind.

The Fredericksburg area was patrolled by pike armed horsemen and, therefore, was an unfavorable range for these raiders. With tactical orders given in German, there was just no telling who might end up on one of them frog stickers. Whistling Dixie didn't help. A fast horse was the only out.

There were nights when these raiders would invite John Scott to come out to palaver in the dark. From his doorway, with gun in hand, he would return the invitation by asking them to come into the lamplighted room.

There were no takers by either party, and these Mexican standoffs often lasted into the wee silent hours. But daylight was avoided by these braves.

* * *

Judging the activities about Blanco City during this period, 3rd Lt. Pleasant Wimberley of the organized homeguard was fortunate to have his bailiwick centered at Walnut Creek near the Llano-Blanco county line.

11

At the Grove

For a time, Uncle Billy (William Nimrod Scott) and his brother-in-law ran John Scott's cotton gin in Lone Grove. One morning they were about ready to start ginning when Aunt Annie came running to the gin in search of little Ruth. The daughter was missing at the house. After a frantic search little Ruth was found asleep in the cotton press. A fate too grim to be imagined had been avoided.

* * *

Just north of Points Peak, a small branch forks from Cedar Holler in an arc across the Schadt survey to head into a small canyon. At the entrance to this canyon, there is a flat of sandy loam of just the right texture to be used as cover in building a charcoal kiln. Because it had ample space for several kilns, was easy to get to with a wagon, and had water nearby surrounded by cedars, the site was ideal for burning charcoal.

John Scott's top crop of boys, Ernest and Leslie, burned charcoal there so many years that they named the branch Charcoal Holler.

In his old age, John Scott fought a running battle with the trimming ants in his orchard. Each time the ants would open a new hole to their den, he would pump their chambers full of fumes from his bee-smoker charged with a mixture of rags, sulfur, and cow chips.

Without his loving care, this orchard soon fell into ruin. The grapes were first to die; the old pear tree on its quince rootstock lingered longest. The native hog-plum thicket held its corner until the Angora goats came scrambling over the rock wall fence.

A network of small gullies carries the topsoil across the old field to form a widening wash that meanders through the pastures toward Board Branch.

With the tall grasses gone, the cedars spread from their brakes into the lowlands where bee weed and mesquite infest the post oak flats.

In the early spring season, there are no tender pokeberry shoots to be gathered near the ashes where John Scott's old home burned. And the droplets of gold from the coins melted in this inferno remain mystic.

From *The Highlander*
April 19, 1979

12

The Tow Boys of Falls Creek

The granite uplift of Llano County is better cow country than the caliche hills of Wimberley, where I now live. Cattle do better up there, but it has produced about the same breed of old-time Texans you used to find around here.

Hope I am not grazing too far from the mill trying to tell you about a pair of them I knew before they passed on — the Tow boys, Jim and Sid. They were neighbors of mine for about thirty years, and to have known them was to know the feel of a handful of good old Texas soil run between the fingers. So if you were not around back in the eighties when they passed through here driving a herd of mast-fat hogs on their way to the railroad in San Marcos, or if you didn't get to burn some saddle leather with them and were not one of the lucky ones who got to chop some of those good cedar posts that grew in the old Tow cedar brakes, well, I'll just have to tell you all about them myself.

Tow Valley, a pioneer village on the Colorado River, was named for old man Tow, and when the waters of Lake Buchanan pushed it back to the slopes of the hills the post office retained the name Tow, Texas. ("Tow" rhymes with "cow," so when you go up there, don't say "Toe" Valley unless you want to be considered a tourist.)

The Tow home place was on Falls Creek. The springs were only a short piece from the front porch, and just behind the house stood a huge live oak, blazed at shoulder height with old marks made when the Llano and San Saba county line was surveyed. The Tows were there before the old oak was blazed with a broad ax.

A whole tribe of Tows was raised here, but Jim and Sid always did most of the riding. After all the other children had married off and the old ones had passed on, these two old bachelors were left with the home place. While they were lads (and to Jim, Sid was always "the Lad"), Jim came in from riding and was at the supper table when the old man asked: "Where's Sid?"

"Out soaking his leg in the horse trough — horse fell on him an' broke it," was all the answer Jim felt necessary to give.

That horse trough treatment, coupled with a short stay in bed, was all the medical attention Sid got. Though the leg was short and warped a bit, Sid was still in the saddle busting cattle out of the brush while most old men his age were riding old rocking chairs on the front porch range.

14

About the time Sam Bass was busy making some six-shooter history for Texas, a band of men with a string of horses made it to the Tow place about dusk one evening in the cool of summer. Their spokesman claimed to be of kin while he asked for and received permission to spend the night in the Tows' horse lots. He was the only member of the band to sleep in the Tows' house, and though he was not much of a hand at saying exactly who he was, he was not a bit bashful about asking for an extra early breakfast in order to make an extra early start.

After a predawn meal the band was gone, and with the light of day the Tows discovered that most of their saddle horses were gone, too — including the old man's favorite, a big blue roan bearing unusual markings.

The thieves made a clean getaway, and the old man worried most of the summer over the loss of old Blue. Months later, Mother Tow was cooking breakfast when she looked from the window to see the horse standing beneath the trees beyond the brush fence out back. A short lead rope with a frayed end hardly touching the ground was tied around his neck. He was gaunt, his ribs showed, his hoofs were worn down to the hair, his color had lost its sheen, but it was old Blue, all right, for his markings were plain to the eye and he nickered as the old man came to turn him in.

News traveled slow in those days, though by word of mouth it had a way of drifting across the land. Nothing was ever learned of old Blue's travels to the north, but over the years his return trip was an odyssey heard at Falls Creek through talk.

First, it was at Cherokee where a horse had been seen passing through on the road: "He was a big blue roan and he walked slow with his head turned aside to trail the lead rope tied around his neck." Then at San Saba the same thing happened. Later at Coleman, the same event. Finally, from the road near Abilene, the same account, except there it was said, "He trailed a new lead rope better than twenty feet long."

Jim was old when he told me the tale. When I asked if he had ever heard any more of his claimed-to-be-kin visitors, his answer was to the point: "Yep, years later, heard he got shot up in Oklahoma Territory — been a sight better if it'd took place before he made it by here."

When the Tow boys were asthmatic old men crowding their seventieth year, with Jim riding a horse about seventeen years old and Sid on one that was twenty-two, I saw these two old codgers push a mixed herd of heat-crazed cows with calves and long yearlings out of the cedar brakes, then keep them bunched and moving as they crossed the slick rock bottoms of Falls Creek, flat rocks and loose boulders, and on into the pens. And when some fool cow or scared yearling tried to break away from the herd, they were shoved back into place with a heated fearless display of real cowhand riding which would have left you stunned with amazement.

Gouging spurs to the flanks and lifting rumps off the ground with quirt lashes and yelling their heads off, they would bust those old ponies across that glade with shod hoofs scraping blue smoke from the top of the flat rocks and sending loose boulders the size of a man's head in all directions. I wouldn't have taken one of those old skates by the bridle and walked him across that particular piece of real estate afoot. But, following one of these wild rides, while Jim stood leaning against the rail fence wheezing and fighting for his breath, when he was chided about the doctor's orders to stay in and take things easy, it brought: "What Dr. Hoerster don't see can't hurt him none—you ain't a-tellin' nothin', see." It figured—for a Tow, that is.

The old Tow place is no more. Jim and Sid are gone. The log house their daddy laid in 1866 has been bulldozed and burned. The pastures are denuded of most of their timber, and the springs run low. It is now a ranch where sportsmen go to shoot tame, corn-fed deer. I don't go there anymore.

From *True West Frontier Times*
September 1970

Birdtown Road

With Riley and Cedar mountains to the west and Packsaddle hard by to the east, the old Birdtown road from Llano to Round Mountain took you across my favorite corner of the Texas Hill Country.

Driving down this country dirt road with its twists and curves, steep grades and cautious creek crossings—sometimes, after a rain, waiting for hours for the creeks to run down—you found ample time to gain the feel of the land, to possess it in the mind's eye.

It is a plain of broken hills and crimped valleys scaped in oaks and mesquite with cedar-covered peaks in the distance.

It's a landscape littered in a geological confusion of contrast and contradictions, where assorted formations, spires, granite boulders, rock outcroppings, sandstone, slate, quartz crystals and sands, gravels and soils of all hues and textures lay in close proximity.

It's a place where the hardrock miner and the rockhound part company and university geology classes gather to make field trips.

It's an area steeped in legend, lore, fragmented history, and whopping big lies.

It's a land to stir a cedarcutter's mind with more wild ideas than a blind cat lost in a fish market to send him in forty directions at once.

Driven by the lust for gold, the Spaniards came to leave their diggings along Honey Creek and secreted mine shafts in the hills. For two centuries these diggings have fired the gold bug fever in rockhounds and treasure hunters and sent scholars searching dusty archives in Mexico and Spain. All the while, the native old-timer merely sits in the saddle with a sardonic grin as he watches their antics.

His folktales of gold and lost treasures are told as entertaining yarns among close friends and turns fool's gold only in the ears of strangers who wish to get snake bit.

But I do agree with Mayme Slaughter in that the fabled sixteen jackloads of lost Spanish gold does, indeed, lay at the bottom of Blue Hole on Honey Creek and you are going to have to present a fair-sized stack of bullion to disprove this fact.

The Kiowas and Comanches came to this plain to raid the settlers, steal their horses, and take scalps. The settlers retaliated in kind and, in the mad swirl of bloodletting atrocities, these adversaries stomped hell out of the remnants of the innocent peaceful splinter tribes. So ran the course of human justice in them good ole days.

Since the day the old-timers rode along with the tall grasses dragging at their horses' bellies as they drove the first Longhorns into the area, the plain of the Birdtown road has been cow country. Today the tall grasses are gone, the creeks are wider and carry more sand, and the soils are thinner on the hillsides.

But should we turn back the calendar three or four hundred years to find our self-anointed ecologist standing there in the wake of a vast herd of migrating buffalo, he'd probably sniff the air a couple of times to come up with this dire prophecy:

"We're gonna have to do something about them dam buffalo or they're gonna fill our atmosphere with enough noxious ammonia to pizen all mankind."

17

In 1854 my great-grandfather, Pleasant Wimberley, and his tribe moved his ranching operation from Brenham to establish headquarters on Walnut Creek near the Blanco-Llano county line. For the next eighteen years he labored to create his domain of thousands of Longhorns and horses on the open range of this plain.

As was the custom of that day, he was his own banker, dealing only in hard cash. When in need of money, he would sell a string of horses or send a herd of Longhorns up the trail. The proceeds in gold and silver were poured into a basket which he kept under his bed.

The Indian depredation period may have had its influence, but with the introduction of barbed wire Grandpa foresaw the end of the days of the open range. Firm in his convictions that Texas range land would never be worth the cost of fencing it, he pulled up stakes to move down to Cypress Creek in Hays County, where he blew his fortune by buying an antiquated obsolete cotton ginning and milling operation.

With an empty basket under his bed, he sent the last of his Longhorn herds up the trail with a trusted friend. That was the last he saw of his herd and his friend.

From that day on it was a hard fight with a short stick — downhill all the way. At the ripe old age of ninety-six Grandpa died, filled with religion and poor as Job.

As an appropriate namesake, the village of Cypress Creek could be known as Wimberley's Folly, or merely Folly.

Ironically, in 1890 James Haywood left his 160 acres on the Devil's Backbone to move his herd of 3,000 Longhorns to Llano County. Extending from the southern peak of Packsaddle to the Colorado River, he established a ranch of some 5,000 acres, now a part of the LBJ estate.

Which all goes to show you don't have to be hell for smart to inherit land or be a cedarcutter.

From *The Highlander*

The Cedars of Texas

Fly in the buttermilk, ants in the honey —
Sometimes, livin' in the cedar brakes
Ain't very funny.

Post gettin' scarcer, grub's runnin' low —
Hardtimes seems to foller me,
Where ever I go.

Guess I'd done moved on into town,
If it hadn't a-been for my ole blue-tick hound.

Now he won't hunt and he can't cold trail,
But he's a mighty fine dog at waggin' his tail.

Back in the hills, this old dog of mine can
*   always be, an awful lot of company —*
When there's nobody else around ceptin' him and me;
The ticks, the snakes, the rocks and the cedar tree.

The Texas cedar has to be our best-known tree for it has created more confused opinions than the fabled blind men's visit with the elephant. Everybody seems to see this tree in his own light and usually comes up with his own name for it.

I have heard the species called everything in the book — from Christmas tree cedars to juniper cypress. You won't have far to go to add a few more names to the list. Back in the Hill Country, damcedar is one word and the accepted label. One summer's day spent in the saddle fighting brush, horseflies, and ticks in the heat of the cedar brakes and you'll wonder just how anybody could look at a damcedar without knowing what it was.

But unfortunately, everybody don't get acquainted with the cedars from the saddle and do tend to have ways of their own in looking at their trees. And there's other flies in the ointment to be considered — the species business.

There are several different species of cedars scattered across Texas with one or more of these species to be found in each of the state's geographical regions. Also, to the untrained eye, some of these species have the same general appearance, while members of a given species can resemble one another little more than kittens in an alley cat's litter. And we're back to the blind men's elephant again.

So if you happen to be a newcomer to the Texas Hill Country, feel free to use damcedar or any name of your choice. Everybody does! But, if you choose to get down to the real nitty-gritty of identifying the species, don't depend upon any old nester's terminology or the general reference books. Do your own looking with an authoritative botanical manual in your right hand. After forty years in the cedar brakes, that's what I done. Played hell with some ideas of mine; yet, I'm pretty sure them fellers must not have spent much time walking through the thousands of acres of old cane brake, loose barked, heart cedars that once stood in motts along the Colorado River Basin between Austin and the west line of San Saba County or they would have left out that "single trunk growing from stump rare in species" bit concerning *juniperus ashei.*

Anyhow, as Turkey Johnson would have put it, "Hit's a mighty good book. Knowed what they was talking about and covered an awfully lot of territory — all over Texas, parts of both Mexicos and other states around — without wastin' a bunch of words doin' it. Shame they don't write in plain English or sort of help you keep on the right track with some pictures."

According to Correll and Johnston's *Manual of the Vascular Plants of Texas,* there are about sixty species of *juniperus* widely distributed over the Northern Hemisphere. These are subdivided into eight major species found in Texas.

1. *Juniperus deppeana* — Alligator Juniper or Western Juniper. Small dioecious tree, to about 15 M. high, Trans-Pecos; W. Tex. to Cen. Ariz. and Cen. Mex.

2. *Juniperus pinchotii* — Red-Berry Juniper, Pinchot Juniper. Large dioecious, usual rarely dense clumps; remarkable for viability for sprouting from cut or charred stumps. Cen. Tex, n. to Plain Country and w. to Trans-Pecos, Cen. Tex. to S.E. N.M. and W. Okla.

3. *Juniperus monosperma* — One-seeded Juniper, Cherry-stone Juniper. Large dioecious shrub or small tree with shrubbly aspect. N. Plains Country and Trans-Pecos; N.W. Okla. and W. Tex. to Ut., Nev., Ariz. and N. Mex.

4. *Juniperus ashei* — Rock Cedar, Post Cedar, Mexican Juniper, Mountain Cedar. Large dioecious shrub or small tree to 6 M. high, centered on Edwards Plateau, extending s. to Zavalla Co., n.e. to Dallas Co., w. to Terrell Co., and n. to Nolan, Taylor and Stephens Co., from Mo. and N. Ark., s.w. to Tex., S.E. N.M. and N. Mex.

5. *Juniperus flaccida* — Weeping Juniper, Drooping Juniper, Mexican Drooping Juniper, Tascate. Small dioecious tree to 9 M. high. Chisos Mts. in Trans-Pecos; from Tex. to S. Mex.

6. *Juniperus scopulorum* — Rocky Mountain Juniper. Large or

shrubbly dioecious tree to 12 M. high. Guadalupe Mts. and Trans-Pecos and in N. Plain Country; from N.D. and Mont., w. to B.C., Wash., Nev. and Ariz., s. to Tex., and extreme W. Okla.

7. *Juniperus silicicola*—Southern Red Cedar, Sand Cedar, Coast Juniper. Medium-sized dioecious tree to 10 M. high. Usually coastal plain and S.E. Tex.—near coast from E. Tex. to Cen. Fla.; n.e. to N.C.

8. *Juniperus virginiana*—Eastern Red Cedar. Medium-sized to large dioecious or sometimes monoecious tree to 30 M. high. East Tex. and in N. Plains Country in Tex. Panhandle; from S.W. Mex. w. to N. N.Y., s. to Can. and S.W.N.D., s. to Kan., W. Okla. and E. Tex. and Ga.

Schooled only at the end of his little double-bit ax handle with travels limited to tours of the West Texas and Arizona cotton patches and back to the cedar brakes, the ole cedarcutter came up with about the most logical names for the Texas cedars to be found in the layman's language. I heard them in the Hill Country cedar brakes, so I'm not exactly patting myself on the back.

Nos. 1 and 3—brush cedars, usually pronounced dam bresh.

No. 2—Johnson Grass Cedar or White Splotched Bark-Sproutin' Cedar.

No. 4—This was THE cedar, Fence Post Cedar, Texas or Mountain Cedar; also class according to growth appearance and wood texture as sap, heart, buckhorn, loose barked, cane brake, and brush.

No. 5—No name.

No. 6—Juniper Cedar.

No. 7—Salt Cedar.

No. 8—Pencil Cedar, Red Cedar, Bastrop Cedar.

And the old cedarcutters knew about the Mexican piñon pines growing among the cedars on the western edge of the Edwards Plateau and the Lost Pines of Bastrop.

From *The Highlander*
September 18, 1975

Cedarcutters and Others

The cedarcutter's ancestor was among the poor-white pioneer stock who came to take up land, to carve their small places among the hills, and to hang onto the stubborn soil by their teeth and fierce

21

BERNICE
BROWN

pride. Restless in spirit, he revolted against the slow ways of the plow or following the herds and in time found his ties to the land with his ax and the cedars. The clan was born of his breed. From woodchopper, railcutter, and charcoal burner to cedarcutter was but a small step, once barbed wire created the market for his post.

The cedarcutter was among the last of the truly independent American craftsmen, and cutting posts was his chosen trade. He possessed a special skill with the ax which he used to turn cedar timber into the most marketable kind of post with the least expense of time and effort. His day's work was done within a matter of four or five hours, and during that time he could produce upwards to a hundred good clean-cut post if he were working in fair timber. Though he always worked standing on another person's property, he lived and passed into oblivion without having ever known the feel of wearing another man's collar — union or boss.

The cedarchopper was a lesser member of the tribe. Though he might be able to chop several cords of oak firewood in a day, he was never quite able to master the cedarcutter's special skill with the little double-bit ax. Any day he produced a hundred good posts, he accomplished the feat by ample use of brute strength and endurance. His ties to the cedar brakes were loose.

The cedarwhacker was a reckless, careless rogue. He didn't give a damn. Using any sort of an old ax, he would tackle his job with wild abandon. He could turn good timber into the sorriest looking post, leave a sloven mess where he made a track, give you the shirt off his back while stealing you blind, have you laughing ten minutes after you had hunted him down to break his damned neck, never around when you needed him, and about the time you got around to thanking your Lord for good riddance of the pest, he'd show up again grinning from ear to ear.

The cedarhacker took to the cedars like a blind beaver with the hiccups but with less favorable results. The pitiful post he produced spelled starvation. Either he developed some skill with the ax in a hurry or turned to brush cutting or became some cedarchopper's grunt. The cedar brakes held no promise for him.

Traveling in the mode of itinerant farmers or squatters in search of new land, cedarcutters had not severed all ties to their pioneer stock. They rode on wagons drawn by willow-tailed ponies, heaped high with their plunder, and topped with ragged children and coops of chickens. Hidden somewhere among the cracked dishes and dirty bedding, there were packets of seeds and roots of vegetables and flowering plants growing in cans, and hounds or feists or cur breeds trotting alongside, and a milk cow tethered behind and bringing up the rear. Sometimes there was also a donkey or little mule that had been trained to drag logs and poles through brush from deep canyons.

At campsites near water they stopped to throw up their rag houses or shanties of tin and scrap lumber and brush, to chop select timber into post so long as the brake suited their whim, to follow hounds at night, to dance barefoot to fiddles on grounds cleared among the cedars, to curse and fight and drink raw whiskey, to take their women and raise their children—all done in strange ways foreign to other eyes.

Though the timber belonged to the cedarman, the cedarcutter chopped for himself. The post he cut belonged to him until they had been hauled to the yard, checked, entered into ledgers, and he had been paid his full fair share of their value. He was his own man, his earnings determined only by his skill and effort.

The cedarman could determine the grade and price he would receive for his post, and the brake boss could set rules for running the brake, but nobody, nobody, could tell the cedarcutter anything he had to do. No anchors held him in place, and he drifted with the first restless wind. He was among the last of an independent breed.

In his time, Snuffy Pruett was a real cedarcutter from the old school. One day his old truck groaned onto the cedar yard under a load of post that made everybody sit up and take notice. Before Snuffy's kids perched on the load had time to climb down, the cedarchecker was a-blowing about the size of this load, how good a grade the post was and how nice they were trimmed—like Snuffy had always done. Even the cedarman got into the show by saying Snuffy's bunch was about the best danged cedarcutters he'd ever had, and everybody around had something good to say about Snuffy that day.

With his chest swelling out bigger and bigger every minute, Snuffy says we hadn't seen nothing yet. He knew where there was many another load of post better than them in that brake and he was going to get every last one of them. He liked this place and everybody around. He had found the pie in the sky; contentment was his.

The cedarman gave Snuffy a swig from his bottle in private and Snuffy demanded everybody have a soda water with him at the commissary store before he headed for his camp.

About 12:00 that night the dogs began to bark and set up a howl along Honey Creek. Also, if you had listened closely you could hear chickens and kids squalling over toward Snuffy's campsite. Around 2:00 A.M. Snuffy fired up his old truck and you wondered why in the devil a man would be going to town at this hour.

The next morning, Snuffy's campsite stood as empty as last year's bird nest. Kids, dogs, cats, chickens, raghouse, washtubs, the pepper plants growing in cans — everything was gone.

The cedarman wanted to know why. The puzzled cedarchecker stood fingering his chin while the cedarhands anxiously offered all sorts of speculations.

If one had been included, any old cedarcutter would have told them the event was no riddle. "Hell, a man's got the rights to his own mind without havin' to have a reason. Ain't he? He jest went; that's all there is to it. Nothin' else."

Honest John was another one of the great cedarcutters during the Depression. In the cool of early morning, John's cedar wagon would take off for the brake with kids in and on and hanging all over his Model-A Ford Tudor Sedan. With a wife who could swing a pretty wicked ax and a bunch of kids who cut their eye-teeth on ax handles, this tribe could stump a jag of cedar posts about as quick as you could shuck and shell a peck of ear corn. By 9:30 or 10:00, a couple of the younger boys would pull onto the cedar yard with piles of poles riding the front fenders, post sticking from both back windows and a four-foot stack racked a-top the rear bumper. Sometimes they would make the second or third of such loads before the Tudor came in on its final run for the day, with kids and cedar posts in and all over it and John's head hanging out to see where he was headed.

Usually there was an armadillo or two lying on the floorboards of the last load. John's wife could grind off a batch of armadillo sausage that tasted, looked like, and ate as good as Mr. Anybody's pork and, if you paid no heed to bone structure, her armadillo shank fried in deep fat surpassed roast pig.

Disaster never seemed to strike these people; they lived with it. One time John was traveling along with his load of kids and cedar when a blowout spat a homemade boot as big as a man's hat from a front tire, sending the Ford Tudor on a swerving course across the ditch to break a rural telephone pole off at the ground and knock three big posts from a rancher's fence. No blood was shed, no cussing hard luck was spilled, and extra dips from the bottle of snuff sufficed. John left the scene with three green stays baling-wired in to hold the fence in place, the phone lines sagging in the air, and his load topped with three new, dry, heart-post and a ten-foot pole — all barked, butted anew, and freshly blazed.

This era — from before the turn of the century through the Depression — was the heyday of the cedar business in Texas. Fortunes were made and lost by the cedarmen, the yard operators. The virgin cedar brakes of heart timber stood much as they had during the Indian days, and timber rights to large tracts of land could be bought for a song. No clearing of brush was involved in these deals; they just harvested the post as they pleased. Within a twenty-year span, the cedars had grown a new crop of four-inch posts; therefore, these old brakes could be reworked again and again, maybe cutting the timber a bit closer with each new operation. Also, with the tall grasses gone the way of the buffalo, new brakes were being grown as the cedars spread to cover new areas of over-grazed lands.

The cedar kings ran a loose herd, for judged by any time standards, it was a bastard business they operated. Each cedarman ran his own show in his own way and none was ever quite able to put his collar on the cedarcutter tribe, no matter what his methods. Any cagey move and hell broke loose and his business could go up in smoke. The succcessful cedarmen, the cedar kings, were characters worthy of their day. Had to be.

During this period, Homer Rogers operated yards along the Nueces River. To tie his operation to the railhead at Camp Wood, he built a narrow-gauge railroad up the river. The track was laid on hewn cedar crossties which, after the project had been abandoned, were sold to be used as fence post in a wide area of Texas. Some of these crossties are still standing in fences on Llano County ranches.

Old Sholton — a name I use here because the old-timers did differ in the spelling and the initials they gave — operated his businesses in the Falls Creek area with yards in the brakes and at Tow Valley (now headwaters of Lake Buchanan on the Colorado River). The railhead and shipping point was located downstream at Kingsland. With a Prussian methodical approach to all matters, he tried to eliminate hauling the post by wagon from the cedar yards to the railhead.

This first try was an elaborate fiasco. Determined to float his post as rafts down the Colorado, he built large booms to fish these rafts from the river near the railroad. While the river ran low, he had the rafts assembled along the banks of the Colorado near old Tow Valley and awaited a freshet. The freshet came and the rafts were on their way. But the old Colorado was a wild and untamed river in those days. The freshet was merely the quiet forerunner to the rip-snorting torrents of a flood. The rafts passed Kingsland like the highball express and scattered Sholton's post down the Colorado watercourse to the Gulf of Mexico.

Smitten but undaunted, Sholton had to have another try. This time, a steam tractor was used to draw six floats loaded with post, traveling a new route from Tow Valley to the Iron Spur, a railroad siding between Kingsland and Llano. To replenish the tractor's water supply, wells were drilled along the way. One of these wells is still in use today at the Hodge Nobles place and another at the Hudson Hereford place.

Another fiasco was in the making. The tractor's iron wheels spun on rocks and mired in mud and the devil was to be paid all along the way. On top of all that, the limestone in the water soon clogged the tractor's boiler tubes and another effort went down the drain. So, Buck Nobles, one of the haulers, was still in business. Using a little span of hard-tailed mules hitched to his farm wagon, Buck made two round-trips per day, earning two dollars and fifty cents each trip. Five dollars was a real good day's wages for a man and his team to make in them good old days.

This last story doesn't have much to do with cedar cutting, but it's about one of the real old-time cedarcutters.

Flatnose Joe earned his moniker early in his career by arguing with one of the Young boys about the grade of a post.

With the post held in one hand and the four-inch horseshoe measure in the other, Joe was demonstrating that the top end of the post could easily be passed between the prongs of the horseshoe without the bark touching either side, and it damn well wasn't a four-inch post.

Meanwhile, without a word Young had eased one of the wagon standards out of its loops and settled the argument with one wild swing that left Joe flat on his back. The Youngs were like that. Joe's nose was never the same.

In addition to the flat nose, the wagon standard must have also given Joe a split personality. While he was Joe, he was a cedarcutting dude. But when old Flatnose came to the surface, he was like a house cat on the kitchen table. If his head wasn't hung in the cream pitcher, he was sniffing at the butter bowl or lapping at the gravy dish.

During the early twenties, Pfieffer ran a cedar yard in old Tow Valley, and Joe was around to give the camp life some color. He was married then and old enough to have some sense, but wife and time had not slowed down Joe's roving eye.

One night, with one hand holding a lantern and the other concealed beneath her apron, Joe's wife prowled the camp hunting for her husband. At the far side of the camp she burst into a stranger's tent to hold her lantern above a bed where Joe lay beside another cedarcutter's woman. Lowering the lantern, she brought the other hand from under the apron to point the barrel of Joe's pearl-handled six-shooter right between the other woman's eyes. She then began a tirade which berated this wench below the level of being worth the price of the powder and lead; otherwise, she would pull the trigger.

While these words flew, Joe slipped his feet from inside the covers into his boots, grabbed his pants and hat, and made a run for it, clad only in his long johns.

As he cleared the tent flaps, his wife got off a couple of shots that were close enough for Joe to know that this time, the old gal meant business. This was not going to be one of those rabbit runs of zigging and zagging and sweet talking. Adding distance between himself and the lantern, he set a course across the old Thorpe place towards the cedars. And found his Waterloo.

The Thorpes had drawn their water from a hand-dug well, four feet in diameter and some twenty-odd feet deep. Several pieces of old lumber laid across this well had prevented any cattle from falling into it. Under Joe's weight they crumbled. With a splash he stood trapped neck deep in water, and the lantern soon dangled overhead.

Joe's best honeyed words were wasted as his wife cleared away the remaining lumber, lay flat on her stomach, lowered the lantern, and took a steady aim with the pearl-handled six-shooter.

About the time the six-shooter barrel steadied, Joe's head ducked beneath the water. When he could no longer hold his breath his head surfaced near the side of the well. As the barrel steadied again, down he'd go again. With little room to maneuver and that six-shooter barrel staring him in the eye every time he looked up, Joe was soon winded. With a final half-hearted plunge, he came up

28

gasping, "My God, woman, hurry up and shoot. Can't you see I'm running out of breath?"

Where Joe's finest words had failed, his anguish struck a different chord. His wife began to laugh, and the more she looked the more she laughed. And laughing she finally left the scene.

Sometime later she did tell some of the hands that her husband had fallen into a well and where he might be found, if they had nothing better to do.

A way of life is gone from the Texas cedar brakes and the hills are not the same. Born hard to die hard, the cedarcutter belongs to the past. Descendant of a tribe spawned during the dying days of the Old West, he now stands a stranger among the people on his native soil, on land the Indian's peaceful splinter tribes were ground into oblivion by the cedarcutter's ancestors. Then he too found his fate. For just as the sands of time have claimed the final fragments of many cultures in the ancient past, today the remnants of his tribe are being worn away—marked only by man's indifference to his own kind.

From *Some Still Do: Essays on Texas Customs,*
Edited by Francis Edward Abernethy
(Publications of the Texas Folklore Society, Number 39,
Austin: Encino Press, 1975)

Jess Carter

Jess Carter lived alone in a Texas-style three-room house on the west bank of the Little Llano River. He used the shed room as a kitchen, slept in the north room during the winter, and on the porch through the summer. The south room held cottonseed for which the ginner had failed to meet Jess's asking price back in 1917.

Though he failed to get along with most of his neighbors, Jess and I used to spend a lot of time sitting and talking in a way that did not burn up words. We were on his porch late one summer evening when I called his attention to the movement of mice among grapevines growing on chicken wire nailed along the edge of his roof.

"Yeah, I been thinking about that," Jess replied. "A rattler has moved in with me. Rats move up to the ceiling everytime one does that. Sack of flour been on the floor in the kitchen over a week

now and nothin's bothered it. Guess I'll have to take a day and scratch through my plunder and find him."

About two weeks later, Jess greeted me from his porch with: "Whimp, I told you I had a boarder. Got a four-foot rattler out of the kitchen and a big chicken snake was working the seed room. Next day I had to put my flour in a lard can — rats had already cut a hole in the sack."

Farther back in the gimp oaks there used to be a clan of hounddog men they called the Harkey Boys or something like that. Armed with a carbide headlight and surrounded by a sniffling pack of pot-lickers busy at cold-nosing everything about them, the Harkey boys showed up at Jess's place one night wanting to go coon hunting. The old suckegg of the pack found plenty of time to rob all the hen nests while Jess hunted up his kerosene lantern and cleaned its chimney — so we were all ready to start together.

With the pack yodeling along behind, the lead dog struck up a hot trail in the creek bottom and the race was on. About an hour later, they treed in a big live oak growing atop a bluff beside a bend in the creek. The Little Llano skirted this bluff with a wide sandy-bottomed pool as it changed its course. High over the water, the varmint's eyes shined through the leaves of the outermost branches of the oak. After taking stock, the elder Harkey decided this was the ideal site for a dandy good coon fight and took charge of affairs.

Wearing the headlight on his hat, Jobie was sent up the tree to shake the coon out while the rest of us gathered the hounds by their collars and dragged them down to where the lantern sat beside the pool. We were supposed to hold the yowling restive pack and loose only a pup or two to fight the coon after it had fallen into the creek, but somehow the best-laid plans do go astray.

We were standing about the lantern with the hounds straining at their collars and the headlight was far out over the water when Jobie hollered down: "This here ain't no coon—hit's a bobcat." Then the hat with the headlight on it came tumbling down to the water and Jobie started squealing like a shoat with its head hung under a gate; then followed his cap with a splash that drowned out the lantern. Dripping wet and in the dark, we forgot to hold onto the dogs. By the time we had beat the hounds off Jobie and pumped the water out of him and some air into him, the bobcat could have been two counties away. The hunt was over.

After Jobie was able to breathe, he explained it this way: "That cat done had his mind set on goin' back down that tree jest the same way he come up it an' me bein' in his way didn't make him no never mind—he just clumb down my frame from head to heels before I got scairt an' lost holt."

There was no cause to doubt Jobie's word, for it was plain to see where that bobcat's claws had blazed their path down the hind-side of Jobie's carcass.

Jess's place on the west bank of the Little Llano River was the sort of place where the chickens roosted in trees, hogs wandered the creek bottoms, goats grazed the hills, and the valleys belonged to the cows. And when they were not penned in the horsetrap, all you had to do was to listen for the old blue mare's bell and you knew where the horses were.

Living the life of Riley, Jess banked from his hip pocket. When the wad in that pocket got a little thin, he would sell his mohair or a few calves or some shoats. Money went a long way for Jess.

On the east side of the Little Llano, there were some sixty acres of rich cultivated land which Jess farmed or grazed, according to the mood he was in that year. In front of his house a windmill stood beside a sizeable garden plot of deep red hickory sand. With a little moisture, most anything could be grown in that old red hickory. Stick a broomhandle in it and you could come back and find green sprouts on it within three days. Jess kept his plot green. When the windmill failed him, he would swing the pump handle to keep the water flowing. But his long suit was his pecans. He had budded all his trees along the Little Llano and the years they made a crop he was in the velvet.

Jess was among the last of the old loners in those parts. For forty years he had labored to pay off the other heirs to his place. Those long years of loneness had left him about as skittish of strangers as a wild cedarbrake boar. Though I had to do all the visiting, he was a good neighbor of mine, after a favorable ten or twelve years of getting acquainted. Afterward, I always managed to be around when the squirrels had begun whittling on Jess's pecans or the does had been jumping into his pea patch long enough to be carrying some tallow.

One summer Jess had a dirt tank built on a deep ravine behind his house. Fall rains filled it to hold about an acre and a half of good water ranging in depth to sixteen feet, more or less. It was his pride and joy. Of course, I found time to help him stock it with minnows, perch, and bass seined from the Little Llano. A grand assortment of frogs and dragon flies found their way to this tank without any help.

Later, Jess decided he needed some catfish for his tank, so we put a barrel in the back of his pickup and headed for Tow Valley. Lake Buchanan was young then and the yokels around old Tow had turned fishermen. The going price was ten cents a pound for catfish on the hoof, blues or yellows, mess or a truckload. As for scale fish, you had to do your own catching.

I figured the barrel to hold something like a dozen or two blues or maybe a couple of yellows in the six- to ten-pound range. No, sir. One of the Alexander boys just happened to have a fifty-five-pound yellow cat that, outside of several scratches across its back which bore remarkable resemblance to trammel net burns, it seemed to be in excellent health.

In less time than it takes to tell, we had the yellow cat bedded down with wet tow sacks in the back of the pickup and headed for

BERNICE BROWN

Jess's roost on the Little Llano. After a couple of unnecessary stops to pour fresh water over the sacks, the yellow arrived at his new home safe and sound.

The following spring was a dry one followed by a long, hot summer. By early August the idle windmills would groan and squeak as they turned to catch an occasional erratic gust and try to make a few feeble strokes before it died. And dust devils danced with the dry sands along the roadsides in the glare of the midday sun. On such a day I chose to go see how Jess was faring the weather. Big as a bear, he was sitting on the porch fanning himself with his hat. He had one worry on his mind: what was he going to do about his big yellow catfish?

"Seen it this way before," says he. "Can't rain a drop now before November and my tank's goin' dry shore's hell. Water's done down to four foot and falling fast. Green scum all over it, he wouldn't be fit to eat. Be a shame to let him go as buzzard bait. Let him go in the river and no tellin' who'd catch him. Wish somebody I knowed would come along and take him off my hands—anybody."

"If that's all you're looking for, I'll take him," says I. "My horse trough is bigger'n a wagon bed four cotton frames high. Many-a-times it's held more pounds of yellow cats than him, for weeks without losing any of them. He ought to be fit to eat after a month or so."

"Good," says Jess, and we threw a tub full of tow sacks and his thirty-foot minnow seine in the pickup and headed for the tank.

The water was low and frogs scattered in all directions as we walked up to the tank with seine in hand. Jess stood at the water's edge as I made a wide sweep into the tank and, with the seine bogged by a huge mass of moss, dragged it into the shallows. And as the water drained from the seine—what do you know? Like a big shoat in his wallow, there he lay in the moss with his belly shining in the sun and pectoral fin fanning the air. In all his regal color, he was a beaut.

With ashen face agape, Jess stood looking. After some long, long moments, he turned to stare listlessly across the Little Llano, down through the gap in the hills to the northeast. I could feel the slow tug as he furtively slid his end of the seine away from the fish.

"Look," said Jess hoarsely, "low, just to the right of Points Peak. Little thunderhead, forming fast. Away in yonder. Must be about over Burnet."

I couldn't see nothing but blue sky. But I looked anyway. Across the Little Llano a whirlwind chose that moment to burst into action. Swirling across the sixty acres it carried a burden of dry corn leaves higher and higher into the sky, only to let them fall crazily back to earth among the cedar-covered hillsides.

"See that! See that!" says Jess with glee. "Whirlwind's surest sign of rain there is."

"Come on," says I, giving the seine a jerk that sent the yellow cat scudding. "Let's get out of here. Left my slicker at home this morning and I'd sure like to get back before the creeks get up."

Epilogue

That Saturday, I went down to the store to see if I had any mail. The mail hadn't come in yet and the sweaters were setting around and Will Templeton was giving his part of the news.

"Yep, you never know what you are apt to run into when you go around Jess Carter's," he says. "I was up at his place this morning and you'd never believe it—he's hauling water out of the Little Llano and puttin' it in that new tank of his! Yeah. Got a big hole scrapped out in the creek, his old pickup full of barrels and hauling

34

water out there like he was fighting fire. From the looks of things he's been at it for several days."

From *The Pioneer Heritage,* by John T. Dailey,
with material by C. W. Wimberley
(Remington, Virginia: Allington Corporation, 1981)

Dave "Crockett" Walters

Hill folks in Texas had a way. Weathered by drought and tempered by hardship, they developed a raw sense of humor of their own brand. They needed it to endure. During the depressed thirties, old Dave "Crockett" Walters summed up his situation with these sentiments: "If I was to die today, the bank would have to shear my goats twice before they could foreclose their mortgage on me — once to bury me with an' a fall clip to pay my lease up to date. Then they could take it all an' have my sympathies to boot."

Crockett batched back in the cedars and was a good Llano County neighbor of mine. To get away from his own cooking, Crockett rode his chuck line which ran from Baby Head across the hills through Tow Valley and on down Old Bluffton way. At any home where he put his feet under the dinner table, he was a most welcome guest for old Crockett always made each lady of the house feel that she was the best little cook in all Texas. The same medicine was used on old Jim when he ate with the Tow boys, Jim and Sid, too.

About once a week, Crockett would ride up to my front porch about the time the biscuits were brown enough for my wife to call dinner. He was never there in time to help cut any stove wood and was always gone before milking time. If you went to fetch him a watermelon or mess of roasting ears from the patch, he waited in the shade of the porch. "'Cause," he claimed, "sun gives me a sick headache." But when you needed him in the saddle, Crockett was Johnny-on-the-spot at the crack of dawn and stayed till the last knot had been tied. His fee was your friendship.

After his old mare had done her do, Crockett kept her for what she had been and looked around for another saddle horse. Ben Wallis sold him a spirited brown gelding with black mane and tail. It had a good head along with the makin's of a real cow pony and had been broke to the saddle; yet he was delivered to Glen Chisholm to have "the rough edges took off him" before Crockett took his new horse home. "On account of," as Crockett put it, "I'm jest too old an' stove up an' brittle to take any chances on bustin' a bronc."

35

Glen barely got to see the brown for, come daylight next morning, Crockett was there to ride him home. A week later we were riding along beside an old field with Crockett a-blowin' about his new mount. Out of the clear blue, the Brown spooked at an old planter standing at the corner of the field, swallowed his head, and went bucking out across a glade that was all cedar stumps and honeycomb rocks with prickly pear growing in the cracks.

Clawing leather, Crockett choked the saddlehorn with one hand and fought at the reins with the other for the first few jumps. Then, giving the horse his head, Crockett sat up in the saddle hanging the spurs to him with each jump and cutting his rump with the quirt every time a hoof hit the ground. Before he was through, the Brown was glad to stick his muzzle into that old planter box or thread the needle back and forth across the planter tongue on an easy rein.

Crockett was sitting with one leg cocked in the saddle and using both hands to build a brown paper cigarette when I asked: "Whatever happened to that old feller that was too old and brittle to bust a bronc? Shore ain't seen him around lately."

Without dropping a stitch in his cigarette making, Crockett nodded towards the glade and says: "Had to ride him — you show me a place out there a man could quit him without gettin' kilt." The Brown made a real cow horse and Crockett got to be pretty wild in that saddle.

Below Hog Hole on Falls Creek, there is a place where the water riffles through deep crevices or stands in the shallow pools on a solid rock bottom. A growth of green algae keeps it slick as glass. Old range cows would go around this place to get to their calves. One day a bunch of wild goats spilled out across this place and were gone, as far as the rest of us in the saddle were concerned. Crockett blasted straight across, headed them before they could make it to the bluff and brought them back the way they had gone. The Brown never faltered on the way.

Over in the roughs of the Everett Ranch, he headed a wild cow by shouldering her to the ground with the Brown, jumped over her, and was standing in the trail before her when she regained her feet. The trail was narrow; any miscalculated timing or distance would have delivered horse and rider into a deep canyon. Angered with fright, I rode over to dress him down for his recklessness. Before I could speak my piece, Crockett's face clouded and he waved me away as he spoke: "I know — I know — I was mad and hot

36

when I done it — an' I'll wake up nights an' be scared as the Devil when I think about it."

Next time Crockett showed up at my place, he was riding a big-footed bay, a docile animal short on looks and long on sense. I wanted Crockett to blow and brag about the fancy price he had gotten for his Brown. I wish he had. Instead, he mentioned the Brown only once after that. With unseeing eyes, he was looking past me across the valley to where Packsaddle Mountain stood blue in the haze and his hands fumbled listlessly as he spoke: "He was a young man's horse — forty years ago, no man's money coulda got him from me."

From *The Pioneer Heritage*

Highland Lakes

Buchanan Dam was completed in 1937. Behind the massive structure of concrete arcs and piers, the vast empty basin lay as a treeless wasteland of vacated homesites bordered by the ragged contours of the 1,020-foot elevation lines reaching into the distance.

The somnolent Colorado thread its way up this valley like a little girl's ribbon lost in the grass and browned by the sun.

The scene prompted one of the Yankee engineers at the damsite to remark, "It will take ten years for that little crick to fill this basin." Old-timers gazed without expression and kept their opinions to themselves.

Come June, spring freshets along the upper reaches of the ole Colorado and floodwaters roared past Tow Valley mid-morning that fateful day. By evening the townsite of Old Bluffton lay beneath muddy waters — never to be seen again until the drought years of the fifties — and waters spread toward the hills. The next morning found all floodgates open at Buchanan but not before some waters had skirted the east end of the dam.

Back to the drawing boards. Concrete was poured another half mile or so into the cow pastures of Burnet County.

And so, the first link in the chain of Highland Lakes had been forged.

Old-timers gathered around the Tow store began comparing this flood with those of yesteryears. Some way or another Uncle Horse Maxwell's version of the time hogs crowded to one side of the Bluffton ferry turning it bottom up in the middle of the river got mixed into the fray. After that, any old codger two days under seventy-five could not have gotten his two-bits worth in edgewise with a hickory ax handle.

A fisherman's wildest dreams had come true and I didn't know about it until I went to wait for the mail to come. None of the sweaters and sitters were about. "Lake's full. Everybody's gone fishin'! Catch 'em too — in broad daylight."

It was like finding a bird's nest on the ground. All you needed was a cane pole and a can of worms. Wade out into the murky waters from most any point and start pulling them in. Cat fishing and throw back the perch. Both blues and some yellows, ranging upwards from big keepers to four- or six-pounders with an occasional eight or niner.

Best fishing was to be had around a heavy growth of submerged prickly pear. It also paid to keep an eye peeled for red ants. Flooded from their beds, they clung to tall grasses or weeds, ready to board any passerby and begin stinging only after having discovered warm flesh beneath soggy clothing. The neck at the collar or a sunburned ear would do for openers.

As the murky waters cleared, the bonanza began to fade. No one seemed to care. Everybody had had his bait of fish and it was getting harder to find anyone who would take a mess off your hands without a binding offer to clean the danged things for them having been attached firmly to the front end of the bargain. "And I don't want any fish heads left laying around to stink up my place."

Night catfishing on the new lake could be a milkrun or long hard nights of distant trotlining with tubs and tubs of fish to dispose of and a neglected housewife left at home. Slats Williams and I chose the milkrun.

By having everything ready I could pick up Slats after he had finished his day checking at the Lone Grove cedar yard, hie ourselves down the old Bluffton Road to Preacher Nobles's place, have a few throw lines set, and be pole fishing off the rocks before good dark. By 11:00 or 12:00 we would have all the cats either of us wanted.

After dumping Slats in Lone Grove and ditching my share of the catch in the horse trough, I could be in bed by 1:00 or 2:00. Sometimes I would just grab the .22 and headlight an old doe and have her shucked before daylight.

Doe ham for breakfast with gravy over eggs and you could sop my mother-in-law's biscuits without one of them ever getting soggy. Catfish for Sunday, and, if folks came visiting, there were always some fat fryers among the half-wild Cornish flock that ran with the quail and roosted in trees behind the barn.

Milch cow in the lot, fattened hog in the pen, and a red hickory sand garden spot that grew about anything you set your mind to. Had to cut cedar post to pay the taxes; but we ate pretty high on the hog for pore folks.

There were times when Slats wished to be delivered to Llano. With a thumb jammed in the corner of its gaping mouth and fingers hooked in the gills, a fair-sized yellow cat hung from either hand as Slats and I parted company.

Down the street a nickel was dropped in the slot and the music box came alive to fill the cafe with a glittering array of revolving beams of colored lights as Hank Williams moaned about his San Antonio Rose and the fiddle sawed into the night.

Then there was the time Ross was out of pocket and it was late before Slats could leave the cedar yard. Slats knew some Lone Grovers were already on the lake, so we decided to join them.

After quitting the road, Slats opened gates and guided the way down cow trails through post oaks and mesquites to a point above Black Rocks where Buck Nobles's boys were camped. Nolan was doing the cooking.

Skillet and lid bread was in the makin' and the coffee was ready. Roy and Earl were busy cleaning fish, and I'm not sure whether it was John D. or Pete Overstreet that was helping Carter Holland clean a yearling doe he had brought to camp.

As we sat about comparing the merits of hand-sized fillets of yellow cat rolled in corn meal then dropped in a pot of boiling lard to come up browned through and through, with those of backstrap sliced thin, rolled in flour and black pepper and fried in an open skillet—you could look in all directions without seeing another campfire and no motor boat hummed about in the darkness.

The distant glow of the lights at Buchanan was the only harbinger of what the future held for this land.

Today the houses along this part of the lake shore have the sameness of a city street. It would take a native-born son to locate our old campsite.

From *The Highlander*
July 21, 1977

Ground Signs

Forty years ago the old Tow place in Llano County was about as far back into the cedar brakes as you could get. It was a good place to see how things used to be in these hills of Texas; that is, if you cared for such.

The Tow boys, Jim and Sid, lived alone on an old homeplace where time had stood fairly still for fifty years. Aged and asthmatic, they were able to do little more than ride the range and, on occasion, make it to town for Saturday evening.

Too many long days spent gazing listlessly across the hills had given them their own brand of peculiarities. You didn't gain much from them through talk, but just by walking or riding about on their ranch, it was easy to see why their old daddy had chosen to settle there in the 1860s, and to understand pretty well how the Tows had lived over the years.

The Llano–San Saba county line passed between the house and the barns, and Falls Creek flowed within a hundred yards of the front door. From the house, you traveled a winding road through the cedars, dodging rocks and stumps and the bigger trees to follow the course of least resistance some two miles to the ranch gate.

About midway, a dim-marked wagon road branched off at right angles to snake its way down a long glade to an old field of some sixty acres, more or less, of cultivated land (depending upon how far from the fence the turnrows were made each year).

During the late thirties, my brother-in-law, Guy Alexander, rented this old field from the Tow boys and planted it in hegari and redtop cane. And he plowed his turnrows close to the fence.

By the time the hegari had matured to the dough stage and the pilfering doe deer were carrying a nice coat of white tallow, we decided to begin protecting Guy's crop by gracing our tables with some grain-fed venison. To facilitate matters and avoid any possible conflict of interest with the Tows, we walked a couple or three miles across the hills in the night and gathered our dubious share of this deer crop by headlight with a .22 rifle during the dark of the moon.

Returning from a visit to the hegari patch one night, we had to walk up the glade empty-handed, outsmarted by a snorty old doe, and Guy was a bit on the irritable side.

"Quit walkin' in the road leavin' tracks," he griped. "Them

40

suspicious ole codgers would take notice if you so much as turned over one dry cow chip on this place."

This overstatement rattled a loose screw somewhere in my cranium, and a quick flash of my light revealed a carpet of thin grass polka-dotted with gray, sunbleached cow chips.

Immediately I set about to enliven this drab color scheme by changing the gray polka dots to an olive green, merely by turning the dry cow chips upside down. Why not?

Erratic quirks of human behavior surely must beget their likes in others, for Guy moaned and groaned several minutes before he faded into the night, leaving me alone in my endeavor. I didn't leave the glade till each chip lay bottom-side up to greet the morning's sun.

Early the next day we were out in the field as farmers, securing a little batch of redtop to haul in for Guy's milk cows. Toward the shank of the morning, we looked up at the right time to see Sid lope into the glade, jerk his old horse to a skidding stop, and stand in his stirrups to look the situation over. Then, after cantering slowly about the glade, like a good hound searching for a lost scent, he busted a beeline through the cedars to the house.

Guy and I stood looking at one another, each waiting for the other to speak. Neither of us had found any words before Jim's pickup came bounding into sight at the upper end of the glade. We watched it turn off on the wagon road and head down the glade our way, with Jim and Sid each trying to outdo the other in pointing his finger at the strange phenomena as viewed from his side of the pickup.

They stopped at the field fence near the gate and sat and looked at us. We ambled over to the fence and stood and looked right back. Everybody seemed to be suffering his own troubles in finding the first word.

"You fellers seen anything wrong?" Jim finally asked.

"Nope. Nope," Guy said. "Gettin' hot an' dry is all I got to say."

"Seen any strangers or city folks around up here?" countered Jim.

"Reckon not," said Guy.

With that, Jim cranked up and toddled on back toward the house. Guy seemed some relieved, but I didn't go for the way Jim had talked to him but looked at me all the while. For that I'd have to make amends.

41

That very night, while Guy toted out an old doe across his shoulders, I stayed behind to turn each cow chip back into its original position.

For the next twenty years, Jim Tow always referred to me as that danged feller from "Saint Marcos er Wimney er summer's else." And that was as near as that incident ever came to being mentioned in words — until now.

From *The Highlander*
Also published in *Frontier Times* (September 1975)

The Way It Was

Though there must be a million of them around, I have never met a hunter or fisherman that didn't have his lie he was aching to tell, and any cedarcutter worth his salt could lie all day without repeating himself.

Some of them were pretty awful to swallow, but I will try to believe all of them. If you will just hold still and listen awhile, I will tell mine.

Forty years ago this Texas Hill Country was the backwoods home of hard times. It's true, the Great Depression lingered in these hills throughout the thirties. Being poor as hell wasn't so bad, long as you didn't know any better.

Besides, hounddogs and fishermen are always too busy living to waste much time worrying about making a living. And worry was about all you could do about it in those good old days.

In the fall of '37, my wife and I moved to my mother-in-law's little place near Lone Grove, where everybody knew everybody else, and busybodies knew everybody's business. The hills were sparsely inhabited by ranchers and small landholders, with the younger generation gone to town, the boys in the Tree Army, and a few old diehard cedarcutters scattered in the brakes.

Barbed wire had divided the range, but some of the finer qualities of the old pioneer spirit still clung to the land. You could run hounds across most of the country without complaints. As long as you didn't make a nuisance of yourself by leaving gates open and violating similar common-sense customs, you could hunt coons and squirrels or fish about any place you pleased.

Of course, it didn't hurt to go by the house to exchange howdies and let folks know you were about. Along some of the county roads you could find a few old trespass signs, posted mostly for the benefit of total strangers and unwanted kinfolks.

Then there were always a few thrifty souls to bellyache among themselves, branding everyone who wasted his time in the woods as a shiftless lot and wondering why they had been called upon to suffer having such for neighbors. But there were always the good years when it rained a lot and everybody could wear a smile.

You had to be a Lone Grover awhile to fully understand their attitude about deer. It wouldn't take much birddogging to come up with a green doe hide near the barn of about any household and at any season of the year.

You could be sitting at the store waiting for the mail when your fool pup came around the corner wagging its tail and carrying a fresh deer hock in its mouth. Everybody grinned when he tried to give you the bone and that was it. Everyone seemed to be eating deer, and no one seemed to care to speak of it or bother to deny the fact.

I guess it was sort of like having to wear an old pair of brogan shoes. You were not too proud of them and you were not ashamed of them, for they were still good shoes and all you had.

Before the day of the REA, a fat doe afforded you with a good bundle of red meat that you could handle without refrigeration. Should it happen to be a big buck in the velvet or a doe and a yearling, and you were caught with too much meat for hot weather, you were still in luck.

Hang the carcass until well drained of blood and glazed. Bone and slice into thin steaks. Fry the steaks until browned well done. Fill fruit jars or molasses buckets with layers of these steaks, pour hot lard over the steaks until the containers are brim-full, then seal.

You are a lazy lout if you left much of this labor for your wife. Now, you are ready for steak and gravy anytime you tire of the usual *frijoles* and black-eyed peas fare.

With city dudes' high-priced deer leases thirty years in the future, most landholders considered deer a pest and a nuisance. It did not take many deer many nights to bite the tops from the hegira or maize field, trim the pea patch, play hell with the melons, and leave the garden spot a shambles. In the pastures the deer were always the furstest with the mostest at nature's crops, leaving only the dead fish and frogs when the ponds went dry in the summer.

If money be the root of all evil — with six-cent hogs, ten-dollar yearlings, the last cotton crop left in the field priced too cheap to pick, and good cedar post bringing a buffalo nickel and a red penny more bringing the best — Lone Grove of the thirties could never be considered an evil place.

From *The Highlander*
July 2, 1977

Gates

Stopping and getting out to open and close a gate has always been a fretful chore to the country traveler. Today it's an impossible task. Nowadays when you can bank, eat, see a movie, or go to church without leaving the car seat, who the devil is going to leave that seat to open a gate? That's how cattle-guards were born. Using the wreckage from several gates, an Edison-inclined owner devised a contraption a car could run over with only minor damage and a cow would have better sense than to walk into, and he called the thing a cattle-guard.

Over in the hills of San Saba County, Mack Yates had a means of slowing the speedsters on his ranch. Like many of the oilmen ranchers, Mack had his herds of cattle, horses, and buffalo, and many western innovations on his ranch, but he is most often remembered for his own brand of bump gates. The gate proper was made of two-inch timber and operated on three of the biggest cedar logs to be found. For years the cedarcutters in that part of the country hauled all their "Yates Posts" — straight heart logs over twenty feet long and with tops measuring twelve or more inches in diameter — to Mack for a premium price. These gates operated well with the proper bump and a smooth follow-through. But, when hit too fast, they would retaliate by denting fenders and smashing lights fore and aft, and leaving deep scratches alongside for any who attempted quick escapes. If the gate was damaged in the incident, Mack rewarded the offender with a boot in the pants. His size twelve's were no idle threat.

Some fifty years ago, when most roads were caliche and cars were automobiles, people didn't have speed troubles. Back in my part of the hills, the "Dutchmans" kept drivers down to a reasonable gate-opening speed. "Dutchmans" were mounds of dirt the old-time commissioners built across the roads at intervals on grades to divert water from the roadbed. After your Model T had hit one of these mounds while your foot was hung in the carburetor, it was always a good idea to stop and count the kids before leaving the scene.

Along these old county roads each property line was usually marked by some sort of gate. Perhaps as old as barbed wire itself, the wire gap was the most worrisome of the lot. With an old harness hame or bowed stick to lever it shut with taut wires, it remains picturesque Old West. As late as the 1930s, by using these "saddle gaps" you could ride from Lone Grove to Tow Valley along the old wagon road to Lampasas. But, as people began to be more concerned about deer leases than neighboring, these gaps were closed. Now that travel in the area is restricted to county roads, deer are more abundant, and old neighbors continue to speak to one another, if they happen to meet in town.

Along about that time, an old saddle gap on the divide between Falls Creek and the Little Llano River was closed under different circumstances. For forty years, Jim Tow had courted a lady who lived across the hills; at least, he seemed to have figured it that way. The lady lived on the Little Llano and Jim lived at the headwater of Falls Creek, and theirs was the last link of an old party-line telephone. After each weather spell, Jim would phone over to compare rainfall and temperature changes in the two locations. Over the years, the affair had advanced to the stage where Jim saved his grease and rancid lard for her to render into soap on the halves. Every month or three, he would ride over with a bundle of clothes to be patched or have buttons replaced and a Sunday shirt to be ironed for a reasonable fee.

For several days following a rain storm, Jim had been unable to raise an answer on the phone, so he saddled up to see if the line was down. He found the trouble not too far from the lady's house. The line was not only down but it had also been rolled up most of the way across his pasture.

At the saddle gap he found "A feller a-tyin' up the gap good and tight with the telegraph wire that was half mine."

As Jim told it, "He looks up but don't stop workin' an' says: 'Be Jim Tow, I reckon, an' me, I'm the man of the house on this side of the fence now, an' I allow my woman won't be washin' er sewin' for anybody except me from now on — so we won't be needin' this gate er phone anymore.' An' I don't say nothin' an' he keeps on tyin' wire. You know, he was the ugliest kind of a lookin' little cuss. If'n she wanted to get married, why didn't she say so to me? I could of beat that for her. He shore don't look like much to me."

During the Depression years, my brother-in-law, Guy Alexander, built some gates that would be a worthy reminder of those moneyless days. Guy was the kind of fellow that could do more with a double-bit ax than most jack-legged carpenters could with a whole box full of tools.

One blade of his ax was dressed thin from the eye to the edge with a file, then honed smooth with a whetstone. The handle was scraped with glass until it had the proper spring-in-the hand when used. Then it was soaked in linseed oil with a washer used to wedge it properly in the eye. No one but Guy used this ax or so much as laid their hands on it. In a tight, I have seen him field dress an old doe with his ax. With a short blow he could sink it to the eye in green cedar. For dry cedar or other timber, he carried another blunt-edged ax.

For his gate Guy selected a cedar with a heavy branch extending at an angle from the body. This tree was cut several inches below the fork and topped at about ten feet. Small cedar poles were used as gate panels, with the forked branch serving as a cross brace supporting the panels. The butt end of the tree was set in a hole beside the gate post and the top was wired loosely to the post, allowing the gate to swing, after a fashion.

Blacksmith and tinker of sorts, Great-grandpa Adare found time in his old age to build gates on his place to suit his taste. Fashioned from slab lumber and hewn cedar, they were something to see. Wagon axles with hub spindles fixed to the gate post served as hinges. This post was tenoned at the top and a long, bowed log with a hole in it was placed atop it. The small end of this log was attached by a chain to the end of the gate, and a trough on the butt end of this log held enough rocks to balance the weight of the cumbersome gate, making it swing quite easily. Each time these gates were opened or closed, the tenon at the top of the gate post moaned and groaned like a tom cat with his tail caught under a rocking chair.

Sitting beside Grandpa Lawrence in his hack and being his gate-opener as we rode from his place on Pin Oak Creek down the old road to Wimberley and on to San Marcos is one of my fondest memories. Grandpa had a way of always making a boy feel right big. He let me open the gates that were easy to handle, and, on the mean ones, he would allow me to drive the team through. The fact that Grandpa could talk old Mox and Bill through a gate from start to stop at a distance of forty feet had no bearing on this matter.

46

The gate at the old Decker place was my favorite and a standard for that era. The lumber used in making these old gates was of a grade that seemed only to weather gray with age, and hardware was usually made from worn wagon tires by some local blacksmith. The hinges consisted of two long strips bolted to the gate and hung by the eye on male spikes driven into the gate post; a figure "4" latch held it shut. At the Decker gate, the top male spike was slightly right of center, causing it to swing open in a rising arc and, therefore, close on its own weight. By hanging on, a six-year-old boy could get a free ride on this gate while it swung shut, and a teeth-rattling jar if he failed to step off before it slammed against the post.

During Great-grandpa's earlier days, travelers going up the Blanco from Wimberley entertained another shade of memories for Bill Adare's pole gate. This antiquated contraption of inconvenience consisted of a series of small poles held parallel to the ground by a series of holes augered through a large gate post standing on either side of the road. After climbing down from his wagon, the traveler had to remove each of these poles by sliding it through one of the gate posts and stacking it beside the fence, one by one, before leading his team through the opening. By the time he had replaced each of these poles to its proper position and had regained his seat in the wagon, the traveler was certain to feel that he had had his dose of self-control for the day.

Being sticklers to the code of leaving a gate as you found it, most people closed Grandpa's gate, with the exception of an occasional Saturday nighter returning from Fischer's Store. Sometimes one of these riders would try to jump the poles, with splintering effects, or would merely leave them scattered about in the dark. Either event could add substance to sermons on the evil of drink preached at Wayside schoolhouse and in Wimberley on second Sundays.

According to my dad's memories, the first attempt to devise a cattle-guard in this area took place at a site some two miles from San Marcos on the Old Wimberley Road during the late, late 1890s. As is often the case, the name of this creative genius has been lost to time and it is just as well.

From logic that only he could fathom, he figured that a steep barrier in the middle of the road would serve to stop and turn livestock. So, he set about to fill one side of the road with a long slope gradually rising from ground level to the height of three or four feet.

Parallel to and at opposite hand, he filled the other side of the road with another slope.

Needless to say, cattle paid no heed to this cattle-guard, but a short-fused teamster did. One run through this cattle-guard and on his return trip, he skirted it, and cut a hole in the fence to create a new bend in the Wimberley Road that remained intact long after the reason for its existence had been forgotten.

The first cattle-guard I can remember seeing was in the Wimberley area. This guard consisted of an open pit four feet wide and three feet deep, extending across the road bed with the fence anchored to posts at either end. Two flat-bottomed troughlike affairs made of two-inch lumber bridged this pit. With a careful, well-aimed approach, this cattle-guard was a surmountable obstacle. Get a bit reckless and you could very well end up with one of your Model T's front wheels hanging in the pit while the other tried to climb an anchor post. In any event, the old milk cows or savvy brood sows soon learned to trot these cattle-guards with more ease than did most drivers.

In time this type of cattle-guard was revised to be bridged with a lateral framework of poles, or two-inch lumber stood on edge, secured at two- to four-inch intervals across the width of the guard. With that improvement you could zip your Model A across this guard at a fair rate of speed without losing the muffler or having a blowout — that is, if it was a relatively new structure. Heavy traffic and age could turn a cattle-guard into a booby trap.

After prosperity began to smile on Texas, the cattle-guard blossomed in all sorts of elaborate forms and fashions. The proven standard and most practical of the lot consisted of a concrete walled pit of various dimensions bridged with two-inch parallel piping set at four-inch intervals. Old tubing from boilers which had seen service in Texas oilfield drilling rigs often did its final service embedded in cattle-guards of this area. The fence anchor posts were often set three or four feet from the end of the guards, with sloped concrete piers or metal grillwork closing these ends to discourage goats and other animals from attempting to skirt these guards.

Cattle-guards were a relatively new innovation in my corner of Llano County when my brother-in-law Herman rode old Blue down to one of the shindigs held in Lone Grove. During the course of the evening he must have visited the jug of moonshine the boys had hid in the bushes a mite too often for, with a hoot and a holler, Herman jumped in the saddle and headed home in a high lope.

Recent rains had left the road in proper condition to record each hoofprint for all the neighbors to see just how old Blue had loped up the center of the road, clearing each cattle-guard with the ease of an English jumper — all the way home.

From *Built in Texas,*
Edited by Francis Edward Abernethy
(Publications of the Texas Folklore Society, Number 42,
Waco: E-Heart Press, 1979)

Fishing with Jess

Jess Carter lived on the Little Llano River and he was among the last of the old loners living in the county. Some of his neighbors said that old Jess was just contrary as hell, but I was never able to see where he had strolled from the path to the Sweet Bye and Bye any farther than most of us.

Jess was in his late sixties, big as a bear, and walked with a deliberate stride. But don't let your eyes deceive you. He was the best fishing partner to be had.

That is, if you wanted to get in some hard-down trotline fishing, eat the very best camp cooking, and, on a real fifty-basis, share all the fun and hardships of an overnight fishing trip.

These trips began about 2:00 in the evening with Jess piling his plunder aboard his pickup. You asked for it and it was there — from coal oil lantern to a tub full of what the garden could afford, as well as a bucket of eggs packed in cottonseed and trotlines galore.

Then he would head for town, where he would buy a bushel basket of groceries. Lastly, and a thing which need only to happen on the umpteenth trip, he would go to the whiskey store and come out carrying a little half-pint bottle. In his great hand this bottle looked as small as the little free samples of cheap perfume passed out by drugstore drummers.

By good dark all lines had been set — just right — and ready to bait. While fishing on Buchanan we always found a place where the trotlines could be set to cover a wide arc, beginning and ending at points not too far distant from the campsite. You see, Jess would not get into any boat with a motor hung on its rear and I never asked to debate the issue.

There was always a good fish fry during the night. Towards morning, allowing ample time to complete running the lines before daybreak when fish would break into a final frenzied effort to free themselves, Jess would kick the coals alive to warm the coffee pot. After scouring two tin cups and waving me aside, he would break out the whiskey. A tablespoon of whiskey to each cup and the bottle was returned to storage for the next trip. Handing me my cup and taking a comfortable seat in the sand, he began to sup.

"This's the way I like my whiskey," he says. "At times like this, there's nothing like a good shot of whiskey to perk up a man and fire him up for the day ahead."

One evening Jess and I went down to the Fitzsimmons Ranch to try our luck on the Llano River. By 10:00 we had enough catfish for a fry—even by Jess's standards. After we had eaten all either of us could get around and sat sipping our coffee, there were still some fish and the fried potatoes Jess had thrown in for good measure left on the cottonsack spread on the ground.

About a quarter of a mile away, Al Wells and his forty house-cats stayed in an old house on the ranch. Al's present chore for the Fitzsimmons Ranch was to milk out some twenty Hereford cows that were giving too much milk for their young calves to handle.

Cat and cow smells not withstanding, Al must have gotten wind of our fish. Shuffling through the bloodweeds like an armadillo, he broke into camp and took his seat beside the cottonsack. "Nope, I done et, but will take some coffee," he says, and began whining about being worked to death for starvation wages.

Shifting to telling exactly what he was going to say to Hugh Fitzsimmons the day he quit, the noise subsided as Al gained momentum nibbling at the food on the cottonsack. After the last scrap had disappeared, he opened the end of a new fifteen-cent loaf of lightbread. Using a slice of bread as his skimmer, he began gathering the cornmeal crumbs from the grease in the skillet—allowing how the crumbs were better eatin' than the fish they came off of.

Leaving Al to his skimming, Jess and I allowed it was about time to run our lines.

When we returned Al was gone, the bread wrapper empty and skillet licked clean as a hound's tooth.

"Better than two pounds of pure hog lard at one sitting has to be a lethal dose for any human," says I. "We'd better hunt up the old cuss and try to get him to Doc Gray before it's too late."

Jess would not be stirred.

"Eat anything a wild hog can and not even get a bellyache," was all he had for the matter and I guess he was about right.

Next morning Al was down in time for breakfast. Put away six eggs and was working at a pound of bacon when Jess stopped cooking.

After pouring most of the grease on the ground, Jess heated the remainder piping hot, dashed a cup of water into it, and let the big skillet fire-burn clean in a flash. But he didn't fool me one bit. His concern was not centered on cleanliness of the old skillet.

Now Jess might not have done much to prevent Al jumping into the river to drown himself or trying to hang himself from a windmill tower. But there was one thing for sure: he knew one more session of grease-sopping would lay old Al away for good, and Jess was not about to let anything like that happen. That is, under circumstances which might make him a possible heir to forty housecats with about nineteen of the tabbies filled with the bright promise to domino in the very near future.

From *The Highlander*
December 1, 1977

Remembering Lone Grove

In the old days, when dirt roads snaked their way through the Texas Hill Country in all directions, there was always some kind of a small community just down the road no more than a good buggy ride away. Any sort of an old slow-trotting horse could make the trip, let you do some talking with neighbors along the way, and still get back home in time for supper.

Today, most of these communities are gone, many leaving little cemeteries and lost gravesites as their only marker. Some vanished without a trace.

Oxford, Click, Hickory, Honey Creek, Teichville, Leiningen, and Baby Head are but a few of the bygone communities in Llano County. But down by the Dreary Hollow Crossing, the post office still stands beside the Little Llano. And the store is open. Everybody who has ever gotten his mail at the Lone Grove Store figures there will always be a Lone Grove, Texas.

The schoolhouse is closed, the churches are empty, and there are few people left to gather at the store and wait for the mail to come in; yet Lone Grove continues to exist and the ghosts of the past live on.

Some say the stage stop was on the other side of Dreary Hollow. I don't know. All will agree that the stage line running from

51

Austin to Llano and points west did, indeed, pass through Lone Grove. And that stage did run, with the old coaches bouncing from rock to rock, up hill and down dale, bogged in mud during rainy spells and hell on horses all the time.

Over on the Blanco-Llano county line, my great-grandfather, Pleasant Wimberley, bred horses for stage use. They had to be light-heavyweights, good on their feet, and had to possess those rare qualities of stamina and endurance the old-time horsemen called "bottom."

The wild and woolies of the Old West had their saloon and gambling hall across the road from the store, but their days were limited.

Lone Grove was settled primarily by dirt farmers, and it was not long before this den of iniquity was razed to be replaced by a cotton gin and grist mill. My wife's grandpa, John Scott, and his sons ran this operation while ranching and farming his place near Points Peak. After selling out, the gin going to the Templetons, he moved to Topsy to establish the same operations anew.

During the boom and bust era of mining operations in Llano County, Pat Mayes came from Bastrop to work in the Heath Mine and make his home in Lone Grove. Paradoxically, this sage old-time hardrock miner became a patriarch in a land of small farms and cow country. Like most old Lone Grove men, he was still in the harness at the far side of age sixty-five.

I once asked Pat how much gold the Heath Mine had produced. Measuring off the length of two extended fingers with a thumb, "Oh, a bar about that big and it wasn't around when the mine closed down. Seems some rascal had made off with it."

Allowing how Pat's hand was about the size of a grizzly bear's paw, the fact remains that gold ingot had to be a pretty meager yield for a 600-foot shaft. Maybe that absconding rascal did posterity a favor. Last mention I heard, that two-finger-sized ingot had grown to the size of a loaf of bread. Who knows? Another sixty or seventy-five years hence, it could be big as a bale of hay and a bonanza in the offing for new investors interested in reopening the old Heath Mine.

Early in the days of the Great Depression, the Heath Mine rendered its last service. Under the auspices of Washington AAA efforts to stem the tides of the Depression, the owners of livestock were paid to destroy a portion of their herds. Cattle from a wide area of Llano County were driven to the Heath Mine to be killed and dumped unceremoniously down the deep shaft.

With prosperity just around the corner, the Depression held its grip. Lone Grove farmers abandoned their plows to work on the Buchanan Dam project, while the younger generation sought the bright lights of city life. Most of their plow tools found their way through scrap dealers' markets to see service in opposing armies of World War ll.

Another Depression-born program initiated the final business bustle suffered by Lone Grove. Stimulated by the cedar eradication program, the old withered trade in cedar posts, no longer tied to the railroads, blossomed with cedar yards on each side of the Little Llano and Dreary Hollow. In the early '50s, Forrest Ross and I filled the "Y" between the forks of the road with cedar posts stacked to the heights of the oaks. Cedarcutters filled all vacant houses in or near Lone Grove. Today, you have to drive to Burnet or Cedar Mountain to buy a cedar post.

Lone Grove continues to appear on most Texas maps and, here of late, has received some national attention of sorts.

A couple of months ago a niece sent me a clipping from the *Santa Fe New Mexican*. This Associated Press story — datelined Lone Grove, Texas — was topped with a picture of the reporter panning for gold in the Little Llano. Days later my brother, living in Fort Sill, sent me the same picture cut from an Oklahoma paper. Then through the magic of TV, I sat enthralled as another reporter interviewed postmaster-storekeeper Mrs. Bill Kerr (Doodle Mayes), then gave us a peek at the Heath Mine from the road and panned a pocket full of nuggets from the Little Llano before heading back to San Antonio.

Now, don't get me wrong. Both of the boys did a fine job. No complaints. It's just a shame they didn't spend enough time sitting around the store getting their homework done.

At first glance, the Little Llano — lots of sand, little water — may not look like much of a stream and set you to wondering why it should always be designated as a river. One spring freshet or a try at maintaining a water gap across it between you and an ornery neighbor and you will accept the label without reservations.

Any Lone Grover could tell you that it would take six boxcar loads of Little Llano sands to yield a minuscule of flour gold whose glitter could only be seen in the smear on a microscopic slide. Had either of these reporters just hung around long enough to gain the confidence of one of the old nesters — a mere twenty or thirty years — he would have felt no need to feign an attack of gold fever in his journalistic effort. After learning the secret of the sixteen jackloads of Spanish gold buried beside the spring on Cedar Holler, he could have suffered the rigors of the gold fever for real.

This brother-in-law of mine lived around Lone Grove all his life. He never did get right down to telling me where he learned about this gold or exactly how he had determined it to be buried by the spring on Cedar Holler, but you know how persuasive a Lone Grover can be at times. So, I am certain the gold is there. Any doubts about it and you can start the fight with him yourself. Not me.

Though he has already dug around every spring on Cedar Holler — from the Whitt pasture to the top of the hill in the Verda Everett, at Little Seep Springs at the head of Zula Everett Branch, at Big Seep in the Schadt 320 on Charcoal Fork, and still takes to the field sometimes — have heart. The gold is there. None of his diggings was deeper than a duck's nest, and that's no way to find gold.

Now, don't you go wandering off down to Honey Creek after that treasure in Spanish bullion lying at the bottom of Blue Hole since the days of the Conquistadors. According to Mayme Slaughter, there are only twelve jackloads of gold in that cache. What man in his right mind would want to sacrifice four jackloads of gold before he has even turned one spade of dirt?

Now, if you insist on being bullheaded on the matter, you may as well go on down to Big Sandy to look for the other lode in the Click country. All right, there is a wide vein of ore exposed across the face of one of the high cliffs near Big Sandy. It is so rich that the Indians picked out the grains of gold dust with turkey quills by pressing the open ends over the big grains until the hollow portion of the quill was filled. In small bands, they kept sneaking back from the reservations to fill a few quills well into the late 1870s. So what? No white man has ever laid eyes upon this vein, and what makes you think you could be the first?

Best you get on back to Lone Grove. After all, the gold there has already been mined, smeltered, and cast into bars worth more than $200 an ounce on the London market. What else do you expect from me, a government subsidy?

Good luck, anyway. Be seeing you in Lone Grove at the store or Cedar Holler or someplace.

From *The Highlander*
January 25, 1979

Hill Country Range Hogs

The range hogs of the Hill Country have their place in Texana. They earned it. A blend of many pioneer breeds, their bloodlines often reached back into Texas history as far as any Mustang or Longhorn. They also developed herd distinctions that old-timers could read as easily as those of cattle or horses; they could tell you what part of the county they came from and just about who they belonged to.

The old spotted range sow was a noble creature. Her only assist from man was to have her ears laced with his mark in matching and mismatched patterns of his choice of cuts and combinations thereof selected at random, from notches, slits, forks, crops, over or under half-crops, over or under slopes, swallow-fork, or grubbed smooth to the head. And, if your heart harbored a little mean streak, you could bob her tail to boot.

With her it was root hog or die. To survive, she ate what she could find — snakes, prickly pear, weeds, roots, grubs, pecans, acorns, and cedar berries. She cooled in creek mud during summer's heat and, to escape winter's cold, found some sheltered cove where she built a huge nest of leaves and grass.

She asked no odds from man. In the brush she ran like a ghost to keep from being seen and came out fighting when cornered. And, in lean years, would starve to death suckling her litter to propagate the species.

From pioneer settler to sore-necked farmer and well-heeled rancher, she was the source of his winter's meat (sausages, ham, and hogshead cheese), his summer's bacon and grease for sop gravy, his lard, his soap, and his hard cash, when swine herds were driven to market or arrived by railcar and truck.

And in her demise, she was not removed from the range to improve the use of the land as the source of mankind's food supply. She was starved and killed to make way for near-domesticated corn-fed deer herds, so that today's Daniel Boone can have a buck tied to his car as he returns from his foray into the wilds.

The hog was the first livestock allowed the freedom of open range. Hog laws, passed at the county level, required the owner to confine his hogs within the bounds of his property. With this final facet, the days of open-range were closed.

Although my mother-in-law considered herself of the landed gentry, she abhorred the hog law, contending, "They are taking from the poor their last rights to the land. If you don't want hogs in the field, build a better fence." And you might remember, most of the first settlers came to these hills to farm small patches and were dependent on an open range to run such livestock as they owned. The saddle was not their home.

Range hogs roamed free when I moved to Llano County. Also, back in the cedar brakes and post oak country, there were some wild ones too — tusked boars no one had gotten around to marking in the ears. Ranging on the reaches of Big Sandy Creek and over towards House Mountain there were herds that would rally, but you had better keep your good seat in the saddle.

The only restrictions on the hog's range were established by local custom in each area.

On the bigger ranches, each owner tried to run about the number of hogs his pastures would support and spent considerable effort to locate them to range on his land. Strays were returned to proper owners at hog-gathering time. Clay Kuykendall, Luke Moss, and their likes could tell you pretty well how many sows and shoats could be found at each waterhole around 4:00 any hot August evening. And Will Stribling's hoghand had better know where to look for each hog on 10,000 acres of land, though he spent ninety percent of his time chasing cows or building fences.

In communities of small landholders, the old chicken-eating sow might often test the mettle of neighbors and ole breakfence might visit the wrong neighbor's field too often to make it home one day — missing, never been seen or heard of since.

A good widow lived in Lone Grove. Her cows ran in the lane, her hogs ran up and down the Little Llano and Dreary Holler as far as the first good water-gaps, and an old Dominique hen raised her three broods of chicks behind the general store. And that's how it was.

Up the Little Llano east of Baby Head, Mike Houston ran a black-and-white spotted Poland China type range hog on the root hog or die basis. Below the south water-gap, Jess Carter raised red Tamworths with some feed when needed.

56

Anytime one of Jess's sows showed up with a spotted litter, those pigs were sure to find an early market—at any price. When one of Mike's had sandy-colored litter, they too were among the first batch to be marketed.

Down in the post oaks, range hogs could be a fair-sized business. In lean, dry years the herds were trimmed by selling off as feeders. But when the oaks hit with a heavy mast crop, thousands of two- and three-year-old spayed sows and barrows were fattened on acorns. When needed, feeders from other areas were also shipped in and all finished for market without having seen a feedlot.

While Old Man Clayt owned the Fitzsimmons, he was big in the hog business. He shipped, by rail, carloads of feeders and finished hogs and brought in the fine Hampshire boars and stockers when needed. But Lone Grovers had it that he got more money from his lawsuits with the railroads than he ever made from his hogs or cattle. So it goes with men who make and lose fortunes, only to bounce back again. Old Man Clayt's track record would fill the pages of a good Western novel. He lost some 60,000 acres of the best Llano country, yet died a wealthy man.

I had a cedar yard in Llano at the time, with Grif Lucas and his gang of cutters camped atop Cedar Mountain. If I needed to see ole Grif, my Burma Jeep was what it took to cross Big Sandy and climb Cedar Mountain.

After you leave Oxford, the only good stretch of the road to Cedar Mountain is a section of the railroad bed left by the aborted Llano to Fredericksburg line. I was traveling down this section at a fair speed when an armadillo darted from the safety of the bar-ditch just in time to be crushed under the left rear duals. A little bump and I thought no more of the incident.

On my return trip, I looked down the railroad bed to see a bunch of buzzards gathered at about the place I figured the arma-dillo to be. But something was amiss. The buzzards took no notice of my truck and I slowed down. After all, a low-flying buzzard through the windshield or just passing close overhead an open-topped vehicle and things could get pretty messy.

Easing on, I was alarmed to see that the buzzards were gath-ered about a spotted sandy sow, laying spread-eagled in the middle of the road. They were gawking and pecking and she was swinging her head, snapping back.

I knew danged well that was an armadillo I'd hit, but here was an old sow broken down in the back in the middle of a road my cedarchoppers and I traveled. And you know who was going to get the blame for any unfavorable happenings along this road.

I stopped a short distance from the scene as the buzzards left in a mad swirl of flopping wings. The buzzards' departure did not much improve the scene. Two pigs were on either side, hunching and fighting to get their heads under their mother's belly, appar-ently anxious to get a last free helping of milk before mama passed.

Finally, the old sow scrambled to her feet to reveal her secret. This sage old sister had been lying on the flattened armadillo to prevent the buzzards getting at it while her brood feasted. After they had their fill, she would have done battle with the buzzards for her share of the remains.

Looking about, she saw me and accepted as fact that she had lost one enemy only to gain another. Gathering the remains of the armadillo in her mouth, she hightailed for points yonder, with the pigs bringing up the rear.

From *The Highlander*
September 15, 1977

Rollie Decker's Yaller Catfish

Don't go telling this tale around Llano, unless you just want to gather a bunch of knots on your head or think you can whip half the people in town all by yourself. Nobody but a feller like ole Rollie Decker could have pulled the likes and got by with it. Even the old people just standing around who saw it knew better than to laugh then. After all these thirty-odd years, they are still pretty sure of their man before they will offer to mention it.

Around Llano it's still pretty much like it used to be here in Wimberley years ago when it didn't pay for strangers to put their two bits worth in without first being asked to by one of the old-timers.

Rollie Decker could feel at home any place where they put saddles on horses' backs — at the polo grounds or about the racing stables and around the old chuckwagon on a ranch. And they always saved him a place to ride in the parade at all homecoming rodeos. He was a horseman.

Though he had retired from the field and lived in town, Deck always wanted to have on hand a young horse or two: ponies showing some promise. Ole Deck could often be seen riding one of these ponies along the roadsides at the edge of town, putting them through their paces to see whether this one had the stuff in him to polo or belonged back on the farm.

One Saturday morning, ole Rollie was riding along the hi-way east of town when a bunch of old friends from San Angelo hailed him from their car and a pickup. They were returning from a two-week fishing trip on Lake Buchanan. They were loaded, and the pickup was loaded with fish.

A brief roadside confab soon took place, with them keeping their seats and Deck still in the saddle. As they were about to leave, one of them ran to the pickup, dragged out a big yaller cat they had caught that morning — about a forty-pounder — and, with it flouncing in the raw, handed it up to ole Deck. With wheels spinning to the tune of the wild laughter at their own joke, they were gone. They failed to stump Decker by a long shot.

59

With his forty-pound yaller catfish hanging from the saddle-horn, Deck paraded down main street across town on a long, round-about way to his house.

Of course, there were the lookers who crowded street corners and those who had to run out into the streets and holler, "Hey, Deck! Where'd you get him? How'd you catch him? Where'd you catch him? Which sort of line did you use? What kind of bait?"

Deck had his answers down pat. He told each and all that he had caught this one down on the river towards the Iron Spur on a throw-line set, without giving an exact location on this six- to eight-mile stretch of the winding Llano River. But with the passing of each city block, he changed his bait from rat-trap cheese to white laundry soap to raw weenies and repeated the process several rounds before quitting the saddle.

At no time did he brag on the size of his catch. Just fair to usual.

By sunset there had been an exodus down the Llano River. Them that didn't have cars walked the railroad tracks. Some by-passed the Iron Spur to head on down to Dead Man's Hole, while the eager beavers kept moving on till they hit the Colorado River. One stayed behind to try his luck under the town bridge, and two more fished in the hole behind the ice plant.

Poolhall closed early that evening, and nobody showed up for the poker game over on Flag Creek that Saturday night.

Town grocers were surprised by the unusual run of single orders for a pound of yeller cheese or a bar of P & G wash-tub soap or a dozen weenies, and they were perplexed by the secretive manner in which each of these customers wished to transact his business. Each seemed to sneak into the store, look around a bit before whispering an order to the clerk, then conceal their purchase from prying eyes and hurriedly leave the building.

To this day, there have been no further single sales of these three items made to local citizens in any Llano grocery store. Yet, there's always that few who ask for the second dose to get snakebit twice.

Several years later, the county was struck by one of its worst droughts. The Llano River dried up, buzzards gorged themselves on dead fish laying about the last potholes, and the town's water supply came from tank-cars shipped in by rail.

Ole Decker comes into the poolhall one day, takes his seat on the sweater's bench, crosses his legs, and starts fanning himself with his straw hat.

"Boys," he says, "took a little ride up the river this morning and run on the biggest yaller cat I believe I've seen in many a day." He pauses till the games slow to a stop before going on. "A big one. Must have weighed seventy-five or eighty pounds."

"An' musta been in somebody's freezer," says one of the wiseacres, anxious to get the balls rolling on his table before his winning streak cools.

"No, no," says Deck, "he was in the Llano all right." He starts fanning again, but he has done broke the ice for the snakehunters.

"Where was he at? Was he dead? What'd you do? Let him get away? Still there?" comes at Deck from all directions.

"He was in that big hole in Slator's and he got away," says Decker, and he starts fanning again with that danged hat.

"You shore? Which way'd he go? Where'd he hide?" and it looks like they are all about ready to jerk that hat from his hand.

"Well," says Deck, laying the hat in his lap, "he was in the shade of a willer tree when I first saw him. Must have been asleep as I rode up the river, because when he sees me, he took off kicking up so much sand and dust in the dry river bed, I couldn't see which way he went. Can't tell you whether he climbed a holler post oak or hid in an armadillo hole. Bee weed's bad up there, too."

From The Wimberley Mill
September 1973

Snakes and Rattle Bean Bushes

Scientific studies of snakes and other reptiles may have produced some valuable data for college professors and their likes, but it sure played hell with many of the wild notions the old-timers used to entertain hereabouts and plumb ruint most of their best snake tales.

Be that as it may. For my part, I have always been able to enjoy a semiknowledgeable state of ignorance where a reasonable bit of superstition and imagination could be used to season a snake story; that is, in about the same proportions as a touch of garlic and a light sprinkle of salt might be used to enhance the flavor of a fine soup. Too much of either and you have a mess on your hands.

Therefore, it seems quite natural that, at an early age, I developed a penchant for determining how well the facts had been salted by merely asking the simple question, "How come?"

Grandpa Lawrence had a visitor. While waiting for Granny to fix dinner, he and the old-timer sat on the porch talking and I sat next to the wall listening.

For a while it looked like Grandpa had him bested with his snake tales. Then he was left in the shade by the old-timer's hoop snake story. With his tail in his mouth, this hoop snake came rolling down the cotton rows to chase a cottonpicker clear to the barn, where the poor fellow saved his life by running into the barn and slamming the door shut behind him—just as the hoop snake impaled himself on the door by slamming his four-inch stinger clear into a board on that door. And there he hung by his tail.

"How come that cottonpicker didn't run across the cotton rows where nobody could roll a hoop if he tried? And how come you didn't leave the snake right there hanging by his tail and call Prof Stanfield at the normal school in San Marcos? He's a teacher down there and he's got all kinds of snakes and lizards and frogs and bugs in big bottles of alcohol down there. I bet he would of—"

My noble efforts to fill the lapse in their conversation was cut short at this point by being sent to the kitchen to see how Granny was getting along with dinner, and I got to eat my dinner in there all by myself without seeing anybody till the old-timer left.

Then there was the time when a whole bunch of men were sitting around talking and somebody had to tell about coming down the big hill with a bale of cotton on his wagon and, about halfway down, he ran over a big rattlesnake—big as a stovepipe—with all four wheels and didn't even hurt that snake one bit. He knew this because the snake was gone after he got his horses to the bottom of the hill and climbed back to where the snake had been.

"How come a snake that big didn't bite one of them horses on the foot?" sez I.

"Oh, he tried to," says my Uncle Tom, coming to my rescue. "Struck right at a horse leg, missed and bit the wagon tongue. And you know what?"

"Wot?" says I.

"Right away that wagon tongue began to swell and swell. Before long it was as big as a barrel and pulling down heavy on the horse's neck and pushing them sidewise in the harness. Why, we had to stop four times to trim that wagon tongue down with an ax before we got to town."

Gosh, my Uncle Tom Adare was a great man. Nobody ever fooled around with him.

One thing about it, those old-timers didn't leave you much room for "how comes" when they named the snakes found around here. One look at a diamond-backed rattler and you knew danged well, for sure, what it was and how it came by its name. The same held true for the copperhead, water moccasin, coachwhip, white racer, and you didn't have to catch a chicken snake in the hen house but once to know who that rascal was.

But nobody but an outsider could call a thunder and lightning snake a coral snake; that is, after your grandfather had told you how dangerous this deadly little creature really was, as you watched the bright bands of red and blue and yellow flash like lightning in the dry leaves where it writhed and fought at the stick pinning its middle to the ground. Right there, you knew for sure that you had as soon be thunder and lightning struck as have one of those little demons bite and sting you with the stinger half as long as your finger that it had hid inside the end of its tail.

However, there remained some itchy silent "how comes" for a pretty little old snake like that to be carrying a big stinger in its tail. So, when I was old enough to carry a knife of my own, I killed one of them little devils and done some exploratory dissecting. The messy operation perished the myth of the stinger in its tail but revealed a delicate set of tiny fangs attached to a venom sac in its head. This left the thunder and lightning name intact, for the deceit concealed within this timid-natured little beauty caused those tiny fangs to appear more sinister to me than the arced blade of the grim reaper's scythe.

In fact, the other day I killed a thunder and lightning snake in my front yard and could find no reason to mention the matter to anyone. But my wife, she had to tell all the neighbors about finding a coral snake in her flower bed. She's from Tow Valley.

Now, I don't know how come my snake tales could have got this long without having mentioned the one the Beal boys used to tell about Uncle Horse Maxwell killing the biggest rattlesnake ever seen in Burnet County.

It was a hot and dry day in the latter part of August, and Uncle Horse had spent most of the evening watching a water hole near Shovel Mountain. He needed a nice big buck to put some good meat on the table for a while. But no deer worth the powder had made its way to this water hole. So, Uncle Horse started walk-

63

ing slowly towards home down an old wagon road, still keeping his eyes peeled for most any sort of deer now.

He was about a mile and a half from the house when he noticed a big log lying across the road and thought about taking a seat on it for a short rest. Then another thought struck: "Strange thing that I've never noticed this log laying across the road here before and I've been down this ole road hundreds of times."

Taking a closer look in the gloom of dusky darkness, Uncle Horse Maxwell realized that he was looking at the biggest rattler he'd ever seen — stretched out motionless across this old wagon road.

Bringing his old "thirty" into action, Uncle Horse blew a goodly hunk of the rattler's head to smithereens and stood ready to give it another. There was no need.

Uncle Horse carried this snake into Burnet, where it was weighed on a set of cotton scales. It weighed sixty-five pounds. The stubbed tail of this monster rattler bore only nine or ten rattles, for the set had been worn or broken off.

Nobody with two grains of horse sense could have a "how come" for Uncle Horse Maxwell's snake tale.

In the first place, Uncle Horse knew when a buck deer was fit to eat, for during August, most any meat of a big buck will be carrying a nice coat of tallow with his meat marbled as good as the best Kansas City corn-fed prime beef and bear none of the funky odors of a romantic billy goat.

In the second place, anybody ought to know that anytime a man like Uncle Horse Maxwell busted a cap on a .30-.30 shell, just to kill a rattlesnake, it danged sure had to be one helluva snake. Old-timers of his calibre just didn't go around wasting good gunpowder for nothing. He might be tempted to use his deer gun to shoot a mad wolf or cure a horse thief of his habit, but for snakes and other pests just smaller than a bear, a good stick or a handful of rocks was all he'd ask for.

Now, if you don't know why a possum is scairt to death of an ax handle, you don't understand one word I been saying.

Without trying to steal some of Miss Hazel Green's thunder, I'm wondering if you have noticed the Lindheimer's senna blooming in wild profusion along the roadsides and across the hills. Through the dry summer season, these innocuous little weeds (bush, if you like) stand dormant with their velvetlike leaves taking on a grayish silvery-haired sheen under the August sun. Then come September rains and — boom — the hillsides are decorated with clear yellow flowers.

Of course, us cedarcutters and local natives got our own name for this weed. Just find one that is loaded with dried pods and give it a shake, then you will have no trouble in relating the name "rattle bean bush" to the plant.

This dry senna can be a pretty mean bush to an old doe hunter, for there is nothing worse than stirring up a rattlesnake in the dark — with your feet.

In the first split second of cold sweat, you realize that the bold hunter is now a cornered prey where any uncontrolled impulse to run from this panic could be fatal. Also, you are fully aware of another nasty fact — the snake knows exactly where you stand and you can only wonder where he is.

As you turn your headlight to search the area circling your feet, there is some relief in finding you have merely walked into a rattle bean bush. But the drumming throb in your ears grows louder and louder. You have broken a cardinal tenet to the challenge of night hunting during the dark of the moon in the month of August. You must be slipping; the tight ground rules of this Spartan game allow no room for any careless act or sympathy. To be a winner you must be first to see the other in any encounter with a rattle-snake and never be taken in by nature's decoys. Otherwise, Saint Peter might hold the only available sympathetic ears for your lame excuses.

Nevertheless, no amount of self-chiding could keep you from finding all sorts of snaky-looking sticks and shadows on the remainder of the way to the house.

From *The Wimberley Mill*
October 1974

Cedarcutters and Range Hogs

Nowadays the white-breasted hawk just sits in a tree beside the road and waits till a fast automobile kills his dinner for him; the coon spends his nights robbing garbage cans; and the corn-fed deer is on medicare and has more legal protection than your Jersey bull. Our Great Society has done brought social security to these hills for man and beast alike. Government-sponsored range programs coupled with soaring land prices have driven from these woods the last wild and independent creatures to inhabit the area — namely, the old-time cedarcutter and the wild range hog.

With his little chain saw, club-of-an-ax, beat-up truck, and empty beer can, the cedarhacker you see today is not the breed I speak of. The old-time cedarcutter was a woodsman. The ax was his tool and he was danged proud of it. When the $6' \times 4''$ post (the price corollary to all sizes and grades of post) had to be round, sound, and straight to be accepted and cut full $6\frac{1}{2}'$ long; measure $4''$ to $5''$ in diameter at the four-way cut top; butts rounded smooth; and all knots and limbs trimmed smooth with the body of the post — at the cedar yard, this post brought the cutter six cents less a twenty-percent brake fee and a forty-percent deduction of hauling charges. Yet, the old cedarcutter was able to cut enough of these posts to survive.

Here of late much has been written about the wire that fenced the West and brought new ranching methods to the world. Strands of old barbed wire have found their place in historical halls of fame, but nothing has been told of the cedar post which held these wires in place from Old Mexico to the Canadian border. And even less is known of the men who cut this timber. Paul Bunyan brought glory to the lumberjacks; John Henry did the same for the early railroad construction gangs; Markham's "The Man with the Hoe" has bathed the peasant with alligator tears for more than fifty years; and our historians have even found a little niche for the bone pickers who cleaned the Great Plains of the last remains of the buffalo herds. But no one has championed the old cedarcutter, and he has not asked for it.

The innate spirit of independence possessed by this species of old-timers was illustrated at the Goodrich Ranch during the food-rationed days of World War ll.

A chopper with a surplus of kids and ration stamps had sold, at bonus prices, some sugar and other rationed items to this grizzled old loner when someone asked him why he did not go in and sign up for his own ration book. This person then went on to suggest that, at his age, he might also be eligible for some welfare funds.

The chopper's answer expressed all the old-time cedarcutter sentiments:

"Who I am, what I am, where I am, an' what I do is my business. All they want to do is get your name on a piece of paper — then actin' like they are tryin' to help you, they'll be tellin' you what to do. Nobody — nobody is gonna tell me what to do. All I got to do is die, an' I'll work to put that off awhile. An' when I get tired of that—it's still nobody's business but mine."

The last of the wild hogs hereabouts were down in Little Arkansas. Gay Harris can tell you some pretty good ones on this subject—once you get him started.

Twenty years ago, the real wild hogs could be found on the hills about Llano, and the woods there were full of range hogs to fill about any description. The wild hogs were of a more primitive breed than the old razorback and must have had their origin during the early days of the Longhorn cattle, for they had been in the area long enough to develop herd distinction of their own.

Over on Smoothing Iron, Goat and King mountains, there were droves of these hogs which were blue in color, often had wattles the size of your little finger on their necks, and many were mulefooted (bore uncloven hooves) on one or more feet. When working their range you had better be on a good horse or ready to take to the trees because these hogs would literally tear you to pieces on the slightest provocation.

Of the four-footed animals that trod the sod, I grudgingly admire most the old black-spotted, sandy-colored loner range sow. Though her ears may be laced in marks of swallow forks, half-crops, under-bits, over-bits, under half-crops, over half-crops and slits to identify their owner, she looked to man for trouble only and tried to stay tohelloutofsight. About all you ever saw of her was a glimpse of her rear as she made it for tall timber in a high-ended gallop, with tail a-spinning like a lopsided windmill facing a norther. Corner one of them and you fully understood the meaning of the local idiom: "to come out like a bitin' sow."

Creek bottoms were her usual home, but during persimmon season she would take to the hills like a ridge-running coon. And through the heat of summer, she would try to beat the coons to the fish and all edibles in the drying water holes. Come fall, she would get fat and lazy on pecans and acorns and might join a herd.

The spring season was her most trying time, for then there was little to eat other than the tender new plants. On such a diet, she grew weed-gutted till her belly nearly dragged the ground, but she looked to man for no handouts except those she could steal.

Range hogs were adaptable, though, for soon after Lake Buchanan had filled for the first time, an old spotted sow on the Maxwell Slough was living pretty high by robbing the camps of unsuspecting fishermen.

The first time I saw her, she was headed for the brush carrying a loaf of bread in her mouth and my camp was in a shambles.

The last time I saw her, she and her shoat-sized litter were headed for the brush — each one carrying a catfish in its mouth. By some means, she had gotten my string of fish which had been staked some distance from the shore in four feet of water.

From *The Wimberley Mill*
October 1966

Deer Roping

Orien Rogers was a helluva good judge of horse flesh and one of the few who had a way with horses. There couldn't be much wrong in a man like that — even if he was my brother-in-law.

Blaze was the quarter-horse type: brown filly with a wide blaze running down her forehead from above the eyes to the tip of her nose, stocking footed on the right rear, black flowing mane and tail, no blemishes, beautiful to look at, and the last real cow pony raised on the old home place. Orien was a plumb fool about her, and she was worth every bit of it.

One morning Orien was riding the pasture looking for wormies when he noticed a deer, a big buck, standing in the edge of a wide glade near Cedar Holler. The buck had a little case of worms behind an ear and was concerned only with fighting at a fly that was deviling him. On the spur of the moment Orien decided to give Blaze a little workout by doctoring that old buck.

Putting the spurs to Blaze, he had his loop on the startled buck before he had cleared the glade. Nice beginnng. Wheeling around, the buck took off across the glade full blast. Hunched on her hind feet, Blaze was ready and busted him good when he found the end of the rope.

But this buck was a salty old cuss. On regaining his feet, he turned, bristled every hair on his back like a bad dog, and charged. Sidestepping him easily, Blaze busted him again. The performance was repeated for the third time, with the buck stopping short of being busted to make his stand fighting at the rope.

Fearing the possibility of Blaze getting boogered up took the fun out of the game for Orien. Pulling over to an elm he quit the saddle, dallied the buck up, and snubbed him to the tree. After it had calmed down, Orien doctored the worms and eased the rope

off him. The buck continued to stand sullen with its head pressed against the elm as Orien walked away.

Fortunately, there was a large live oak — one with low hanging limbs, easy to climb — growing nearby, for the buck came to life in a flash and put Orien up this oak, fanning his shirttail with a horn till he was out of reach.

For a while it was cat and mouse. Each time he thought it was safe Orien would start down the tree, only to bring an angry buck out of the brush in a rush shaking its head. After sitting very quietly for a period that seemed to last hours, Orien was able to leave his perch.

Bill Wilbern lived across the hills on the Little Llano. His back pasture lay on the north side of the Zula Everett. We usually saw one another in town on Saturdays.

One Saturday he showed up looking like his horse had dumped him head first into a pile of dry brush then ran over him. I would not ask any questions, but I would guess that he took all the pains to spill all the beans just to get that silly grin off my face.

"Got me a buck, or maybe it would be more like it if I turned that around . . . a buck got me," he says.

"Lately, every morning, when I rode up to the gate at the back pasture, there would be a big buck standing out there in that big flat some place. He'd just stand looking at me till I got the gate open, then he'd run down that flat and jump the fence into the Everett. Every time, he'd run to the same place to jump the fence. Must be laying up in those cedars. Plenty of them in there.

"This had been going on for about a month. Always jumps the fence at the same place. Sometimes there's a doe or two with him. They just fade back into the brush on my place, but that old buck always makes it for the Everett.

"Riding in one evening I decided to break him of the habit. Fixed the gate to open without leaving the saddle. I was ready.

"Next morning the old buck was at the far end of the flat. Eased through the gate — waited till he made his move — jumped my old pony out for the middle of that flat. Not a bit of trouble in putting my loop on him 'cause that old buck closed the gap without changing his course an inch.

"Next thing I know he's up in the saddle with me, flailing hell out of me. Then he's down running across the flat, jumps the fence into Everett, dragging my rope behind him.

"Told ole Crockett about it. He's always riding the Everett. Said for him to be on the watch for that deer 'cause I'd shore like to have my rope back.

"You know, Crockett looked me over, then he said he'd be on the lookout all right and if he found that deer and it was dead he would bring me my rope. But if he found that buck while it was still alive, he'd just send me the word and I could come over and get my rope myself."

The incident revealed nothing new. The person and time involved may have determined that I value it as a sentimental memory.

Rancher, cowman, and cattle broker, the late Damon Smith was a man I am proud to have known as a friend. He was one of the old-timers who had the knack of saying or doing the right thing at the right time. During the gloomy days of World War II, when the Battle of the Bulge had put the final chill on the Christmas season, Damon placed a candle and lay the opened family Bible on a red velvet tapestry in the window of his office.

The bold print could be read from the walk: "And the angel said unto them, Fear not; for, behold, I bring you good tidings of great joy, which shall be to all people."

I know of no better place to seek the true spirit of Christmas or begin the season of good cheer.

From *The Wimberley Mill*
December 1971

Table Meat

In the days of dirt roads and getting your mail at the post office in the general store, it was sop gravy on cornbread most of the time, biscuits on Sundays, and hardtimes all the time.

Using salt pork, fresh onions, sweet milk, and lots of black pepper, my Grannie Lawrence could make the tastiest white gravy in the hills. She had plenty of practice, for making good gravy was the culinary art of hard times. Sometimes there was only hog lard for starters; bacon's gone. And now we remember them as the good ole days.

Fresh beef seldom reached many tables back in the hills, even in winter. During summer, the flow was nil. Most communities were too small to support much of a general store and meat markets, or butcher shops, were confined to towns of some size.

71

Everybody had some sort of cattle, and that may well have been the source of some of the troubles. Beef clubs were organized whereby each member, by rotation, would furnish a beef to be butchered periodically and shared with all club members. Sounded good, but usually ended in squabbles.

"Mine was a prime Hereford steer an' what did I get back? A bunch of Jersey neck and some flank with more hair left on it than went with the hide." That's the way some told it. And hard feelings lingered among neighbors long after the club had been forgotten.

While I was a kid visiting kinfolks around Wimberley, I felt pretty big when I helped bring in a mess of squirrels. Squirrels were table meat then. Anybody could fry a young squirrel to a brown crispy delight, but it took folks like Aunt Susie Pyland or Aunt Ethel Schneider or Rhoda Cowan to turn the old ones into a bowl of stew or pot of dumplings or pan of dressing for Mr. Anybody. And my mother was no slouch in cooking your squirrels any way you wanted them.

In 1937, Texas Hi-way 29 was a paved road from the state maintenance shed down the hill to Ford Street in the city of Llano. And that was the only mile of hard-surfaced road in the county.

Local politicos had it that the hi-way engineers down at Austin didn't know there was a county as well as a town named Llano printed on most Texas maps and left it off theirs. Could be. From the county line it was sand, granite, gravel, rocks, sharp turns, twists, concrete slab creek crossings, few culverts, and rickety bridges all the way. And those rub-board county roads were doozies too.

(Today's exodus from the cities would have zeroed in on Old Llano County to get away from it all — far away. Then each new immigrant would have set up his howl for immediate delivery of all city facilities to his front door before the paint had begun to dry on his fine home. "And don't you dare try raising your taxes on me. I'll never stand for such. Why do you think I came out here?")

The squirrels were working the first rows nearest the back fence in the corn patches along the creeks around Lone Grove when I got there. And I got with it. Sort of, at first.

Squirrel hunting in my corner of Llano County was not a rerun of the old days in Wimberley, even after the edges of being an outsider had worn down some. There were no miles and miles of big cypress trees and pecan bottoms as those of the Blanco River and Cypress Creek. The floods of '35 had left the Llano River a treeless

72

waste of driftsand and granite boulders, and the timber along the Colorado had been cleared for the Buchanan Lake basin.

Jess Carter had a pretty good little pecan bottom on the Little Llano River. Pretty good squirrel hunting in the fall and still better on the years he had seen fit to farm his fields. Most of his trees were budded, and I usually found a welcome.

One July evening Iolene and I took a notion to go over to Jess's to kill a squirrel or two and fry them for supper on the banks of the Little Llano. Jess was on the porch and hoped us luck — ladies were always welcomed at Jess Carter's, provided they stayed in the car until he knew they were about, kept their distance, and didn't try to peep into his house.

After making a little round without any luck, we decided to call it quits and head for home. On hearing this news, Jess tells us to just sit tight a minute or so and quits the porch with his .22 in hand. After awhile and a shot or two or three, here comes Jess carrying a couple of frying-size chickens by their legs, still a-flopping.

"Here," he says. "Now you all go on back down yonder an' have your fry."

I didn't insist he join us, for old loners make their own decisions and no good will ever came from prying on their shell.

A lot of water has passed under the bridge before this day.

Hunting the creeks and hollows in the post oaks and cedars north of Lone Grove was more like hunting with Logan Roberts in Sink Creek Hollow or Purgatory Creek. To get many squirrels, you needed a couple of good dogs like this old Streeter and Jack and my Shep.

My first Llano dog was a bob-tailed fox terrier named Bruno. I gave Bruno his name, and that was about the limit of our relations. He hadn't run around the house twice before he had decided he was my mother-in-law's dog and never strayed far from her heels. Their friendship left no room for squirrel hunting with me.

Will Templeton had a good squirrel dog, but there were always enough Templetons around to keep him busy. Birke had two and Leroy was always gone with them. Elbert Moor solved the problem. He leased the Everett and had a couple of curs that were pretty good squirrel dogs and better at varmint hunting.

From *The Hays County Citizen*
August 27, 1977

73

Cedarcutters and Hounddog Men

I never knew a Texas cedarcutter who wouldn't recommend himself pretty highly, or saw a hounddog man who wouldn't brag on his dogs, or found a horse trader I could outtalk or catch in a lie. Everytime I thought I had one of them hemmed-in on something a little hard to swallow, he would explain things in a way which would make me feel plum sorry for doubting his word in the first place. Guess they've got a way of seeing their facts in a different light than most folks.

One time a horse trader palmed off an old mare on me, and to this day I have yet to figure out how he did it. All he really did was guarantee the old mare to be worth more money than she actually looked like she was worth. My mother-in-law was a fair judge of horse flesh, and with one look at this mare she said, "Poor old thing — not worth two cents in Mexican money." Then, looking straight at me, she added, "When the word gets around, you are goin' to be the laughing stock in this end of the county for some time to come."

Sure enough, next day my brother-in-law shows up with a gloatin' grin on his face and starts in before he even gets close to my old mare. "Blind in one eye," he pronounced. "Be as gray as a rat when that brown shoe polish is washed out." Looking her in the mouth, he cheered me up a little more, "Pretty a job as ever I seen on cuttin' new cups in old teeth. Must'a used dentist tools."

He didn't waste any words on the firecut front foot or the fistula on her back, but began probing her left shoulder with his fingers. "Ah, here it is — had the sweeny, an' they put a hot dime in the shoulder muscle here to cure it. Feel."

Now I knew why that horse trader's guarantee was good; and for once my mother-in-law had let one get by her. My old mare was worth a good American dime, and had a lump in her shoulder to prove it!

Back when cedar posts were dirt cheap, the cedarcutter they called Honest John taught me another little lesson. Blowing about how he could handle an ax and cut forty dollars in cedar any day, he offered to bet me that he could go out into the middle of my pasture, chop down twenty dollars worth of post, and have them in the cedar yard before dinnertime, or I could keep the post he had cut. Figuring on getting some post cut for free, I called his bet.

I was in the cow pens the next morning when John and his wife went by with all nine of their kids in and on and all over his Model A sedan. By the time I had done the chores and saddled up, here comes that Ford back down the road, and it was a sight to see. Held by baling wire, a bundle of long post rode each front fender, with ends sticking out both sides of the car. The rear windows were crammed full of post. Racked on two posts extending from under the rear end and over the back bumper, more were piled to the top of the rear window. Occupying the front seat were two of John's three-foot-high kids — one was handling the steering wheel, the other was taking care of the gas, gearshift and brakes, and they were not wasting any time on the road.

Over in the pasture, I found John's tribe scattered like a bunch of Spanish goats in a peach orchard. Two of the biggest girls were spotting the best post timber and taking care of any underbrush in the way. Five or six licks from John's four-pound Kelly felled the tree, and by the time it hit the ground John's wife or one of the big boys was on it, trimming and cutting off the top. Then two of the little ones would grab the post by its end and go kiting it out to where the Ford was being loaded. Had there been a squirrel in a cedar tree that day, he would have gotten a ride to the cedar yard before he could quit the tree.

When John sees me, he says, "I'm choppin' 'em down an' puttin' 'em in the yard, ain't I?" And the next time I saw Honest John in town, he was a-blowin': "Cut more'n twenty dollars worth a cedar in less'n half a day — all by myself an' not half tryin'."

Always was a cur dog man myself. When I hear my dog bark I want it to be "here 'tis," and have him on a limb when I get there. Hound music is pretty all right, but it usually don't put any meat on the table. Got no truck with a pack of dogs who will yodel "yonder he goes" all night long and come in the next morning whining "he got away." Guess that's why me and one of my second cousins can't see eye-to-eye, for he's a hounddog man from way back when.

About forty years ago, I was sitting on the side of Joe Wimberley Hill when down the trail comes a jackrabbit, coasting along on three feet with one ear cocked down and looking back over his shoulder to see if he needs to shift over into four-footed full speed ahead. Then here comes my cousin's Walker foxhounds, a-burnin' the breeze an' makin' all kinds of tenor music. Carrying bass and bringing up the rear was his Kentucky-bred, black-and-tan imported coon-

hound. Hightailin' it off that hill, I jump this second cousin of mine about what I had just seen his fine fox hounds a-doin'. He looks down his nose at me and says, "You set right there in broad open daylight an' let that fox get by without seein' him, but you did see the smartest jackrabbit in these parts. That rabbit knows my dogs wouldn't bother him, an' he also knows while he's running along with my dogs there's not a fox or coyote in Texas that's goin' to bother him, either."

Ought to know better than to jump him because he had straightened me out about his hounds four or five years earlier. That time, he and I and my daddy were camped under the big pecan tree on the other side of Cypress Creek, just below old Dripping Springs crossing. This country was about all in cedar brakes then, and Phylos's place down the creek was the only house between there and Blue Hole.

About 9:00 the first night out we were busy setting throwlines along the creek, while over towards Joe's Hill my cousin's hounds were tuning up for a race. Then all of a sudden a couple of them dogs yelped like they had run onto a rattlesnake and everything got quiet. We stood listening, and here came them hounds a-bustin' the brush. They swam the creek and gathered around underfoot, whimpering like they were scared half to death. About that time a panther screamed over across the creek and we set out for camp in high.

Nearly every other step, somebody fell over a hound. The lantern went out too, but we made it to camp in nothing flat anyway. Daddy got his old shotgun out, and we built up a big fire and sat there with them durn hounds underfoot. Once in a while one of 'em would walk to the edge of the dark with his hair all bristled up and growl low-like, then come back and try to crawl into somebody's lap. Nothing else happened. Finally, I said to myself out loud, "If them hounds were any account, they'd be out there a-puttin' that cat up a tree."

Second Cousin snapped back, "Wasn't for these dogs bein' right here, that panther would of already been in here and tore this place all to pieces."

From *True West Magazine*
April 1972

Hog Droving

On one of my trips to visit with my folks in San Marcos, I stopped at Fischer's Store for a chat with Mr. Herman Fischer. Our acquaintance stemmed from the days when I rode in the hack with Grandpa Lawrence from Wayside to this store and returned with my pockets filled with Red Fox Beer caps bearing Reynard wearing coat and cap printed on each top.

On learning I then lived in Llano County, he told me of the time the Tows had passed through driving a herd (500 or 600) of mast-fat hogs from Tow Valley to the railroad in San Marcos. Spent the night camped at Fischer's, must have been in the 1890s.

Jim Tow was a boy when he walked this route. Spent one night at the springs beside the Devil's Backbone. But he, too, was hazy with details and I didn't take notes. Cool weather did favor them all the way.

After having his craft capsized in the middle of the river by hogs crowding to one side of his ferry boat, Uncle Horse Maxwell refused further transporting of hogs at the Bluffton Crossing of the Colorado.

This fact may have determined the Tows' choice of San Marcos as their railroad shipping point rather than Austin. In any event, the 125-plus-mile trek of a 600-head swine herd drovered by two boys with their dogs, one mounted horseman and led by one driver on a wagonload of corn and plunder, could be considered a pioneer odyssey. And it happened less than a hundred years ago.

Forty years ago these Texas hills were full of old men who rode pretty tall in the saddle during their day, but it was hell getting them to talk.

Weather had no favors for the hog drive Robert Lewis was on years later. The drive had passed Lone Grove and headed for Llano when troubles found them.

It was warm and the hogs were getting hot as they passed the Mrs. XXX place. On finding the moisture where the Mrs. had been watering her flowers in her front yard, the herd moved in one wave towards this house.

The best defenses the drovers could offer were overrun in a sweep as the herd pushed on to flatten the yard fence in mass formation. Spearheading in all directions, they entrenched themselves in wallows among the flower beds, under the house, and in all tree-shaded areas. There they lay in positions they would not yield for hours.

The Mrs. stormed from the house to beat hogs across their backs until her broom handle broke. A hog or two grunted and one flicked an ear as the only response she gained for her efforts.

Turning from the hogs to the drovers, she shook the remains of her weapon in each face as she blessed him to the depths of purgatory where they and all hogs in the county should remain until the day of the big freeze. Then she stormed back into the house.

All offers of cash compensation for damages were refused and answered with, "Don't you set a foot on my place again." Those drovers, the hogs' owner, and those who found it a laughing matter when it's told down at the store — all of them should be thrown in jail and out of the church.

Nobody could keep a hot hog in the sun, but I side with the Mrs. in this case. Her hollyhocks, and zinnias, and marigolds, her cocks comb and morning glories were her pride and joy, and she had drawn water from the well all summer to keep them fresh, even the trumpet vine growing along the picket fence and arched over the gate.

I have always had a special feeling for old ladies who loved to grow flowers, no matter how fussy they be. They did bring beauty to many drab places and, once they were gone, it didn't take long for an old homestead to go to pot. A sad sight, indeed.

Addendum

The Davis Ranch was a working ranch dating from the days of the Longhorn. The original oak log cabin still stood, and Hiram lived in the ranch house when I got acquainted with the area.

The four walls of the vestibule to this old home place were covered with the finest collection of mounted deer heads to be seen outside the Buckhorn Saloon at San Antonio. Eighteen- to twenty-foot pointers — all taken on the big hunt the Davis boys had made on their return from World War I. To talk old times with one of these brothers was to gather Texana at the fountainhead.

On one of the rare good occasions when I found Hiram in the mood to sit and talk a bit, we were in the living room, when I took notice of a number of boxes of the old .22 special shells about and got this account.

No dates were mentioned, but it must have occurred during the twenties or thirties. The area involved lay from the eastern slopes of Cedar Mountain at Big Sandy and extended southward in a wide band towards Gold in Gillespie County.

In any event, the ranchers living in this area were of the old breed: raising hogs on their range was secondary only to cattle. Therefore, when deer first began to populate this area in an over-abundance, these men took notice of the damage done to their range.

Deer robbed the cattle of the forest green pickins in the spring or after each rain, and they kept the pastures clean of acorns and about all the basic edibles the range hog fed on. Only cockleburs and sunflowers grew in the field beside Big Sandy where Jerry Allred had grown near-waist-high oats in a strand so thick that when ripe for harvest, you could sail your hat out from any point and it would come to rest, laying atop the grain-laden heads without bending the stalks.

Taking matters into their own hands, these ranchers formed a block and set a date whereby each member would begin to systematically kill all deer on his property.

This plan had progressed to the point where the Davises had bought several slide-action .22 special pumps and a gross of shells for the job. Somewhere along the line, a member or two balked at the last moment, perhaps getting cold feet by theorizing how the state of Texas might look at the matter.

Anyway, the plan fell apart. And due to the strong pioneer spirit of keeping harmony among neighbors, the matter was soon relegated to the forgotten past.

And it may have been just as well. Because, with the invasion of white brush and mesquite into the area, post oaks are no longer the dominant species. Without their occasional heavy mast crops, raising range hogs has to be a poor business — literally and figuratively.

The ecological loss was not total. Mesquite and bee weed (white brush) provide the finest flavored honey to be had. And after each summer's rain of any consequence, the bee weed bursts forth in blossom to fill the air with fragrance — or had you noticed?

From The Hays County Citizen
September 24, 1977

Bragg's Cats

They are gone. Most of the cedars have been destroyed and the desolate, cleared land is now inhabited by a people and cattle whose lives are dependent upon food delivered to them in paper sacks.

In the old days the trees sheltered a much hardier breed. Uncle Ben Johnson and the Braggs lived as neighbors in these cedarbrake hills. A widower for many years, Uncle Ben usually had a string of cattle scattered from the head of Miller's Creek to the river and spent most of his time in the saddle. With a good team tried and true, Mr. Bragg farmed most of the land on his small place while his good wife did the other thousand and one chores which afforded them a comfortable home. Each found contentment with his lot in life.

One day Uncle Ben rode by just as Mr. Bragg was bringing his team from the field, headed to the house for his noon meal. As was the custom of the day, he insisted that Uncle Ben have dinner with him. After he had properly tended his team and Uncle Ben's mount stood in the shade cooling his back under a loose cinch, they made their way to the back porch of the house. There a fresh bucket of water with dipper in it, a tin wash basin, soap, and several clean towels awaited them on a table. By the dozen, in assorted color combinations and ranging in age from kittens to old toms, Mrs. Bragg's gentle housecats sat patiently on the steps and along the edge of the porch.

Stomping his boots and kicking, Uncle Ben waded in, slapping right and left with his old Stetson. Weighted with several pounds of sweat and grease, his hat served as an effective weapon to send cats a-sailing far out into the yard. After clearing the deck he washed with considerable ceremony, then threw the suds into the faces of a bunch of cats that had been bold enough to venture back to peep at him from the corner of the house.

Even on short notice, Mrs. Bragg's table did reflect the abundant wholesome goodness of simple foods during that grand era when the old wood-burning cookstove dominated the country kitchen. In addition to two meats with gravies there was potatoes, beans, squash, okra, garden fresh greens, onions, tomatoes, and peppers; cucumber pickles, pickled beets, pickled peaches and a relish; jam, jelly, preserves, and a honey pot; buttermilk, sweet milk and/or coffee; and a dewberry cobbler topped with sweet cream. Corn pone would have done for every day but, for company, brown biscuits were served hot from the oven.

Uncle Ben neglected none of the dishes set before him but did show a considerable favor for the large bowl which held a big pot of fresh firm butter. Each of his hot biscuits was sandwiched with a goodly sized slab of butter and was consumed before the golden nectar had time to do much melting.

Mrs. Bragg did not sit with the men. As they ate she scurried to and from the kitchen, keeping a constant supply of warm biscuits on the bread plate and seeing that all dishes remained bountifully filled. After Uncle Ben had complimented her cooking by disposing of a fair share of her biscuits and the dewberry cobbler had mellowed him further, Mrs. Bragg gathered enough courage to speak.

"Uncle Ben," she says, meekly fingering her apron. "How come you don't like cats?"

"Why, 'pon my word, Miss Annie," says Uncle Ben, "I does laks cats. I laks 'em wild."

Now you have no cause to doubt Uncle Ben's word. That is, if you are an observant person and have visited his home.

Because, as you approached the house, you would have gained a fleeting glimpse of Uncle Ben's cats as they hightailed it yonder for the tall timber. And you certainly would have noticed the three big scuttle holes cut in the bottom of his kitchen door. For when

Uncle Ben Johnson said "Scat," he meant S-C-A-T — and he wanted no dilly-dallying around hunting an exit.

From *The Wimberley Mill*
April 1971

The Rock Fence

The craft belonged to the old-timers. Built without the use of mortar, the old rock fence was held together by the thrust of the weight of each well-placed rock in its structure. Although there were many miles of such fences built on old surveys hereabouts, Gay Harris is the only person I know of who could build one from scratch or, for that matter, do a commendable job of repairing one of them. His old daddy taught Gay the craft while there remained a considerable open range north and west of Wimberley.

Back some years ago, W. T. Rogers expressed his sentiments on the matter. He and his son Orien had finished repairing the old rock fence that skirts the lower slope of Points Peak and stood looking at the results of their labors when the elder Rogers spoke, "We have lost something here. It will never be the same. The blamed goats have torn this old fence down an' we can't rightly put it back together again."

Today this old fence is all that remains of John Nimrod Scott's labors in taming the raw land he had come to settle during the 1850s. His orchards and fields are cow pastures now. The dug well is dry and filled with rubble. The cedar cribs and log barns have long since been reduced to fence post or kindling wood. Taking a host of pioneer treasure with it, fire destroyed the house — a home where tired, circuit-riding preachers were welcomed to spend a day or week or months before journeying on. It was the place where cattle buyers came to leave their money belts of gold and saddlebags of silver lying on the porch while they traded in the hills making up their trail herds of Longhorns. It was at that doorway where, a night during the Civil War, Old John stood, shotgun in hand, to defy renegades who tried to lure him into the darkness where he could be murdered as they had killed some of his more docile neighbors. All are gone. Yet, after these hundred years, sections of his old fence stand without change, except in the aging color of the rocks and having caught eroded soil to its height in low places.

Horse-high, bull-strong and pig-tight, the rock fence met all requirements in protecting the pioneers' crop land from livestock.

And where patience and perseverance prevailed, miles of these fences crossed hills and valleys to enclose range for grazing. This was the first truly successful fence to appear on our frontier in these hills. Down on the coastal prairies, the McCarty rose has turned acres of lowlands into thorny jungles to mark the only lasting results of the missionary *padres'* early efforts to grow hedgerows of this plant introduced from Formosa. The bois d'arc you have observed growing in motts along old fence rows on the blackland prairies or out on the plains are the only remains of early Anglo pioneers' efforts to divide the open range with hedges grown of this timber. In its many forms, the rail and picket fences well served the purposes of Eastern farmers and stockmen who raised their livestock by the inherent English methods of herdsmen. But in Texas, the cradle of American ranching methods, these fences found limited use on the western range. Here, these types of fence did yeoman services in enclosing cultivated lands and were developed into sturdy corrals for handling range cattle.

Barbed wire brought an end to the era of the old rock fence, but the introduction of angora goats to the area made them obsolete. By playing atop them, goats have ruined more old rock fences here than all the latter-day rock masons have destroyed in their search for suitable building stones to be used in modern structures. Tons of rock that the old-timers laboriously carted by oxen to fence sites have since been trucked to distant points in Texas, as can be attested by the Hughes tribe, from Great-uncle Nathan Emory to Cousin Curlo, and too many masons to mention.

Many boyhood memories center about these old fences; of twisting cottontails out of the fence where Tip and Chum had treed them; of killing a big rattler in a fence without the use of a gun at a time when most pople felt duty-bound to kill every rattlesnake they found; and of Mell Greene's not exactly face-to-face encounter with a civet cat as he tried to see what his dog had found in a fence on the Old Summie Allen place (he bawled, "I'm goin' blind!" and gave away his gun and other things useless to the blind while he was being led to the creek, where he promptly forgot the whole transaction as soon as the musk had been washed from his eyes).

Defamed as snake harbors, pack-rat nests, and polecat dens, the old rock fence remains a neglected landmark, lost in the hills.

From The Wimberley Mill
February 1969

Black-eyed Peas and Venison

Done my hunting back during hardtimes when the deer were wild and meat was scarce. Made those long, lean years on a steady diet of black-eyed peas and venison.

Any time I felt the need for some solid red meat, I'd hunt up a deer in good shape to eat and that was it. While I lived in the cedarbrake hills, getting a mess of fryers from the half-wild flock of Cornish game chickens that roost in the trees around my barn could be about as exciting a chore as killing and dressing an ole doe or velvet buck.

Usually I would let the ole gun hang above the fireplace mantel during the legal season and leave the buck hunting to the city dudes. Once in a while their eagers might rub off on me and I would make some half-hearted efforts at horn hunting. A couple of these are worth remembering.

There were always some pretty good bucks to be found on the Tow Ranch. One season I figured I needed some horns to show the dudes, or a better appraisal might be that I just wanted to join the clowns.

Jim and Sid Tow had planted the sixty-acre field across Falls Creek in oats that year, and the deer were grazing those oats most every evening. About 3:00 one evening I took my stand in a big post oak that grew in the corner of this old field. It was a good stand, for it afforded a full view of the field and the dense cedars from which the deer approached the fence to jump into the field. Also, the tree had a hollow trunk where I could spit my tobacco juice without advertising my location.

Wasn't long before a little yearling doe jumped the fence and began grazing about the field. Eagerly, I watched for more deer to join this little ole yearling. But she must have been the lonesomest deer in all Texas. After eating her fill, she spent the remainder of the evening wandering aimlessly about the empty field — all by herself.

Well, close to sunset she headed towards the post oak where I sat and began nibbling at the young winter grasses growing along the fence row. Finally, she was grazing beneath the limb where I sat. The devil got me; I spat a goodly gob of tobacco juice that landed squarely between the little doe's shoulder blades.

At first she twitched her tail, flinched the hide on her back a time or two, and continued to graze nervously. Perturbed with the

85

results of these vain efforts, she tried to reach the source of irritation with her nose and tongue. On finding herself unable to reach the spot with her first effort, she spread her legs wide apart and heaved her head about in a mighty effort. Success was hers. Just as the tongue found the tobacco, the eyes spotted me and off she went across the field bounding in ten-foot leaps—snorting and whistling each time a foot hit the ground.

Behind me in the cedars was pandemonium: a herd of deer broke brush with white tails flying in all directions.

No horns that day.

The late Lometa Yates's middle pasture consisted of some 2,000 acres of rolling hill country with oak and cedar motts growing on hill tops and along the creek bottoms. It was a natural environment where the deer were protected but neither pampered nor fed. Some real old mossheads roamed this range.

One December this country was gripped by a three-day blue norther. While the winds howled incessantly, Ole Man Winter could not make up his mind whether to give us freezing rain, sleet, or snow and settled the matter by intermediate delivery of small samples of each, thereby creating three days of Texas weather at its worst.

After two days of restlessness about the house, I decided to try for one of those mossheads. I could hang his rack over the barn door, for my wife didn't go for such trophies in her house.

Bundled in nearly all the clothes I possessed, I hied myself to the south fence of the middle pasture and set a zig-zag course northward into the wind, from brush mott to brush mott. In this bitter weather, with the wind whisking away your scent and drowning any small sounds you might make, it was a simple matter to creep undetected by the deer seeking shelter in these motts. Worn by weather and hunger, their senses were also dulled to some degree.

Cattle were huddled in the first long ravine, so I skirted it and headed for the hill tops. A herd of hungry cows following me was the last thing I needed that day.

Several does, some lying down while others stood humped in the cold, were found in the shelter of the lee side of these motts. After flushing them from cover, along with a couple of bucks that did not come up to my measure, I saw that I would have to start looking in the right place for the right buck or have the whole pasture alerted to my presence. Circling, I headed for the high peak near the big windmill.

A large mott covered the south slope of the hill. Entering from the south fringes, I eased toward a huge live oak which dominated the side of this peak. A dense growth of small cedars surrounded this oak. As I was about to enter the cedars — there he stood, humped and head down, ole Big Boy was caught napping. With neck swollen as big as a nailkeg and gaunted by the rutting season, he carried a rocking chair rack of horns. For a fleeting moment I studied the scars of battle on his neck and shoulders. Then he was gone, faded into a brush like a large fish disappears in deep water. Moments later, in a mad scramble, he broke brush on the opposite side of the mott.

Satisfied with myself and the hunt, I headed home. Come August, when ole Big Boy would be carrying a nice coat of white tallow, his meat would be marbled and bear no funky odors — that's another story.

Anyway, I never could figure out how you would go about cooking a set of horns anyhow.

From *The Wimberley Mill*
December 1975

Big Sandy

To the casual visitor's view, Big Sandy Creek is little more than a broad expanse of drift sand traced with a thin trickle of surface water and pocked with an occasional shallow frog pond along the way. And that trickle grows lean under the summer sun.

Big Sandy is a stream of no great consequence, except to those who know her.

From the far reaches of the Enchanted Rock, the course of Big Sandy arcs through the hills of Llano County, passes between the towering cliffs of Riley and Cedar mountains, then skirts the south slopes of Packsaddle Mountain to empty into Lake LBJ.

This watershed drains an area where old named ranches stem from the days of the Longhorn, a land where Indian lore lives on, and the Spanish Conquistador's quest for gold lies unrequited in the shrouded mist of the past.

The Llano boom of the 1890s brought the gold bug back to the banks of Big Sandy. In the vicinity of the old Birdtown Road crossing, a bargelike craft was launched upon the sands where it sat and sat and sat.

Mad professor and Rube Goldberg talents were incorporated in the production of this mechanical fiasco. Theoretically: by pumping the water-laden sands aboard at the bow a body of water would thereby be created to set the craft afloat and, as these sands were being processed for gold, the tailing sands were discharged at the stern where, as this fill grew, the craft would be pushed forward to new sands.

It didn't do so good. The tantalizing minute traces of flour gold held by Big Sandy remained beyond its reach.

Now don't you fret. One of these days, this flour gold will go glittering across computer screens to send the gold bug fluttering back to the banks of Big Sandy on a bit more sophisticated set of wings — you can bet on it. Got my stakes set at the old Jess Carter place on the Little Llano River between Baby Head and Lone Grove. Lots of the same kind of sand over there, and it's closer to the house.

The rusted remains of the old contraption were removed from the sands of Big Sandy during one of the early scrap metal drives of World War II.

After the war, the Texas Highway Department decided to do its bit in stimulating the economy by awarding the Hill Country with a direct route to Austin — State 71.

The engineers were busy staking out the west approaches to the proposed bridge across Big Sandy the day Sam Tate rode up and sat in the saddle studying the situation.

Finally he ventured, "I thought this was going to be an all-weather road."

"That it will be," said one of the engineers. "Data dating back to the 1880s has been researched and at no time has the floodwaters reached this level."

"In that case," said Sam as he turned in the saddle to point high into the tree tops to where a tangle of barbed wire and up-rooted cedar fence post hung among the uppermost branches of a big live oak, "I'd like for you to tell me how those post got up there."

And back to the drawing board. "Due to the steel shortage, construction of the bridge across Big Sandy Creek will be post-poned, blah, blah, blah — " was how they put it in the next week's issue of the *Llano News*.

With minor cuts and a whole bunch of fills, the bridge across Big Sandy extends from hilltop to hilltop. And if you happen to be headed towards Llano on 71, you can look down into the tree top of Sam's live oak as you approach the west end of this bridge. Two of the post were still hanging there twenty years ago.

Lake LBJ was still known as Granite Shoals when, during one of the spring flood seasons, the reaches of Big Sandy received one of those ole time water spouts. The bottom dropped out of the clouds.

At the Fowler Ranch a-top Riley Mountain, Hudson emptied the rain gauge three times before going to bed. Next morning it was full again.

According to the book, Granite Shoals is a constant-level lake. But during that night many of the new residents in the Kingsland area were awakened to find water lapping at their doorsteps. Their boats, docks, and small buildings along the shore were being floated from their moorings.

Damon Smith had a boathouse of sturdy construction. His boat was crushed through the ceiling.

In answer to all frantic calls, the night man at the Granite Shoals station assured everyone everything was in order. The flood gates had been set in accordance to the monitored flow from Buchanan via Inks and the floodwaters of the Llano River. No problem.

The culprit, Big Sandy, was considered too small to be moni-tored — an error corrected soon thereafter. Needless to say, more flood gates were thrown open the next morning before Granite Shoals returned to its 825-foot level. And there was fuss and feathers a-plenty for this incident. But the Lower Colorado River Authority has always been fortunate enough to have had a few good men of Orville Buttery and Warren Kuykendall's caliber on their board of directors, men who could soothe ruffled feathers or kick proper butts with equal ease and dispatch.

With her flow of sands and water Big Sandy was, indeed, the wayward daughter of our Texas weather, with some unpredictable whims and added marvels of her very own.

There were times when water holes were dug deep into her bed of sands and kept deep to prevent thirst-crazed cattle from getting their bellies filled with sand and gravel by drinking from shallow seeps. And with the chunk-floating rain it was time to seek high ground and come back later to assess damage, hunt cows, and patch water gaps.

With most seasons, the waters of Big Sandy teem with min-nows and some fish are to be found in the deeper holes. Through the lush seasons, big schools of minnows of many species inhabit the shoals and deep pools, and there is always some to ripple the shallows where their dorsal fins cut the water.

The most numerous and most interesting member of these spe-cies grows hardly as long as his zoological label when written in a lazy longhand: *Killifish genis cyprinodon.*

With layman's logic Pete Wooten, our Lone Grove minnow merchant of long standing, gave this species of minnow a more col-orful moniker, a name any fisherman could learn to appreciate: the rockroller, naturally.

Most minnows when dropped on a sandy shore will flounder about and lay gasping as they die. Not so with the rockroller. As soon as it hits the warm sand it goes into action. Wriggling and rolling about in the sands and rocks, it will flounce through the air in wide arcs and, with an astounding stamina, repeat this action until it reaches water or dies in the effort.

Most of the time it darts about or hovers in place, fanning the sandy bottom with its fins. But when the need arises or the urge strikes him, the rockroller can navigate the sandy creeks with the skills and determination of a salmon on its spawning run. Flat on its belly with its back above the water, this tough-skinned little cuss can root its way through wet sands, pushing gravel and rolling rocks aside, as it makes its way to deeper water and, after several

failures, with a sudden burst of lasting energy spurt up sheer falls where a mere trickle of water dribbles down the smooth walls of granite boulders.

You can't find a fish in Buchanan Lake or this end of Texas that will take a hook baited with the rockroller. So, when seining for minnows in Big Sandy, Pete leaves the rockrollers behind. No matter how grudgingly, you gotta show some respect for the rockroller. He's a survivor, this amazing, bander-bellied, jugheaded, black-spotted, copper-colored, magnificent little inhabitant of the shallow, sandy-bottomed creeks in the granite uplift on the Edwards Plateau.

As a spell of hot, dry weather lingers on, the waters of Big Sandy slowly recede into the sands, creating conditions to make the minnows and such fall easy prey to the cranes and probing paws of the coon. Their tracks along the muddy shoreline tell the tale.

And when the water stands low in shallow potholes, the old range sow will stop by to clear each of them of all forms of living matter. First she will eat most anything to catch her eye — and she's got a sharp eye. If it crawls or hops or swims it goes well with her weed salad. And an impudent roadrunner could please her palate or lose a whole bunch of his tailfeathers by messing around too close to the dinner table.

Then, with porcine grace, she will wallow the last bit of moisture into a brackish mire of mud before moving on. She, too, is a survivor, this incorrigible rebel to man's domestic effort.

Hunger is not the gentle shepherd when the creeks run low.

But with the first flow following a good rain, nature replenishes her stores and the minnows return to the reaches of Big Sandy with the rockrollers riding herd.

Llano County was known for its fine cattle, deer hunting, and good fences. These fences had to be horse-high, pig-tight and bull-strong to be considered good fences. Nine strands of barbed wire stretched fiddle-string tight, stapled to six $\frac{1}{2}'' \times 5''$ cedar posts set in 18-inch holes nine steps apart, with two $2''$ stays wired-in between each post. Or five barbs with $36''$ netting might do. No less.

But these good fences would end at corner post and anchor post, set points above the flood plain of Big Sandy. Below this flood line the fences were patched-up affairs or water-gaps of various and ingenious designs strung between anchor post set at either side of Big Sandy.

After each big rain, these fences and water-gaps were inspected for damage and any need for repairs. Good neighbors met at boundary line fences and water-gaps to make these repairs and, after some of the bigger floods, build a new one where Big Sandy had gathered up the old one and took it yonder. After these labors had been completed, it was time to count the cows and see to it that each was on its proper range.

Sometimes there was this neighbor who could always find an urgent business to call him to town or be confined to the house until all these repairs had been completed. He would be the first to holler about a missing cow and for somebody to "come get this stray off my property."

When Olan decided to build new fences on his share of the old Click Ranch, he set his corner post at Big Sandy several hundred feet up the slope of Riley Mountain from the point where the original corner post stood.

With the first big flood, Sandy cut new ground to snatch away Olan's corner post, leaving the fences to end in a snarl of broken barbed wire.

Olan could not believe his eyes: a select corner post of good heart-cedar, measuring eighteen inches near the top, set a full five feet in solid ground, braced and deadmaned each way to hold nine strands of new barbed wire taut, had vanished.

Big Sandy must have her whims. Across the way, on the Kothman Ranch, she outdid herself in her inexplicable manner.

Nearly fifty years ago, Forrest Ross built a new crossing on Big Sandy for his cedarcutters to travel while they worked the cedar brakes a-top Cedar Mountain.

Choosing a site where the banks on either side of Big Sandy were gentle slopes, he laid a ramp of flat rocks across the sands. As the weight of the cedarcutters' trucks pushed these rocks into the sand, new layers of rock were added until a stable slab of rock lay beneath the shallow water and a thin cover of drift sand. Floodwaters swept over this primitive effort, allowing it to remain intact for years to come.

Below this crossing Big Sandy flows in a long arc before reaching the rock-cragged walls of Cedar Mountain.

After one of the big floods, receding waters left the south bank of this arc lined with a vertical wall of white sand a mile long and ranging in height to ten feet.

Sage old range cows would walk around this chopped-off sandbar to make their way to water. A few possessed with less wisdom would wade across the sands to its brink, where they were unceremoniously delivered to the waters of Big Sandy in a heels-over-head landslide of sand. Some bones were broken, but most people were able to limp away, a bit wiser from the experience.

With the next flood Big Sandy whisked away this mile-long deposit of sand as if it had never existed. Old cow trails leading to water were the same again.

Big Sandy passes through some rugged country as it flows down its torturous course between Riley and Cedar mountains with the bygone villages of Oxford to the west and Click to the east, if you are one to remember such things.

Out towards Big Sandy they have their own way of saying things.

It is good cow country, some of the best, but dry weather can bring hard times to the cowman no matter where he lives. Prolonged drought brought disaster. It took raw courage and a dry sense of humor to endure some of those years.

As those long, dry days of the 1950 drought years hung on and on, everybody talked about the weather. Most of them living in those hills listened to WOAI radio for the morning news, hoping each day Henry Howell would end his report without having to use the same old weather forecast, "No change in the weather expected today." Henry, let it rain.

And the dry weather was the dominant subject for discussion at the Corner Drug Store in Llano, where the usual gathering of seasoned old ranchers and cowmen of sorts spent their mornings talking and swapping a few lies over endless cups of coffee.

One morning, after everybody had gotten in his say about the weather and the talk had worn thin, Lanham Wallis came up with this one to table the subject for the day.

"You know," he says, "last time we had a spell to dry things up like this, Ed Mansell planted a corn crop right down the middle of Big Sandy," and before an eyebrow could be raised, "brought me a good mess of roasting ears, the only ones I saw that year."

Well, there are times when you find it's pretty hard to swallow one but you never doubt a man's word in this cow country. This was one of those times.

Ed must have planted that corn during the night and worked it with honey child holding the lantern, because everybody knew how Ed and honey child spent all their daylight hours running the store at Oxford, Texas — population two, Ed and wife honey child (Lelia). Though business was usually slow, you could always find Ed at the store, sitting and waiting for someone to drop by to talk with, even if he had to do some of the listening.

Ed and honey child Mansell were one of those grand old couples of another era. Their store and Oxford have withered into the past. Only the cemetery remains.

Now, if you had spent much of your time a-hanging around the old Corner Drug, you would have known right off that Ed's corn patch in Big Sandy was planted the same year the Llano River ran dry. And the catfish got so use to dry weather, they were all drowned when it finally did begin to rain again. And all the river turtles had seed ticks on their backs.

Owned half-interest in an old Jersey milch cow and had a brand new cedar ax on hand at the time, so you might as well swaller this one too. Cow people don't lie. We just happen to see our facts a little different than most. Cedarcutters is another matter.

Epilogue

The old-timers said the first settlers to ride this way rode through a range covered with tall grasses to drag at their saddle stirrups and found the creeks to run clear, cool waters free of silt and drifting sands . . .

Sort of makes you wonder just when did Big Sandy Creek begin to gather her burden of sand and tear the trees from her banks —what are we doing to us?

September 1987

Epitaph for Lone Grove, Texas

They are gone. Gone or dying in the dust. Art, Teichville, The Chapel, Oxford, Click, Honey Creek, and Baby Head (this name should live as a grim reminder of the stark horror the Comanche raids dealt our pioneers), Purgatory Springs, Hays City, Cypress Mills, Naruna, and a host of small villages that were scattered across my Texas hills are gone.

Lands where children played, where families gathered to worship, and men performed their life's labors are now turned into cow pastures and empty fields, where needle grass waves in the sun. Buildings that once were homes, schools, churches, and post office-general stores have been reduced to scrap lumber or filled with hay and cottonseed cake to winter cattle on, or stand listlessly wasted in the winds of time. Most of the old folks have died and the young have moved on, and with them a way of life is gone.

No longer can I go to Templeton's General Store, where for thirty years I received my mail, bought canned goods and a cut of tobacco, kerosene for my lamp, an ax handle and file, or just sat and talked with old friends. They have closed this post office and another village is dead.

So, with my epitaph for Lone Grove, Texas, by Little Llano River, let us toll the bell for all lost villages of a bygone era.

The stagecoach line from Austin went to Burnet, across the Colorado River to Llano, and on to the Far West—a line that brought Lone Grove its first prominence as a community. Bugtussle (the original and real McCoy), located across the Little Llano on a hill beyond Dreary Hollow, was a close contender. But by being blessed with better facilities, Lone Grove was selected for a stage stop. Beside the stagecoach inn, a grist mill and cotton gin were erected to serve the needs of the pioneer farmers. Old Man Lockhart ran the blacksmith shop, and they named a granite hill "Lockhart Mountain" in his honor.

It was through the old ones that I knew this land. Hodge Nobles showed me the place in Behrns' pasture where beneath a post oak a nameless cowboy was buried "on the trail" with only a piece of white quartz to mark his grave. Aunt Dollie Rogers directed me to the location where the foundation stones are all that remain of the log cabin in which pioneer women were massacred by Indians while their men were away.

Scalped and left for dead, the sole survivor made her way to a neighbor's home, where she was greeted with more terror. As the occupants fled, the wife shouted: "You can stay in the house, but don't lay on the bed."

Pat Mayes told me of the mining boom, when eastern investors in search of gold spent a fortune at the Heath Mine to sink a shaft 600 feet in near solid granite, only to be flooded from the lower chambers. This Herculean effort produced but one finger-sized bar of gold bullion which no one could account for when operations ceased. During the Depression years, the shaft was filled with carcasses of cattle slaughtered by the government in a senseless effort to raise prices by reducing food surpluses in a nation of hungry people.

Granite dust finally claimed Punch Templeton, but not before he had told me much about the quarrying business. He once showed me a fist-sized lump of pure molybdenum which he had found in a huge piece of red granite that was being cut into jetty stones for Galveston Bay.

I was present when the wild hogs were driven from the range. The last old razor-tusked boar was killed in Fox Smith's field, and I am not proud of the feat. To whom do these hills most belong — this old self-sufficient boar, or today's corn-fed deer, cows that won't defend their calves and goats that stand to freeze in the rain?

Cedar post sold to bootleg truckers who peddled their wares across the west and north to the Canadian border — this was the last business to give my village a new lease on life.

Every dog has his day. With the war boom, the 6' × 4" top posts at eighteen cents and 8' × 4" top corral poles at twenty-five cents paid at the yard — and the cedarwhacker ate high on the hog. He moved into the sore-necked farmers' vacant houses, ate the biggest steaks, drank the most beer, and made more down payments on second-hand cars than anyone from that neck of the woods ever.

Too soon, the timber was gone. Paved roads invited trade to towns now only minutes away, and REA was not enough incentive to keep the young on the land.

It is gone — the Lone Grove I knew.

From *The Wimberley Mill*
January 1968

Part II:

San Marcos

Hayburners

The Old Gray Mare she ain't what she used to be,
Ain't what she used to be, ain't what she used to be,
The Old Gray Mare she ain't what she used to be
Many long years ago.

So goes the ditty of "The Old Gray Mare," the national anthem of old Southwest—from normal school to teacher's college. Though the Aggies stole her thunder, a rousing rendition of "The Old Gray Mare" was the original twelfth man on a football team—the Bobcats, no less.

With a student body numbering about 800, R. A. Tampke augmented the Bobcat Band with local talent: Herbert Finney, postman, tuba; Leslie Cooper, baker, baritone horn; Claude Brown, granite mason, trombone. So, "The Old Gray Mare" was always well groomed to open the collegiate football season at San Marcos in those days of yore.

The song was appropriately tuned to the era. Though there was a horse trough on the south side of the courthouse and hitching rails about the square, this period did mark Dobbins's finale as the last stragglers of his breed faded from the streets of San Marcos into the shadows of the past.

With the assistance of Eddie Serur, Houston Ellis, Nolan Bragg, George Martindale, Gene Posey, Tula Wyatt, John Lundy and others, we attempt to give a perspective of their era.

Friday Ellis

For what it's worth, I'd like to dedicate this article to my old friend Friday Ellis. Jockey, bronc buster, cowboy, muleskinner, dragman, and rodeo performer—Friday has done them all. During his life, Friday made a hand about anyplace the horse or mule was used in the Old San Marcos scene.

Horsemen

There were some old horsemen—the last of their breed—who, while attending affairs of their own, never traded their seat in the saddle for one in an automobile. Any time you saw one of them in an automobile, they were traveling as guest as a matter of convenience for the occasion. Sam Kone was such a man. He rode an iron gray gelding, sat straight in the saddle, his big white Stetson flat-brimmed, handlebar mustache, coat with heavy gold watch chain across the vest, and boot tops inside the trousers — Old South Texas style. Ironically, he owned the Gulf filling station across the street from the Palace Theater.

Will Donalson rode in from Westover on a big bay, which he tied near the horse trough on the south side of the courthouse. Will had been an oilfield contractor and road builder, but as horses and mules were replaced with trucks and tractors, he turned rancher. He sat in the saddle western style.

Each Sunday morning, Tom McCarty, dressed in his Sunday attire, rode a little blaze-faced, stocking-footed sorrel down Hopkins Street on his way to church. As the sorrel single-footed along, Tom often sat easy in the saddle reading the Bible.

Near the intersection of Blanco Street and the Wimberley Road, Bob Hill ran a general store and bred Walker hounds. He kept a bay and a gray to ride to the hounds with. The city limits only a block away, Bob would often loose a hundred hounds and head for a wolf chase on Crawford's Prairie. He and his companions carried hammers, pliers, and a supply of staples with them for, as was the custom of the day, they would lower the wires of a fence to allow their mounts to cross into another pasture when there was not a gate handy. After the horses had passed they repaired the fence before moving on with the chase.

Bob also kept a buggy, which he put to use when his wife wished to go anyplace.

From an earlier era, Mr. DeLouch added color to local horsemanship. Each Saturday he would ride into town to wet his whistle at the saloon on South Austin Street near the M.K.&T. depot.

Towards evening, when the city marshal came nosing around, the race was on. Out the back and into the saddle, DeLouch headed for Westover and the city limits, cussing, spurring, and whipping his old pony with his hat for all he was worth. On crossing that fatal line, he'd wheel his pony to wave a bon farewell to the marshal before ambling on towards home at an easy pace.

Sometimes, due to a delayed start or mishap along the way, the marshal would spoil the ritual by overtaking his victim, gathering the reins from his hands to lead the pony back towards the pokey with a very dejected Mr. DeLouch slumped in the saddle.

Well, you can't win 'em all, but you can't blame a feller for tryin'. Mr. DeLouch was just born before his time. Today he could have stymied the law with everything from charges of police brutality to attempted horse theft and got his picture in the papers with him pointing his finger at the damage suffered by his hat.

While attending training school, Vernon Biggs rode a donkey which he parked beneath a spreading oak that stood in the area now covered by the north wing of the science building at Southwest Texas State.

I often wondered who was bored the most, the donkey waiting all day under the tree or Vernon having to ride it back and forth to school. Guess I wondered too much about the matter. Vernon got his doctorate while I was still sitting at the back of the class getting ready to become a first-class cedarcutter.

Horse Trade

Horse-trading was often a test of wit as a contest in the fine art of judging horse flesh.

Virgil Cowan and Vaughn Scott were local horse traders who, while practicing their trade, often did a little swapping with one another.

One day Vaughn stopped Virgil on the street with, "Say there, Virg, you lied to me about that pony you traded me the other day."

"That I did," says Virgil, "an' you're going to tell quite a few lies yourself before you get rid of him."

Drayman

Bob Johnson was the best known among the last of the town's draymen. His usual stand was at the southeast corner of the square beside Serur's Mercantile. With Dan and Nellie in harness, his wagon stood in Austin Street as Bob waited for customers to come his way. As time rolled on, fewer and fewer customers came. Bob finally had to close shop.

Mike Rutliff was also a drayman, but Bob Atkinson with a single horse spring wagon was the most colorful of the lot. With his stand down about E. B. Dobbins place, the mainstay of Bob's business was to meet the trains and haul the college students' trunks to their boardinghouses on The Hill at the going rate of two bits each. When a co-ed was unusually pretty, Bob would often forget to collect the fee. Bob finally betrayed his clan and bought a Model T truck.

Other Teamsters

Ben Green, now living in Redwood, was the last driver of the horse-drawn hearse for the A. B. Rogers Funeral Parlor. The matched team of dappled grays were sold to the ice company.

Ivey Smith made the deliveries for Southern Wholesale Grocery in a wagon until the chain stores wrote their finis.

Matched Percherons were used to pull the ice wagons about town. Three routes no less — Westend, the square, the college and academy hills. Tom Cowan, Ed Morris, and Jim Smith were the regular drivers, with John Lundy as relief man.

Professor H. A. Nelson's Holstein Dairy had the last milkwagon. A brown horse called Bell often pulled this spring wagon. But Alice, a speckled gray Percheron mare weighing in the neighborhood of 1,400 pounds, could trot the full route with ease.

With a boy to work each ride, Alice's pace gave just enough time to deliver the quart bottles to the door and pick up the empties. On collection days, Alice was allowed to walk. Gerhardt Schulle could add more to this account.

Buggy and Surrey

From out McCarty Lane way, Emma Wilson drove a buggy to town for years. That is, when she didn't take the notion to walk. She finally bought a car from Ed Dobbins and retired her black buggy horse. She was the only lady I knew who could wear an overcoat in July. After Miss Emma's death a small fortune in five-, ten- and twenty-dollar bills was found sewed between the linings of her old overcoat. There was no F.D.I.C. in her day, and this greenback was real money — certificates of deposit redeemable in gold coin at the Federal Reserve.

It would be my guess that Isaiah Bradley owned the last surrey used for practical purposes on the streets of San Marcos. Florence, his wife, took their children to school in this surrey and tended her affairs while Isaiah was busy training horses or cowboying for some rancher. Only a damn fool would consider a black cowboy to be a rare find on the old Texas scene, for they could be found about anyplace there were cows and horses.

While superintendent for the U.S. Fish Hatchery, Mark Riley kept a gray and a brown which he rode or worked to the buggy, according to his need. These horses and his milk cow were pastured on the Fish Hatchery grounds, since at that time it was enclosed with a cypress picket fence.

There were no horses or cows about these grounds after O.N. Baldwin accepted the helm of the Fish Hatchery.

Lawmen

Sam Perkins was our last city marshal to do his marshaling from the saddle. He was a horseman from the old gentry; no cowpen flavor to his dress or the way he sat in the saddle.

Today it is customary for county sheriffs to wear a white Stetson and high-heeled boots and own a saddle horse. Sort of props their ego. Bill Jackman was our last sheriff of the horse era to do his lawing from the saddle, and he didn't need props of any sort.

Too bad he isn't around today to drop his loop about the shoulders of our beligerent drunks. There would be no kicking or cussing or hell raising when Bill Jackman brought them in. That's for sure. Sheriff Jackman's prisoners had the choice of walking without resistance to the jail or being dragged along the way.

While Massey was the last pound man and cut quite a cowboy figure when riding his little paint pony, Willie's legal duties were to impound all stray horses, mules, jacks, cattle, or swine found within the city limits of San Marcos. In other words, should your milk cow get out, you would have to go to the pound and pay a dollar fee to get her back. And you might thank Willie for putting her there.

Bob Hyatt's milk calves always managed to make it to the thicket behind the academy before Willie could throw his loop; otherwise, they would have earned him more pound fees than their worth at the meat market.

Mules, Mules, Mules

While cotton was king, the prairie below San Marcos was the blackland home of cotton and mules. And it took some hefty mules to turn that soil, big Missouri type, fourteen to sixteen hands, and weighing twelve to fourteen hundred pounds.

When the crop had been laid by, men like Norman Martindale and Jim Lacy would gather all the mules on the farms in the area, leaving only one span to pull a wagon, and send them to pasture on the Parks and other ranches towards the Devil's Backbone. The mules would remain on grass until needed to break the land for a new crop.

Something like four or five hundred mules on the move was a sight to see. First there would be Jess Posey leading a gray mare that wore a bell about her neck. Following the mare would be mules, mules, and more mules strung out for a quarter of a mile, all jog trotting and swinging their heads, docile as sheep.

Bringing up the rear, George Martindale and John Posey were pushing any stragglers and warning motorists.

Their usual route, starting at the railroad, followed one of the streets east of Cedar Street, skirted the college, then up North Austin and across to the Wimberley Road, and latter streets then being county roads.

Sometimes the mules pastured in the Purgatory and Gary Springs country would take to the brush like wild Mustangs. When this happened, the services of some brush-popping cowhands, the likes of Isaiah Bradley, Hoochie and Friday Ellis, were called upon to corral these mules for their return trip to the farm.

The fall of King Cotton ended this mule pageantry.

College Mules

Along the latter part of the twenties or early thirties, Prexy Evans bought several spans of mules for the college, primarily to be used to build roads about The Hill and haul dirt about, creating some level spots on the slopes.

Prexy was an exemplary educator and an easy mark in the mule trade. Those mules were old enough to vote but, considering the caliber of drivers destined to handle their mules, the trade may not have been too bad. Had the mules been young and in their salty prime, it would have taken a seasoned muleskinner to put them through their paces and the fat would have been in the fire.

Sure as shooting, there would have been that day when one of these old muleskinners would have brought his wagon close by Old Main. Right there those mules would start to cut a caper and set the muleskinners to popping the ends of his reins with crack equaling that of a .30-.30 rifle while scorching the air with some good old mule cussing, and school would be out on The Hill for the remainder of the day. Of course, Miss Brogden would report the matter to the State Board of Regents and phone the governor.

According to Gene Posey, the county sold the last of their mules in 1937. And that about wrote the finis to mules being seen on the streets of San Marcos.

Craytons

Baylor Crayton or his brother Bruce owned the last span of hinnies I remember seeing in San Marcos. The hinny has the same kinfolks as the mule, differing only that its paternal parent is a horse and the maternal a jenny and more readily distinguished by always being a zebra dun.

Baylor and Jim continue to farm with a team over about Westover way and keep an old cow pony or two about the place. And like the Old Gray Mare, they too ain't what they used to be or, maybe, they just allowed Johnson grass to grow up among their crop in the corn patch so's to have a little extra hay on hand.

Trivia

While the old Austin Road was a highway, a low-water wooden bridge spanned the San Marcos River above the present Sewell Park. A short distance upstream from this bridge there was a ford for horse-drawn vehicles. Well into the thirties, this ford was used often enough to keep it free of any aquatic growth.

The hollow sound made by their hoofbeats while crossing this old bridge would often spook horses and mules, especially those from rural areas.

Many animals would shy at the approaches to the bridge and refuse to budge another inch. There I have witnessed a team of mules with tail tucked, ears layed back, and twisted in the harness as they were beaten into pussy-footing onto the bridge. Well onto the bridge, they broke into a wild runaway gallop that took the wagon kiting down the road with the driver fighting at the reins for dear life.

With hooves flailing the air, a buggy horse once fell in the harness and literally had to be dragged from the bridge to be quieted.

Teams such as the ice wagon horses or the college mules rumbled their wagons across this old bridge without a detectable change in pace. No trolls under the bridge for them.

Gypsies

Clear Springs Apartments now occupies the area once known as the gypsy campgrounds.

Traveling in vanlike covered wagons, bands of gypsies would camp beneath the huge willows on these grounds and an air of mysticism prevailed while the gypsies were in town.

One morning they would be there. No one seemed to be able to say when they arrived, why they were there, or where they had come from. They were just there and, at all hours, there was some activity about their campfires, where a constant odor of food being cooked filled the air.

During the daylight hours the men silently scattered to the four winds. In twos, threes, or small groups the women invaded the business section of town. At the door of any one a gypsy woman might appear. When this happened, it didn't take a Pinkerton detective to spot another one or two lurking in the vicinity.

The only work credited to a gypsy man was to have groomed his horses and plaited the manes, which was quite evidently a labor of love.

Days or weeks may have passed. Then one morning the gypsies were gone, leaving only cold ashes of their campfires to mark their departure. And the mysticism cooled too.

By evening tide, rumors were adrift. Mrs. Murphy's hens hadn't laid one egg and her milk cow had gone dry while those gypsies were around. Items ranging from an alarm clock in the bedroom, a tidy sum tucked between the pages of the family Bible, three fat shoats or a gaited mare on pasture were reported as missing. And old so-and-so says that big black stallion he bought from the gypsy, well, he broke the latch on his stall last night and can't be found anywhere.

But nary a soul could present one iota of hard evidence as proof positive the gypsies had been involved in any of these matters.

And this horse opera could go on and on—until somebody
hollers, "Aw, shud up."

From The Hays County Citizen
October 1, 1977

Aquarena's Miller

Editor's note: During the sixties C. W. Wimberley operated a
grist mill at San Marcos Aquarena Springs on the beautiful, crys-
tal clear San Marcos River. During that time, he wrote a book
and called it *Stone Milling and Whole Grain Cooking*. Professor Tom
W. Nichols of Southwest Texas State College in San Marcos wrote,
in his portion about the author, "Truly, as J. Frank Dobie once
said about the author, 'C. W. Wimberley belongs.' His family
name connotes a whole region of pioneer folk where as Dobie
says, 'the town and the land far out from it are still marked by
the earth and the original settlers.'" By way of dedication of his
book, C. W. wrote a short story:

They Came

Where the coastal prairie and hill country meet, nature has
created a natural attraction for men at the San Marcos Springs.
Texas history has marched through these gardens. Following the
buffalo, the Indians found campgrounds here where the squaws
raised a crop of corn while the braves hunted. The *padres* established their mission on the first slope of the hills, but Spanish travel
was held to the Camino Real on the prairie because the Comanches
continued to hold the hills. After passing through this area in August
of 1821, Stephen F. Austin described it in his journal as the most
beautiful he had seen and recommended that the waters of the San
Marcos River needed to be harnessed for mill power and irrigation.
During the period of Anglo expansion, Gen. Edward Burleson and
Col. Jack Hays (for whom Hays County was named) made the area
safe for the settlers who gathered at the mill. While San Marcos
grew from a frontier village into a city of schools, men from all
walks of life trod the shores of Spring Lake. But it was a native
son, A. B. Rogers, whose dream it was to make the place a traveler's mecca, where the many wonders of nature are preserved and
the historical settings perpetuated. Through the efforts of his son,

Paul J. Rogers, the dream has been fulfilled at Aquarena, where it continues to grow. For this reason I deem it appropriate to dedicate this account to those old friends of cornbread land.

The Mill at Aquarena

"If you get the wax in your hair, you'll never get it out." So goes the old saw of the cedarchopper's trade. Some people I know seem to have the same trouble with mill dust. To be satisfied they need a little corn meal in their hair. My dad is seventy-five and living in retirement, but in his back yard there is a shed with a little grist mill inside it. When the mood strikes him he will fire up the mill and grind off a batch of corn meal for himself or to share with some old friend. Uncle Hick, in his eighties, comes over from time to time, just to sit and watch the danged thing run.

For my part, I blame this state of affairs on the old-time meal sack. When Dad was a boy, the mill room wall was often lined three deep with meal sacks filled with corn awaiting their turn at the mill. Many of them were freshly washed and spotlessly clean, while some bore sweat marks from the horse's back, and others had been used as cushions on wagon trips to town. Dad said then, "If I ever get married, one of the women with a clean meal sack is raising the girl." My Grandma Lawrence always washed her meal sack and dried it in the sun before it made a trip to the mill.

A fourth-generation miller and the last of the tribe with meal in his hair, I have taken a stand beside the trail which used to lead from General Burleson's house to his mill. Up the trail apiece are the mission ruins which mark the outer reaches of the Spanish *padres'* efforts to civilize the Indians of this area. Down the hill a bit, the clear springs of the San Marcos River flow.

The beauty of this location has always captured the traveler's attention. Trooper H. H. McConnell, 6th U.S. Cavalry, rode this way after The War and described the scene as it appeared near one hundred years ago.

> One evening we camped on the San Marcos River — one of the most beautiful streams in Texas. At the point where we crossed, it was perhaps ten yards wide and two or three feet deep, as clear as crystal and cold as if drawn from a shaded well, although the vertical rays of the July sun shone on it. The latter was a surprise to us, until we learned that the source of the stream was only a

hundred yards distance on the mountain side. In the cool of the evening I strolled out to see the springs from whence it flowed, and found, when high on the hillside, thousands of them at least, forming a good size pond, overhung by gigantic trees, whose thick foliage eluded the sunlight. From the pond the San Marcos emerged a full-fledged and mature river without going through the intermediate stages of rivulet or brook.

Now at the depths of Spring Lake, these springs continue to fascinate travelers who view them from Aquarena's glass-bottomed boat ride.

Birds and squirrels find a natural habitat around the millhouse where they share some of the corn. Beside the millhouse, clear, cold spring water turns an overshot water-wheel made of cypress timber. Native ferns and vines grow beside the millrace to cover the traditional pile of worn mill parts stored there. Relics of the trade are displayed nearby. The grist mill with twenty-eight-inch French buhrstones is operational and of the same model used by my great-grandfather. But the meal bin is not located at the chute beside the mill where Grandpa sacked the meal with a dipper-board. Here, the meal is carried by a conveyor belt to a single-screened corn meal bolt that serves as a sifting unit. One might consider this unit the acme of Yankee salesmanship, because it was sold in the frugal days after the Civil War. Though it served its purpose well, this contraption is an example of an early-day mechanical device that was designed to do a simple task by employing the most complicated and elaborate means possible. Except for the chairs, which belong to my Grandma Lawrence, and my good wife behind the counter, this mill could duplicate the operation at the old Wimberley site. Meal bin, toll box, iron power shafts, laminate wheels, homemade idler, wooden-shoed clutch, pulleys and belts used to deliver power in the mill room are all authentic down to babbitt bearings and grease cups.

A modern vacuum cleaner collects dust which the old feather duster used to scatter, but in most procedures there has been little change. J. A. Woods's name is listed with my toll customers, just as his father and grandfather have their names in the old Wimberley Mill ledger from 1880 to 1890. And the other day Jessie Foster of Seven Sisters made a hurried 200-mile trip to this mill. His aged mother craved some real hot-water cornbread for supper and wanted to use meal made from new corn she had prepared for milling out of the "left over" corn gathered in her roasting ear patch.

For those who have no corn to be custom ground, the mill carries a fresh stock of old-fashioned whole-grain meals of its own grind; white corn meal made of white sure-cropper corn; yellow corn meal made of yellow dent; and whole wheat flour made of recleaned miller's wheat, where the meals have been sifted (only) and the flour is the unbolted product. At this date Harper's Seed Farms of Martindale, Texas, raises the two favorite strains of "meal corn," and, with their modern plant and equipment, prepare the grain for mill. It is then stored and refrigerated until needed. In this way that fresh "new corn taste" in meal can be preserved the year around.

If you have no corn and need no meal, come visit the millhouse as a most welcome guest, just to look and talk. The mill is located in the Hanging Gardens at Aquarena. From the millhouse, you can see the swans as they glide about the beautiful waters of Spring Lake and the Treehouse offers you an excellent back-stage view of the Submarine Theatre activities.

Milling is MY job and people are fringe benefits of the trade. Wearing Homburgs, turbans, sombreros, snap-brims, crew-cuts, and military caps, they come to this mill from all lands. While sitting at the doorsteps here I have, by conversation, traveled across our nation and around the world in less than a day. Here, some of the past is kept alive and the miller's golden thumb, mentioned in Chaucer's *Canterbury Tales*, has survived the years. The meal is thumb-tested to set the grind, but the sack you buy with a label—one and one-half pounds—will tip the scales at two pounds net.

From *Stone Milling and Whole Grain Cooking*
By C. W. Wimberley
(Austin: Von Boeckmann-Jones Press, 1965)

A. B. Rogers's Horse Trade

Don't you go putting too much stock in local folklore, unless you are just looking for entertainment. By the time you have listened to an old tale being told for forty years from forty different directions, you don't have to be hell for smart to figure out that the storyteller is usually more concerned with coloring his version of the yarn than revealing the facts of the case. So, instead of telling this one "like I heared it," I'm going to do a little painting on my own.

Cotton reigned king on the blackland farms and cattle roamed in the hills when A. B. Rogers's furniture store first opened its doors at San Marcos. In those days a businessman had to be a pretty fair hand at horse-trading to stay in the saddle. Mr. A. B. prospered in an era where today's super salesman would have wilted in the first heat of the long race.

You might say that this episode began when a well-to-do cotton farmer's wife put the bee on her husband to buy their daughter a piano. It took a considerable time and effort from these ladies before they were able to dry-herd this tight-fisted ole cuss into the store for a look at the instrument of their choice. He didn't dally too good. One look and without asking the price, he asked Mr. A. B. to drop by his place next time he was out their way. Maybe, they could talk trade.

Days later Mr. A. B. was riding on the prairie in his buggy with his faithful handyman, Oscar, at the reins. Our cotton farmer just happened to be at home when they reached his place and he greeted them from the yard gate. The two sat on the gallery steps of the home to do their talk while Oscar sat in the buggy looking at his hands folded in his lap. Across the way towards the barns a big sorrel gelding stood tied to a hackberry sapling, switching his tail rather listlessly at an occasional fly. His hide glistened with all the luster a curry comb and brush could give horse hair and he bore all the bloom a good coat of fat could give an old horse.

Brushing aside the small talk about boll weevils and weather and cotton, the farmer got down to business.

"How much do you want for that piano my wife's been looking at in your store?" he asks.

"Seven hundred dollars is the price of that particular piece of merchandise. Now, I could show you another—"

"No, no, no," he injects, waving his hands as if to clear the air before he could continue. "That big sorrel you been looking at tied to the tree out there, I've been asking one hundred dollars for him. Tell you what I'll do. I'll give you him and six hundred dollars —cash for that piano. What you say?"

"Well," says Mr. A. B., measuring his words, "if you'll come in and get the piano in the morning, it's a deal. I'll send Oscar by to pick up the horse sometime tomorrow evening."

"Trade is made. I'll get you your money," the farmer states, and he has gone into the house and returned with the money before a protest could have been uttered.

On their way back to town, Oscar fretted with the reins and twisted in his seat until Mr. A. B. broke the silence.

"Out with it, what's bothering you, Oscar?"

"Ain't none of my bother. Bother's all yours. You the one what gives a hundred dollars for a tradin' hoss and don't bothers to take a close look at him first," moans Oscar.

"Couldn't afford to. Might have spoiled the trade."

"Mister Arthur, I's afraid you done 'forded more than you thinks you 'forded on that old hoss."

"Oscar, I would have taken the $600 if it had been a broom stick he had tied to that hackberry. So, what does it matter that the big sorrel is old and stone blind? Surely you are not complaining about leading a blind horse to town; or had you rather deliver a piano?"

"No, sir, Mister Arthur."

Silence prevailed as the buggy rolled on a mile or two before Mr. A. B. contributed the last bit of the conversation.

"You know I don't wish to be bothered with a blind horse, you said as much back there. Suppose you just take our trading hoss and do some trading on your own."

Years later, John E. Parks and A. B. Rogers were reminiscing about the things hound-men and horse people like to remember, when John got around to it.

"Arthur," he asks, in all manner of mock seriousness, "what ever became of that blind horse you and Oscar traded a piano for?"

"I'll never know," replies Mr. A. B. "He was still tied to that hackberry when last I laid eyes on him. I have never heard a word nor have I seen hide or hair of him since. About a week or ten days after the trade, Oscar came in and handed me a roll of bills. Sixty-five dollars, I believe it was. Anyway, when I asked him what it was for he said, 'Hit's your part from our hoss. Done spent mine.' He did not offer to say more and I damned well didn't care to ask."

"Can't blame you there," says Parks quite seriously. "In your shoes, I wouldn't want to know either. Might have been worse than one of those times when I took Po Baby and Bear Poindexter with us to make the races in Bartlett.

"Bear had religion at the time and couldn't gamble, so he gave his money to Po Baby and tells him which horse he thinks ought to win. Po Baby puts the money on another horse and danged if they didn't leave Bear's horse in the shade with Po Baby's horse coming in to win by three lengths at the finish.

"Bear saw it all and when Po Baby hunts him up to give him the money, Bear won't take a cent, then tries to give Po Baby a whipping for not doing as he had been told to do.

"That was one time when we all sure wished to hell I'd left both of them in San Marcos."

From The Hays County Citizen

Fish Hatchery Creek

Editor's note: The following is a letter to the editor of the *San Marcos Record* when Walter Buckner was its owner and publisher. The date is not shown.

Dear Walter:

Unaware of the fact that the creek in question bore a label, The Branch, we must now cede the issue. So, my faithful Sancho, pray abandon me to my fate and turn the noble Rozinante to pasture for, alas, I again find myself unhorsed while tilting at windmills on pre-empt soil.

To overcome the gnawing penchant for naming this particular geographical feature, a willful habit developed over a period of more than fifty years, I must lament the occasion with a swan song all my own.

During the period when Malcolm Fleming, Bill Stockton, and I with a rag-tag following of tow-heads built miniature dams along this creek, the main watercourse was referred to by us as Vogelsang Hollow, the branch extending to the adobe bridge on Walnut Street was known as Haynes Hollow and — at a later date — the branch beginning at the end of Peach Tree Street was given the name Windmill Schmidt Hollow. Until about A.D. 1930 the lower reaches of this watercourse was inhabited by prawn and numerous crawfish and this section of the creek where there exists a constant flow of water, afforded a choice of names, such as Fish Hatchery Creek, Prawn Branch, and Crawfish Holler.

During this prohibition era J. T. Yarrington and my brother, Stanley, discovered a bootlegger's cache of several dozen quart-size Mason fruit jars filled with moonshine hidden under the earth-filled bridge on North Austin Street—now LBJ. Parental authority aborted my efforts to re-name the creek Whiskey Hollow.

Then there were the days when such stalwarts as Jack Neal, R. S. Conner, Talmage Murry, Logan Roberts, Stanley Leffingwell, Fred Wills, Wayne Lewis, Joe Haynes, Edward Gary, the SWTTC freshman football squad of '32, and Sarita Lewis failed in the preliminaries while John Tom Dailey and I successfully suffered the rigors of learning to chew Days Work tobacco sitting on the banks of said watercourse near the site of the Old Evans Field. By the time we had become proficient enough at this manly art to spat in a housecat's eye at five paces, and ground a grasshopper in full flight, we contemplated upon re-naming this watercourse Tobacco Hollow but lost interest in the project on learning that Prof. H. M. Greene could, by removing his false teeth, consume a full cut of Brown's Mule in a single chaw, forming a quid which lasted him all day and a feat which eliminated our Olympic standing.

Later, as familiar old landmarks were being lost to man's endless destruction of the natural landscape, I found new interest in this watercourse. At one time there was a narrow ravine on the watershed of this creek which extended up the side of the College Hill, passing between the girl's gym and the power plant to head at an arched ledge of limestone in the shadows of Old Main. Several mortar holes in this ledge marked the millsite where Indians pounded their acorns and maize into meal. Coupled with the extensive campsites exposed during the excavating of the Fish Hatchery ponds seemed to justify the name Indian Creek.

While walling the river banks at Riverside Park (now Sewell Park) my father, Rufus Wimberley, discovered the remains of the waterwheel (a turbine type, hewn from black walnut) which powered Gen. Edward Burleson's gristmill—San Marcos's first, circa 1840. Based on his past experience in such matters, Dad surmised that the millrace which delivered water to this wheel must have begun its course at confluence of this creek and the river where the first dam on the San Marcos was erected—probably a low-water, makeshift affair constructed of logs, brush, and rocks. Hence, the name Millrace Creek.

In a less facetious vein and speaking for a host of old boys past fifty who caught their first fish and learned to swim in the cold clear waters of the San Marcos, I feel safe in saying that we need no new marker to remember Peter Vogelsang by; for he too loved this river as did the late Paul Rogers, Mark Riley, and my father. And that's good enough for me.

At this point I rest my case—provided some effort is forthcoming in placing a Historical Marker at the original site of the Burleson Mill. Tula Wyatt, Minnie Knispel, Al Lowman, do you hear?

Yours,
C. W. Wimberley

P.S. Thanks to Miss Irma Bruce's English translation of the German name Vogelsang—birdsong. I can now belatedly fully appreciate the logic expressed in each unit of the Vogelsang Lodges having been named for a species of song bird.

> **Editor's note:** A Texas State Historical Marker honoring the Burleson Mill was dedicated September 18, 1987, by the Hays County Historical Commission. The marker is located at the entrance of Peppers at the Falls Restaurant.

Whiteracers and Lizards

To sit quietly in a woodland nook till nature's little creatures resume their normal activities is one way you may get yourself involved in the dangdest mess you ever heard of—an old Indian saying I just thought up, especially for this occasion.

The first breath of crispness in the autumn air heralded many things to a kid some fifty years ago when the woods belonged to a boy and his dog. Squirrels had come down from the hills and quit bothering the nester's little corn patches to begin working on the pecans along the creek bottoms, and no school on Saturday afforded an early start for an all-day hunt.

So far, things had not gone too well for me on this particular Saturday morning. Since early morn I had sat beside the road at the creek crossing below the old Vogelsang field waiting for Logan Roberts and his dogs, Streeter and Jack, to show. It was getting hot as I sat slumped with my pump .22 across my lap, my back resting on the bar ditch and my barefeet sticking out into the caliche roadbed. Once in a while I would peep from under my straw hat to look across the creek up the road to the corner of the field where ole Streeter and Jack should show up first with Logan in tow. Each time, the white caliche roadbed held nothing more than the smooth twin paths made by the wheels of many sparse days of light traffic. Somewhere up the hillside a yellowhammer flicker drummed endlessly on a dead elm and a lost gust of wind rustled among the dry corn leaves in the field. I looked up to catch a scene that my mind refused to accept delivery from my eyes.

Traveling in tandem and in the cobra stance as always depicted in old posters advertising the cheap carnival's snake pit, two snakes swirled around the corner of the field with arced heads held some two feet in the air. But the cobra image faded from my mind as the two oversized whiteracers faltered to sway in the sun. Then, still holding their unusual stance, raced down the near wheelpath of the road towards where I sat transfixed.

Before the pair had traveled fifty feet I saw that they were chasing a striped-back lizard who was trying vainly to add more mileage to the distance he had gained on the corner. As the gap closed, the lead snake lowered his head to pick up his victim, but the lizard had other ideas. Quitting the road, he darted into the briars of dewberry vines growing along the field fence row.

Sliding to another halt the snakes again swayed in the sun, momentarily. Then one of them left the road to tread his way through the vines as the other moved slowly down the path — watching all the while. Teamed in this manner, they worked their way down the length of the berry patch as I sat intrigued.

At the dry creekbed the snakes flushed their quarry. Narrowly favored by the element of surprise, the lizard crossed the creek with one snake hot on his tail while the other cleared the dewberry vines.

In his race with death the lizard passed the shadow of one of my feet in the road only to wheel at the other and zip up the leg of my overalls. Impulsively grasping this leg of my overalls about the ankle with both hands in an inept effort to prevent an event that had already taken place, I inadvertently prevented disaster; that is, for the moment. On reaching the scene the first snake lowered his head and began probing my overalls leg with its nose, trying to follow the lizard's course. In the next instant the second snake slid to a halt, steadied his cobra stance to look me dead in the eye and sample the air with his tongue — inches from the tip of my nose.

Too much is too much. Grabbing my gun, I made a wild swing which sent it and an impudent whiteracer skittering far down the road in a tangled mass. Meanwhile, the other snake had disappeared — yep, up the leg of my overalls.

In an unprecedented display of acrobatics, my clothing was shed falling to the ground over a wide area. Dazed during this per-

117

formance, the whiteracer hung limp from the depths of the vacated overalls. Grabbing it by the nape of the neck, I flailed the road with it a couple of times then threw the dead carcass sailing end over end into the weeds.

Standing naked as a jaybird while trying to regain my composure, another thought struck home: where was that danged lizard? Hidden deep in the folds of my undershirt I found the little cuss playing possum. With eyes closed and limp in body, only a slight pulsation of the rib-cage exposed the act. Gathering him gently up I lay the little body in the sun beside the road — a tacit act of mercy stemmed from my Grannie Lawrence's great love for such creatures. She called toads and lizards her bug eaters and encouraged them to make their homes in her flower gardens. Years later one of them, old Rusty, would take food from her hand and lay sunning himself on the porch near her rocking chair in the twilight summers of her life.

After putting on my clothing and unraveling the lifeless body of the other whiteracer from my gun, I returned to the battleground to recover the .22 shells that had spilled from my pockets during the melee. Before I had finished this chore I noticed that the lizard lay where I had placed him — still playing possum.

By nudging him with my great toe I tried to stir some life into him. He came to life, all right. Zip — and again he zapped right up the leg of my overalls.

Not so gently the lizard was again removed from my clothing and, this time, tossed unceremoniously into the weeds in the same general direction of where the whiteracer lay. Also, the .22 shells were left where they lay scattered in the road, for I didn't choose to waste any more of my time at this place. Sometimes it's tough to be a lover of nature.

From *The Wimberley Mill*
November 1972

Gold Fever

Tales of hidden treasures and lost mines are legion and legend. During the lean years of the twenties and thirties they were a popular theme, and every old codger bold enough to predict Texas weather had his very own authentic version of a dozen or two of them. Though these accounts made more dubious use of historical fact than an

118

alley cat's pedigree, the faith in "Thar's gold in them thar hills" prevailed.

Of course, had you desired a tangible and more reliable reference on the matter, this could have been accomplished readily by crossing the Rio Grande to take a seat in any border town saloon where these desires were aired rather freely. Fluent Spanish or Tex-Mex was not a prerequisite to acquiring a priceless Spanish Treasure Map.

The penmanship and the quality of parchment used to produce your map usually reflected the number of pesos involved in the transaction and/or your capacity for absorbing tequila.

In any event, I was satisfied with the story of the fabled sixteen jackloads of Spanish gold buried in the hills of Texas. I was also satisfied that this treasure was buried at the trunk of a big live oak growing on the slope above the head of the San Marcos River where a Comanche had shot his arrows into the ground to mark the spot after the massacre of the Spaniards. And I was also satisfied to let it be.

But the location of the sixteen jackloads of gold was not my secret, and gold fever is a strange malady that affects normal people in most unusual ways.

A couple of our local worthies spent most of one winter digging holes at the base of all sizeable oaks growing on the hill above the San Marcos River. The most unusual facet of their venture was that they often broke through virgin layers of rock in their search for buried treasure.

On the west slope of this hill there is clay deposit beside a small draw. Persons unknown once dug two gravelike pits into this clay — one about six feet deep, the other about ten — to bedrock. Until a prolonged rainy season created mud slides to fill them, these pits were death traps to many unsuspecting armadillos.

While I was a youngster, this area was my old stomping grounds and the scene of some bizarre endeavors of gold fever victims. On one occasion, I discovered an old man dowsing for the jackloads of gold with a water witch's fork impregnated with quicksilver. He was quite certain of finding the gold, for he had more confidence in his witching fork than in a railroader's watch.

All the predecessors of the modern mineral detectors must have made their trial runs on this hill, for I have witnessed mineral rods of all descriptions being used to scan the contours of its slopes.

119

A bearded old man wearing an army overcoat had the most elaborate Rube Goldberg contraption of all. This machine, which he wore strapped to his chest, was about the size of an apple box. The top was covered with dials and assorted controls. Two long copper rods held in either hand were connected to the machine by extension cords. After adjusting the dials, he would tap these rods together, then proceed to scan the soil by probing the area with a knitting-needle action.

On discovering he was being watched, he would close the great coat about his machine and stand silently. Keeping my distance, I'd sit and look. Though handicapped by his coat he would sweat me out, and was never fooled by my ploy of a bold departure and sneaking back for another look.

In the fall of '37 I moved to Llano County and, before I got around to meeting all my wife's kinfolks, I learned that the elusive sixteen jackloads of gold had not made it to San Marcos — it had been buried somewhere in the northeast corner of Llano County.

Yeah, one of my brothers-in-law had his diggings near the springs at the head of Cedar Holler. Being a hounddog man, this brother-in-law of mine didn't devote much time to his diggings, and for about twenty years you would have thought he had abandoned the project.

Meanwhile, a pair of my Lone Grove neighbors, Frank Beal and Lee Hazelett, took up the chase, scouring the whole county and doing considerably more sighting for sites than digging. The only find they would divulge was two antique smoothing irons — tailor's model, near two feet long, heated by miniature built-in charcoal furnaces. The date these irons were cached in a mott near the top of Packsaddle Mountain remains speculative.

With the twenty years behind him, this brother-in-law of mine renewed his effort with vigor. After pulling up stakes on Cedar Holler, he set up shop in the Calvert pasture where, during a prolonged survey for promising dig sites, he discovered some sort of rare quartz which was going to make us all rich someday.

Another twenty years have passed and we are still waiting for that day.

From *True West Magazine*
December 1978

Joe's Charcoal

Nowadays, you pay six bits for a little shirttail full of synthetic charcoal that was manufactured in Kentucky, sold to your grocer by a firm in Chicago, for which he pays an account to an IBM machine in Houston, Texas. And if you are quite adept with matches, you may be able to burn these synthetic soot balls with a single can of dollar-ninety-eight-cent starter fuel while you turn a goodly pile of nice steaks into a grim heap which any self-respecting hound pup would turn his nose up at. But there is no way to head off a town dude when he gets that Daniel Boone gleam in his eye and hies himself to the hinterlands of the backyard barbecue pit. The local dispenser of soothing medication for the stomach is the only person who can truly love this guy.

Back when the charcoal furnace did all the household heating chores now done by dozens of electrical gadgets, Ney Oldham would answer his telephone at the general store with "Charcoal City, who do you want to talk at?" or some similar greeting. And when good cedar charcoal went as high as four bits a towsack full, there were enough charcoal kilns going around Wimberley to smoke the mosquitoes off the Blanco from Little Arkansas to Bendigo's Crossing. Four-bit charcoal was easier money to come by than six-cent cotton or six-dollar yearlings.

Much of this charcoal was sold to Old Man L. J. Dailey at his Grocery and General Mercantile Store, located on the southwest corner of the courthouse square in San Marcos. And in his time, Joe Blackwell delivered his fair share of charcoal to Mr. Dailey's firm.

On one occasion, Joe had the misfortune of being caught in a heavy downpour at his kiln when his wagon was loaded with freshly sacked new coal. The fact that damp charcoal had about the same commercial value as wet matches on the open market or the fact that his broker would have to make refunds to irate customers and/or be thrashed with a parasol and/or find a dead cat had been thrown into his water well never entered Joe's mind. He merely drove to the house, got his wagon sheet, meretriciously tarped his soggy load, and made his way on to San Marcos through drizzling rain. At the front of his store, Mr. Dailey waved Joe on to the rear, where he unloaded the charcoal into a shed.

Weeks later, Mr. Dailey caught Joe in town and asked: "Why

did you cover that last load of charcoal with a wagon sheet when it was already wet?"

"I knowed it. I knowed it," says Joe as he moved on.

You can bet the scales were balanced in Mr. Dailey's favor further down the line, for these old-timers did have their ways.

From *The Pioneer Heritage*

Mexican Mockingbird

Editor's note: The following is a letter to Bob Barton, publisher of *The Hays County Citizen,* from C. W. Wimberley in October 1975, while living at 1107 Chestnut Street in San Marcos, Texas.

Dear Bob:

Euell Gibbons is too busy listening to bullfrogs while hunting wild hickory nuts in his Grapenuts and my wife won't let me write Ann Landers anymore since she's got to be a grasswidder — Ann, that is — so, again I must turn to you with my problems.

How come all them bird-watching people have such a hullabaloo when one of them sees an unusual bird in their area and just look at me sort of strange like when I do about the same thing?

For example, back in July, bird watchers from all over were coming up to Wimberley, just to see a little ole Mexican Vivletear hummingbird that was hanging around on the Blanco River up there when it ought to a-been away down in Old Mexico where he belonged. Well, at that very same time, I had a Mexican mockingbird that stays in my front yard all the time. And nobody ever came around to look at him. In fact, whenever I tried to tell any bonified bird watcher person about my Mexican mocker, they'd just shy away from me.

Just so's you won't think I'm making all this up, I'll explain some about my Mexican mockingbird so's you'll understand my problem better.

To begin with, I got a nice big chili petine pepper plant growing in a washpot setting on my front porch. Comes in pretty handy-like all summer long, for anytime I need a few red chilies for my breakfast eggs or frijoles, all I have to do is step to the front door and pick a few from this bush.

This summer this bush afforded an abundant crop of lush red chilies. About ten o'clock one July morning my wife called my attention to a mockingbird sitting in my chili petine bush. He was

122

MAS CHILIES
¡OLE!

BERNICE
BROWN

putting away those red chilies like a kid eating jelly beans. Well, I figure this little feathered friend was in for a surprise come tomorrow. But I was the one in for the surprise—he was back again the next day for another bait of chilies and has been feeding on those chilies—the red ones—all summer, a fact which proves beyond doubts that this mockingbird is migrant from far below the Rio Grande. Had he been a native Texas mockingbird, after the initial bait of red chilies, he would have spent the next days flying backwards and/or cooling it in the bird bath.

Now, how come bird watcher persons can't follow my logic?

Yours,

Cedarwhacker

Windmill Schmidt

Early in his career, Windmill Schmidt learned a couple of don'ts in the windmill repair trade—don't work on a mill without first securing the fan, and don't stand on the platform in front of the wheel. Either error could cost you your life.

On this occasion, he heeded neither. He did not turn off the mill because there was not the slightest indication of a breeze in the air when he climbed the tower to mount the platform and stand before the wheel. The windmill was a twenty-footer, so to reach the top of the gear housing, he stood on the circular rim that reinforced the blades from the front, and worked his arms through the opening about the wheel's hub to reach the housing. Engrossed with his labor he realized, too late, that the wheel had begun to turn. Clinging on for dear life, he rode spread-eagled on the huge wheel three revolutions before it stopped, fortunately, with him again standing upright at the bottom of the arc.

Now that the new waterworks about covers the place and the REA lines run all over the country, some people might find it pretty easy to forget what a wonderful piece of machinery the old windmill was in its days. But, if ever you had ridden till you and your horse were dogtired, dusty, and the sweat on his withers had turned to crusts of dry lather, then made it to where the old lone windmill creaked and groaned as she lifted clear, cool water from the depths of the good earth — there are some things you don't forget very easily.

You don't forget how your horse plunged his nose deep into the water past the nostrils before you could remove the bits; how, through the long moments without breathing, he drank in huge drafts that sent visible swells surging up the length of his neck each time he swallowed; and how, after the thirst was gone, he chafed at the bits and took dainty shallow sips near the pipe where the fresh cool water ran into the trough. Then as you loosened the girth to let the cool air under the saddle and his innards expanded and gurgled in adjusting to its new burden of moisture, you knew for sure that water was indeed a precious commodity. Barbed wire may have brought an end to the days of the open range, but ranching would have held an empty promise on land fenced into dry pastures without the manmade water holes that were filled by the old windmill.

Now that the cow pastures along the Cypress and Blanco have become suburban real estate, it's a little hard to remember the endless chore of carrying drinking water from the well or the onerous task of keeping the water trough filled during the dry season, when a cedar rail was the pump handle attached to a deep well cylinder. Cattle may have been thin and a little skittish in making their way to the trough, but every old cow was swelled into an ambulatory rawhide tank of water before she waddled off, drooling and fighting flies. And it took a lot of strokes on the pump handle to do it.

In this era, when most yards were swept with a broom till they were clean and lifeless pans of raw earth, my Grandma Lawrence's yard was devoted to flowers and shrubbery, which she kept green by her own hand with water she pumped and carried from the well in buckets. Sweat and callouses paid the water bill in those days.

Now that all the creeks are lined with summer homes of city workers, retirement homes of people who won't quit working, and the whole place has become a vacation land, it is a good indication that long hours and low wages are almost things of the past. Back when it was hard work from sun to sun to make a living hereabouts, there were some men who gained the respect of all who knew them because of the stubborn pride they took in their workmanship and the quality of services rendered.

Mr. R. M. "Windmill" Schmidt was such a man. Though he now lives in retirement, he is no stranger to the old-timers here, and everyone has a good word for him. From the days of the spring wagon through the period of the Model T truck, he was the windmill man for Hays and several adjoining counties. Dawn to dusk, his overloaded vehicle traveled the wayside roads as he installed new windmills or repaired old ones, for the ranchers trusted and depended upon him to see that their cattle had water, and he never failed them. Since the days of the Republic, Texas has leaned heavily on the shoulders of good German stock for skilled craftsmen in many trades, and Windmill Schmidt is one of her finest sons.

He was a blacksmith and tinker of the old school. Among his creations, there was a six-mule-hitch rooter plow for removing rock from new land, a haybaler of his own model and, before the days of the hammer mill, he made a corn mill with which corn meal could be ground or the whole ear ground into livestock feed. On the walls of his shop there is an array of tools of his own design made for fishing pipe, sucker rods, and other objects from the depths of a well. And there hangs a pair of chain puzzle-locked hobbles used by pioneers in the Fredericksburg area to prevent the Comanches from cutting the hobbles and stealing their horses.

But Windmill Schmidt is most often remembered as a doctor of the waterworks. After a look-see and an ear to the pipes, he knew what to do for an ailing windmill and could repair almost any of the old contraptions used for handling water. Likened to the country doctor, his range was wide; his hours were long; and, for his faithful services, he charged nominal fees which afforded him a modest living. He was a master in the art of improvising when it came

125

to fixing things in an emergency. One time he was hurrying to a job when his overloaded Model T stalled on the side of the Devil's Backbone with the clutch bands smoking and nearly burned out. Unperturbed, Windmill chucked a rear wheel with a rock, gathered a handful of bark from a cedar post, crushed it, stuffed it into the clutch bands, cranked up, and was on his way. Someone needed water—he could overhaul the Model T later.

With his working days behind him now, Windmill Schmidt is one of the few old ones left with whom it is good to sit and spend time renewing that lost art of talking. Not long ago, we rehashed the accounts of August Schubert's hunting and trapping exploits —about the half-grown bear cub he caught in Colorado which later escaped from his home on the Blanco near Fischer's Store. The last time it was seen, this bear wandered up to a water hole near Mt. Sharp. Windmill closed the subject in his rich German accent something like this: "Some say a bear like dot will always go back to where he was born. Don't you put much stock in dot. If what they say is so, dot bear was edder crazy as hell or just plain don't give a doom what he was doing. From the other side of Fischer's Store to Colorado—Mt. Sharp's not the way to go. That's east. From here to Colorado it northwest."

From *The Pioneer Heritage*

Hofheinz Gardens

In its day Hofheinz Gardens was known as The Rock Garden of Eden on a Texas Hill. Fifty Mexican artisans skilled in the craft of Spanish masonry spent more than a year in building the dry-stacked rock walls and adobe structures. The Gardens were in ruins when I first saw them sixty-odd years ago. These are my memories. Daniel Hofheinz was a prime builder of old San Marcos. In the 1870s he brought lumber from Bastrop by ox wagon in order to build his first hotel and be established in the business with the arrival of the first railroad train.

—C. W. W.

All too often our old landmarks fall victim to the bulldozer's blade and without ceremony the last vestige of another facet of our local history is erased from the land. And all too often without record this bit of our heritage is gone forever with the last faded memories of a past generation.

Hofheinz Gardens was one old landmark to suffer a less destructive fate. With fragments of its former grandeur, this unique facet of 1890s San Marcos lingers on in legend and fact. Frances Stovall gave these gardens a proper niche in the book *Clear Springs and Limestone Ledges, A History of San Marcos and Hays County.*

Fortunately, Charles J. Suckle has seen fit to maintain the section of the hillside terraces beside his hilltop home. Unfortunately, the remaining portion of these rock terraces are falling into ruin. And the last veteran quince tree is gone from the scene.

On the opposite side of the hill the incomplete terraces were redesigned and the long stock pile of thin flat rocks put to other use.

Bluebonnet Drive circles the oblong hilltop on the selfsame course of the legendary Indian racetrack. Beneath the asphalt the basic features of this geological lateral remain unchanged since the heyday of the Comanche horseman. (Another of these Indian racetracks is marked by Mimosa East and West on Rogers Hill. A small band of Comanches did race across these hills in the 1840s — to make good their escape with the horses they had stolen from Gen. Edward Burleson.)

At the Belvin Street home of Elizabeth Hofheinz Martindale a rose from the Hofheinz Gardens lives on, a family heirloom of sorts. A cutting grown from the original rootstock Daniel Hofheinz planted at his gardens near a century ago, this favored annual of yesteryear continues to grow and rewards Elizabeth's efforts each spring season with lavish clusters of pink blossoms reminiscent of the Old South.

Hofheinz Gardens lay on the east side of LBJ Drive between Forest and Lamar, with the main entrance gate located a few rods south of Walnut Street. By leaps and bounds of old surveys the 37¾ acre tract encompassed the flat hilltop and the slopes to either side.

Along the roadside to the west the bounds of the garden tract were enclosed by a rock wall which also extended along the south bounds to the top of the hill and a short distance along the north. The remainder of the fence was barbed wire of a vintage to become a collector's item.

At the main entrance a red picket gate hung between tall cedar posts tied together at the tops. From this gate north, the rock fence was an earth-filled, double-walled affair with barbed wire strung to cedar poles down its middle. Planted at close intervals along the way, an old and hardy variety of climbing rose formed a wide hedge, a marvel of its day.

On the gentle slope near the gate these roses survived the years without a gardener's care. The old fence was pink with blossoms each spring. As seen through many eyes, these roses webbed the old landmark with a mystic aura of conflicting tales. In reality the roses only reflect the aesthetic touch of its builder, Daniel Hofheinz.

During the early days of the railroad, Mr. Hofheinz owned and operated one of San Marcos's finer hotels on the first block of East San Antonio Street. While the passenger train and the coded chatter of the telegrapher key kept the old depot the focal point of the town's business activities, Hofheinz Hotel prospered as the gracious host to the traveling guest and center of the town's social activities.

To grace his tables with fresh vegetables, fruits, and fine meats, he acquired the garden tract. Gardeners may ponder his choice of a rock hilltop to the north of town in preference to the nearby fertile blacklands of the river valley. The answer rests with the creative mind of Daniel Hofheinz.

With artistic design he structured the gardens for the production of all manner of farm produce, from smoked sausages and hams to pears, peaches, and parsnips. A berry patch and grape vineyard of 500 plants was planted at the top terrace west. Though never fully completed, the old garden remains as the dead dream of a visionary man. With his death the gardens fell to the ways of the new century.

The decision may have been by his heirs or caused by the refrigerated freight car's ability to fill the market place with the marvels of produce from fields afar in an abundance. In any event, gardening efforts at the site were closed.

The abandoned facilities were boarded up, stock pens stood empty, and slowly nature began to reclaim her land.

Shrouded by a mantle of growing cedar brakes, Hofheinz Gardens stood through the decades as an idle relic of the past and a specter of another era.

Unscathed by vandalism, the plank buildings were allowed to weather away with the passing years. Built by craftsmen of the trade, the dry-stacked rockwall pens and fences were slow to fall apart. They became rattlesnake dens and were a good place for cottontails to hide from rabbit-chasing dogs. Sometimes young hunters would tear at the rocks, but more often they would scold the dogs to leave

128

the rabbit be with the logic of "Who wants a danged old cotton-tailed rabbit? Anyhow, Mama wouldn't cook it for me."

In years to come the confines of Hofheinz Gardens were looted for building rocks and carted away by the truckloads by a breed of men who would have explained to Saint Peter that it wasn't really stealing when "Ole Walter didn't care. Rocks all over the place —laying there just going to waste, an' he didn't need the money —had more'n me anyway."

Though perturbed by the matter, Walter Hofheinz endured these trespasses to his property with the quiet dignity of the gentry. It did present an ugly vein to the scene of pleasant memories.

Scrub and heavy underbrush covered the hilltop to invade the gardened terraced slopes. Bordered by cactus and scrub timber, patches of buffalo grass and bare earth marked the oblong course of the Indian racetrack about the hilltop. Here the thin soil flats of the wide lateral continued to resist the inroads of time and change.

Hofheinz Gardens became a pasture for milch cows during an era when dwellers of town households clung to the land with a cowpen, chickens, and vegetable garden in their back yards, and flowers to the front for folks to see, with a fence to keep stray dogs out.

At the north end of the hilltop, cows watered at an earthen tank dug into the clays of a bygone seep spring. It held water like a jug. Beside it a square pit lined with rock, dug for unknown reasons, held water only during rain season an' not for long. Near this end of the hilltop a decaying pumphouse held an old hit-and-miss gas engine facing a jackpump above the well. The drive belt was gone.

The last traces of any irrigation system were lost in a meaningless disarray of low mounds of earth and sections of half-filled ditches extending to the south along the hilltop. Near the far end of the hilltop a shingle-roofed pavilion stood askew. It was a place where cows gathered in its shade to while away the time chewing their cuds, switching at flies with their tails, and looking at you with doleful eyes as you walked by.

Nearby, the adobe walls of the smokehouse dominated the scene. A plank door hung wedged ajar at the only opening in the two-foot-thick walls. With the sky for a roof the heavy beams of the ceiling joist still hung in place high above the caliche floor.

At the slope of the hill there was a caliche pit where armadillos dug into the remains of an old kiln. At this site smoke had been generated, then tunneled into the smokehouse to cure the meats.

129

East of the racetrack the ruins of two buildings lay hidden by the scrub trees of a prickly pear flat.

At one site a moldering rubble of limed caliche mortar and broken stone lay in low heaps where the walls and chimney place had crumbled back to earth. It had been looted for building stone. At the other, low gabled rockwalls stood naked at either end of a sunken floor pitted between mounds of caliche rubble. Cactus and agarita guarded the walls where cedar elm grew from the sunken-pit floor.

On first visit you left the scene with the feeling of having found an unmarked tomb. In reality, I had found the ruins of the green-house. On the opposite hand to the west of the hill, two dilapidated lumber buildings stood falling to staves among the cedars. Built on the order of the Texas two-room shack—boxed with full meas-ured 1″×12″ boards without paint—the smaller one had shed only its factory-built door and window sash. It still housed a pedal-powered machine. Gingerbread trim and beaded boards littered the area about the other, and winds had torn away the thin tin roofing to leave great holes in the ceiling deck.

Between the two lay a gaping hole where an underground cis-tern had been chambered deep into the bedrock. A cover of cedar brush and scrap lumber warded man and beast from the hole.

Logan Roberts and I would often visit this cistern and caverns in the area to gather white cave crickets to be used as fish bait —one on the hook for hand-sized bream and perch, or gobs for bigmouth bass and bluecats. We were late teenagers before any weeds grew in our paths across Hofheinz Gardens.

Most barefoot boys and some shoe-clad sissies of old San Mar-cos town at one time or another made exploratory expeditions into the wilds of Hofheinz Gardens. The tales of their exploits are still growing.

There was a rattler ten feet long an' big around as a stovepipe. He must a-been the one that bit Mrs. Travis's bulldog and made him die when he had already been bit eight or nine times by other ordinary rattlesnakes and only got sick every time.

An' the time R. K. Shafer got bit by a real rattlesnake and Mrs. Moore drove him to Dr. Edwards's office in her Model T because he couldn't walk anymore.

An' the time Buster got Mr. Vogelsang's old .45 pistol and wasted three whole boxes of bullets just shooting holes in prickly pears, tin cans, and such for Constable Tom Tate to hear about too late to do nothin'.

An' don't ever mess with a polecat because you can get perfumed all over without ever seeing a single drop coming at you.

An' found a big arrowhead that the Indians lost on a battlefield or at least shot at a bear or a buffalo.

An' turned the smokehouse into an adobe fort where a hundred bluecoat troopers guarded the frontier.

An' dug shallow holes in search of the fabled sixteen jackloads of Spanish gold buried somewhere in these hills.

An' saw side oat grama and native larkspur growing in stands of whippear cactus and found the first anemone to bloom in the spring.

An' walked around the clay tank just to see the frogs jump into the water with a squeak and splash and wondered where they went in winter.

An' waked up way in the night to hear Alan Mayes's hounds chasing a fox around the racetrack and then went out of hearing — bet the fox got away. But Alan did kill a big alligator over at Fern's Bluff one time and fed his poor dogs donkey meat sometimes.

Yeb Harle was one of those who pastured his milch cows in Hofheinz Gardens during the day and returned them to his barnyard for the night. Each morning the cows followed him to the red picket gate and that evening he followed them on the return trip to the barn.

The rose bushes were still growing in the rock fence when Yeb and Hester lived across the road in a rambling two-story house decked at the front with sun porches. This grand old couple made a pair you would find easy to remember. Hester managed the home as a rooming house for young ladies attending college. Yeb kept a dairy herd consisting of three or four good Jerseys and a heifer or two which he judged to show good promise.

Dailey's Grocery Store handled the butter. And in the predawn light of day, Yeb walked a short route delivering quart bottles of fresh sweetmilk to porches and picking up the clean empties (didn't stop at our place: we had Mutsy an' didn't need any more milk).

Yeb Harle loved cats, called them his mousers, and kept them by the dozens. Cats were everywhere. There were enough of them to make forays through the neighborhood and an elite dozen or so he allowed into the house to patrol it through the night — his Waterloo.

Hester tolerated Yeb's mousers with stoic indifference held proper to a good wife. That is, until the night Yeb forgot to fetch in the kitty litter box and the legion of cats found his hat lying on the floor. This event Hester gleefully shared with every housewife living on the hill.

At one time the Hofheinz Gardens might have become a part of SWTSU campus. By 1920 SWN had grown to become an institution too big for the confines of Chautauqua Hill: SWT; SWTC; SWTTC; SWTSTC; and all that alphabetical soup.

Had Walter Hofheinz been a more persuasive person, the thrust of this expansion may have been across the hills to the north. But his best efforts failed to concern College President C. E. Evans with the purchase of Hofheinz Gardens hilltop tract at a purported price of $3,500.

Prexy's interest lay with the flatlands to the east of the river — a college farm, no less.

So be it. But just you try to imagine LBJ Drive as the University Drag; the SWTSU Agriculture Department managing the fulfilled dreams of Daniel Hofheinz at the garden, and the stadium between the hills to the west.

This would be easy to do had you been around since the day San Marcos Baptist Academy Cubs beat the Bobcats by about 44 – 10, and during the night the cadets painted this score in boxcar letters on the normal school's water tower for all to see. Canary yellow added insult to injury.

The next morning Prexy came to the power plant, sputtering with indignation, "Rufus! Rufus! What are we going to do about it? What can we do about it?"

To quiet his boss's fury, my dad climbed the high steel tower with a broom and a bucket of paint tied across his shoulders. At the catwalk about the tank he brushed away the offensive yellow from its walls with a new coat of olive green.

Finale

And we dare leave the era with only honorary mention of another old landmark lost to time — our last grand emporium of sweet tooth delicacies, Hofheinz Confectionary, located on the east side of the town square.

Complete in detail, with elegant marble soda fountain bar and oval mirrored wall, lazy ceiling fans, and genuine Joseph Salomon

wire furniture, this confectionary was a turn-of-the-century classic
— straight from the pages of a book.

At the sidewalk entrance the aroma of the eye-catchers lured
the trade.

On the left, a fresh stalk of yellow bananas hung from the ceiling by a rope. On the right stood an elaborate glass-windowed popcorn machine topped with a revolving peanut roaster. Every passing boy had to gaze in wonder at the little red-capped mechanical
clown laboriously turning the crank on the peanut roaster a-top
this museum-worthy contraption.

Mister Voges, the manager, belonged to the old school of businessmen who could wear vest and gartered shirt sleeves with distinction.

From *The San Marcos Daily Record*
January 18, 1987

Part III:

Wimberley

The Old Wimberley Mills

Wimberley Mills is representative of stone-milling operations common to Texas; the village, named for Pleasant Wimberley, is atypical, however, in that it neither grew nor died. It remains a village established by an old millsite.

Pleasant sold his Longhorn cattle and ranching interest in the northern end of Blanco and Llano counties (now known as LBJ country) in 1873. The following year he bought with gold a mill tract on Cypress Fork of the Rio Blanco. At that time the waters of Cypress Creek turned the turbine to power all mill operations. The building housed a grist mill, a flour mill with twenty-eight-inch buhrstones, a sawmill, a shingle mill; and on the second floor, a smut mill for cleaning wheat, and a one-stand cotton gin. Partnered with his son Zack (my grandfather), a thriving business was conducted at that location.

Then about 1890, a four-mule hitch pulled into Wimberley with the first load of Harry Landa's roller-milled flour, priced at seventy-five cents per hundred-weight in the general store. The white bleached flour immediately caught the housewife's eye, and the race was on to see who could have the whitest biscuits, and the whitest cream gravy when it came her turn to feed the preacher chicken dinner on Sunday. Tinged by minute particles of stonecut bran that no bolt could remove, the stone-milled flour never stood a chance.

The demise of the stone flour mill had its "time marker" for the Wimberley family. In 1893 Grandma Wimberley made her daughter, Nellie, a dress from the silk screening cloth cut from the mill's flour bolt. My aunt was thirteen and the dress was dyed pink. But corn meal was still in style, so the grist mill was unaffected.

Like most streams, Cypress Creek began losing volume with the passing of the frontier. To cope with this situation, many changes occurred around the mill. Uncle Hick, who had done his turn as millwright and miller, now began his engineering career. First a millpond was added to the millrace; then in 1890 a smaller turbine was installed. But by 1899 it was necessary to harness steam for supplementary power.

Using the live steam from the boiler and drip lye from wood ashes, Uncle Hick gained local recognition for his ability in making barrels of good corn hominy. He also added another mill to the site by moving the sorghum molasses operation to a place where the cane crusher could be water-powered. "Water- squeezed cane mo-

The Old Wimberley Mill

lasses," as such, made no great splash — except with the old horse that had pulled the cane crusher.

In 1912 Uncle Hick installed an old "one-lung" gasoline engine to turn the grist mill — a chore the lean flow of the Cypress could no longer perform. A small hydraulic ram, used to pump water to the house, made final use of the water power derived from the mill-race.

After the engine had been installed, some of the customers complained that their meal was "different" and didn't taste right. These complaints could have had a logical origin only if the miller had set his gasoline fuel too close to the meal bin, or for some similar reason.

An engine-powered mill could grind with a more uniform texture because a steel-ball governor control (belatedly applied to water wheels) and the inertia of heavy flywheels increased or decreased the power output while the engine turned at a constant speed. Without these controls the miller was constantly fiddling with the treadle control, sometimes resorting to opening the stones in order to keep a uniform power demand at the mill. With power output determined by the water level in its buckets (and/or flume), the water wheel would surge while changing water levels to meet new power demands and sometimes would gallop from balk to balk, sending the grist mill spinning from stop to stop.

Another unfounded claim was that the engine turned the mill fast enough to burn the meal. The old stone mills were not designed for such speed. Turning that fast, the buhrstone would be in real danger of flying apart, or the mill shaft might jump from the ink (open pivot bearing) and spin to new disaster. Dull stones could heat the meal, and new corn not fully cured would generate heat by clogging the mill. Wheat could be fed into the mill too fast or, heated enough by dull stones to taste scorched, would subsequently ferment in storage.

So everyone had his ideas about milling, and Grandpa had to listen because he had to stay around to do the milling.

Following World War I, the Wimberley Mill prospered for a while, then a changing economy brought it to the end of its time. The custom mill depended upon the local trade of people who derived their livelihood from more or less self-contained farming units. With the increase of farming for the cash market, there was a steady decline in farm population and fewer customers for the mill. The Wimberley Mills were razed in 1934, an idle relic of another era. The only surviving memento is the French buhrstone grist mill which Rufus Wimberley had learned to operate at an age when he had to sack the meal while standing on a box for height. He kept it.

So the old mill is gone — but there are facts still to be related and tales to be told.

In its day the millroom served as a local town hall where all the men gathered on Saturday. Young men in a hurry came to learn the news or to give their opinions before moving on, but the old ones came to sit and whittle and enjoy a companionship that would be warm without burning too many words.

While the boys played in the mill yard, the ladies visited with neighbors and looked and traded at the general store; or, all too often, they stayed at home. There was a time when veterans of The War, Rebs and some Yanks too, came as neighbors and customers to this old mill. The raw humor which had carried these men through America's greatest tragedy lives on in this area, mellowed some by the years.

Health Department inspectors never came to the old mill and, during Aunt Mandy Justice's time, their visits would have been unnecessary. Aunt Mandy rode to the mill side-saddle with her sack of corn before her. The miller always helped her down, tied her horse, and brought the corn inside for her. By the time he had reached the mill she had given the millroom an inspection. If conditions there did not meet her standards, it was thoroughly cleaned on the spot — before her corn was ground. And no one knew for sure just when Aunt Mandy might come riding up.

Nature herself provided the mill with pest control, for when rats and mice became too numerous, a rattlesnake or two would den up beneath the floors. Mr. Rattler's presence would soon be revealed by the rodents' abandoning the millroom to find loftier quarters where their activities were limited and marked by silent cautiousness.

To have burned the ill-constructed old building to the ground would have been the only means of ridding the mill of its new boarders, so between men and snake a policy to live and let live was adopted. The rattlesnakes stayed in their dens under the floor during the daylight hours, and any necessary after-dark visits to the mill were made by lantern light with a slow and noisy approach, giving the snake ample opportunity to retreat. The snakes were obliging and rattled only when crowded, for neither party relished the ordeal of an unexpected encounter.

A welfare office of sorts was established in the mill by a custom attributed to my Great-Uncle Joe. Near the grist mill stood a support beam, braced near its top by four short pieces of lumber nailed at angles to the floor. When Uncle Joe was doing rather poorly, he would bring his empty meal sack and leave it hanging from one of these braces. Grandpa would fill it with a peck or two of meal ground from the toll corn, and then set it near the door where other customers' sacks waited to be claimed. Over the years other old men in need, and too proud to ask, would leave their empty sacks hanging beside Uncle Joe's. A spoken word was never used in these transactions, but Grandpa always found some meal for each sack. I guess he was just that kind of man.

In the days when land was checked with a bull-tongue plow, the seed dropped by hand, and the corn cultivated with one horse hooked to a double-shovel plow, life was hard and humor harsh. Those times are remembered better than they were lived.

In the fall of the year the miller at Wimberley was plagued by the green walnuts floating in the millrace. Enough of them would always escape the screen to clog the turbine from time to time. When this happened, the miller would have to close the wooden floodgate, take a bucket with him, and climb twenty-two feet down the dark flume of the penstock to the bottom. There he would dislodge the nuts from the turbine blades and gather them into the bucket, one by one. In this damp, close chamber, a man could get mighty nervous thinking about the innumerable dangers of his task.

One fall season my Uncle John Will was the miller faced with this chore. Three fingers shortened by gin saws may have influenced his caution, for after Uncle had closed the floodgate, he ordered a bunch of youthful spectators from the scene before he entered the flume. When the thud of walnuts being dropped into the tin bucket began echoing up from the flume, Coleman Holt emerged silently from the shadows of the mill and dipped a five-gallon bucket full of water from the millrace.

Holding the bucket in one hand, he began shouting frantically into the air, "Hey, you kids! Get away from that floodgate! Don't you know there's a man down in that hole? Get away from there! Hey, stop it! Oh, my Lord!" And he dumped the bucket down the flume.

Seconds later, when Uncle's dripping head appeared above the flume-top, Coleman had crossed the garden patch, the creek, and was then crossing the village square, heading south, but his wild laughter could still be heard at the mill.

Without federal advice and "givermint" aid, the old-time farmer around Wimberley tried to raise enough corn each year to fill all his needs for the next: to feed himself, his team, and most everything that lived about the barn; to fatten a hog or two; to have a carryover in case of drought; some to sell, maybe, and for darn sure enough seed corn to start the whole process over again, come next spring.

An old-timer set much store in the kind of corn that went into his cornbread. He usually had a "cornbread patch" where he planted a strain which might well be the same kind planted by his great-grandpappy. Necessity could have been responsible for this practice, but it had a certain logic because the strain of corn determines the quality and quantity of the kernel's content of soluble soft starches which, in turn, determines the flavor and richness of the meal. The grain's hard starches contribute little more than bulk and color to the quality of cornbread — no matter how fine the texture of the grind.

According to Uncle Hick, old man Joe Russell was about the first to bring a sack of "Hickory Cane" corn to Wimberley Mills. This was a white flint corn that grew with eight rows of kernels to the cob. Many of these kernels were as large as a man's thumbnail, but they had a hard starch outer shell which meant that the mill had better have sharp stones. Anyone with a grandparent born south of the Mason-Dixon line is apt to agree that this corn made the best hominy to be had, and some swore by its meal and roasting ears. This claim may have to be qualified in certain areas, because south of The Line some people are still pretty touchy about their cornbread. In the South it used to be "*nearly* all right" to use soda in cornbread, and a forgivable sin to add "just a *little*" baking powder to the mix — mind you, not too much. But when it was learned that north of The Line the Yankees were grinding the meal into powdered dust and adding sugar — well, things got to popping sure enough. "Damn Yankee" was heard in the kitchen, and if you are looking for any Lost Causes, don't overlook cornpone bread.

One year Grandpa Wimberley ordered Hasting's "Seven Ear Wonder" and, on land irrigated from the millrace, grew corn that fulfilled the catalog's promise. But most old-timers usually saved their seed corn from their last year's crop. Then too, many of them had their own strain of corn which was not listed in any breeder's book.

The battle of the Pea Ridge was recent history when Mrs. P. L. Kirby lived in a log cabin near Searcy, Arkansas. One spring, drought and other misfortune had left her with only a stunted ear of her favorite corn for seed. In the kitchen she shelled the nubbin, counted each sound grain into a pint measuring cup, and got forty-eight, all told. Under such circumstances, she decided to plant this corn in the garden close to the cabin where it could be more carefully tended.

Leaving the cup on the table, she went to prepare seed-beds in the garden; when she returned, the cup, unmoved, was empty. After considering all possible ways for the corn to have vanished, the solution to the mystery suddenly dawned upon her. Several thoughts crowded in her mind: "That old laying hen . . . she flies through the window and pokes around the kitchen . . . should have cooked her with dumplings a long time ago . . . but she's too good a layer."

A quick search about the yard and, sure enough, the laying hen's craw was bulging a lot bigger than that of the other chickens. After catching the culprit, Mrs. Kirby opened the craw with her buttonhole scissors, retrieved the corn — all forty-eight grains — and stitched the opening together again with white sewing thread. The old hen recovered from her operation without complications or loss of laying habit, and Mrs. Kirby grew a new supply of seed corn that season.

My Grandpa Lawrence had a white "squaw corn" he liked in cornbread. The kernels were rounded and a thin shell of hard starches held a copious cavity of soft starches about the germ. Weevils were fond of this corn too. During the winter season, they could turn a log crib full of this particular corn into a mass of dust-filled shucks and empty cobs by spring. Such an experience did much to create interest in hybrid corns.

Rawhide Weaver lived in the cedar brakes over on Lone Man Creek, where he raised a little strawberry corn in his older days. Strawberry was a soft corn with large, bright-white kernels streaked in swirls of blood-red. One spring Rawhide brought a little sack of this corn to the mill. Grandpa Pleasant poured it into the hopper and was about to dip out his toll when he stopped. "Why, Rawhide," he said, "this corn won't do for meal. Weevils have about eaten it up."

"I know, Grandpa," replied Rawhide, "but it is all I got." Pleasant Wimberley added corn from the toll box to that in the hopper before he started the mill.

In "them good ole days" the weevil ate pretty high on the hog. And he still keeps a lot of men busy just to control him.

From *Old West Magazine*
Spring 1974

Twin Sister Peaks

Today we are going to talk about that valley on the Blanco now known as the Wimberley area. And we are going to talk about those two peaks that rise from the rugged plain lying between the Blanco and Cypress creeks — the peaks which dominate the scene when viewed from the Big Hill bounding this valley on the south.

The Twin Sisters is their name—not "ole Baldy" and "the other 'un."

To give a proper perspective, we turn the calendar back more than a hundred years. We place a bullwhip in your hands and you stand beside your ox wagon piled high with its load of new cypress shingles that you are freighting to San Marcos for dray charges. The sweat trickles down your brow and you are a proud man for you have just ascended Spoke Pile Hill without a hitch.

True enough, the canyons have echoed with the crack of your whip and the leaves on nearby trees have wilted before the fire of your curses and violent language. But you have urged these stolid brutes to Spoke Pile's top without resorting to cruel blows or vindictive slashes, which is more than most wagoneers can justly claim.

While the oxen rest solidly in their tracks, you turn to the boy who followed in the wagon's wake to see that the trailing chuck log was always in place, ready to block the wheels should the oxen falter or you wished to stop. And you say, "Good job, well done, lad. Climb aboard and ride a spell." Then you unhook the log from its chains and cast it aside to be recovered on the return trip. And after checking your gear, you are ready to move on, but you pause —long enough to look back into the valley you have left behind.

Using the Twin Sister peaks as focal points, you calculate time and distance you have traveled from Winter's Mill to where you stand. And last of all, your eyes move from the peaks to a speck seen through the blue haze, the home place where your children and their mother await your return. Theirs is the greater courage. At that time, the pioneers called these peaks the Twin Sisters.

We move the calendar up to or near the year 1900, and you are in the driver's seat of your wagon drawn by a team of horses, both good and true. You have spent most of your "cotton money" to buy essentials for the home and tucked in some little extras for each member of the family, and you are at the crest of Townsend Hill on the way home with this load. You stop here to let the team blow and check your gear before tackling the hill—harness in proper shape and brakes in working order—for you are not one of those senseless creatures who continuously curse their hard luck each time they have a needless accident that could well have been avoided. Before climbing back to the driver's seat, you look down across the valley below and, using the Twin Sisters as a benchmark, you locate the home place and "figger to a T" where the sun will be when you pull up to the big gate at the crib and watch the kids come a-running to see who gets to open the gate. At that time, the old-timers called those peaks the Twin Sisters.

And now, World War I is over and done and the men who fought to make the world safe for democracy are the angry unemployed. To create jobs for them, new roads are constructed. One of these is the new road to Wimberley, coming off the Big Hill at a new location. The mode of travel is much faster, and from this new vantage point the view of the Twin Sisters is a bit oblique. But all the natives of the area continue to call these peaks the Twin Sisters.

Today the road is a highway graded for speed and few people slow down for the view at the top. The roadside park overlooks the Little Arkansas area of the valley, but if you will slow down before Leath Hill obscures the view, you can still see the Twin Sisters as they should be seen. Flatlanders call the one on the right "Ole Baldy," but those who have a feel for the soil continue to call them by their proper name, the Twin Sisters.

Naming the geographical features of our land has, by tradition, been the respected prerogative of the pioneers who passed on before us and the old-timers who lived by the soil and, therefore, is a heritage of the land. From such thin fibers the fine cloth of folklore and legend is woven. Any belated efforts to tamper with them usually stems from the rags of commercialism. Convince Cousin Curlo and Uncle Emmett that I am wrong on this account and I'll eat your crow, feathers and all.

From *The Wimberley Mill*
July 1967

Old Haunts in Wimberley

Possum sleeps in a holler log,
Raccoon lays on a limb.
Better stay in shaller water,
Till you learns to swim.

Went wading in the millpond and fished in the tailrace behind the old mill. Learned to dog-paddle in Thorn Hole and been in swimmin' nakid at J.P., Black Log, and White Log. Boys wore knee-breeches and Daddy drove a Stoddard-Dayton automobile to Wimberley when I was a kid. And old Blue Hole was a fur piece up Cypress Creek in them good ole days.

144

Blue Hole has not changed much since the early 1920s. John Dobie no longer lives on the hill past the cemetery and Mrs. Parks Johnson now lives on Miss Minnie Roberts' place across the creek. But the water still runs deep, clear, cool, and clean — as always in the old Blue Hole. The big old cypress seems to cling a bit more tenaciously to the creekbank and has canted slightly towards the water. On Miss Minnie's side of the creek, floods have reclaimed the huge cypress log which once lay with one end on the bank and the other extending far down into the upper reaches of the deep water.

No longer do the people living in the bend of the creek ford Cypress in the shallows at the lower end of Blue Hole on their way to Wimberley. And no longer does the main body of water flow from Blue Hole down Miss Minnie's side of the creek to a jerry-built dam where it was diverted into the millrace which served the Wimberley Mills.

Uncle John Will Pyland was the miller in those days. He and Aunt Susie and their girls lived in the rock house on the hill. Even if you were a boy, those were the days to visit Aunt Susie. When you were not helping Uncle John Will at the mill, there was all sorts of things you could find to do along the millrace and creek.

With a stubbed big toe that made a legal excuse for carrying my shoes under my arm, I was deposited at Aunt Susie's for one of those weekends. My plans centered upon the new white linen line I had rubbed green with peach leaves and a dime's worth of new fish hooks I carried in my pockets. But they were not to be.

When there was a revival meeting being held under the brush arbor, everybody at Uncle John Will's house went. Singing in the evening and, after the kerosene torches had been lit, the hell's fire and brimstone preacher scorched the sinners and wrasseled with old Satan till 1:00 in the morning and prayed awhile longer.

Sunday, while the preacher and his entourage were feasting on Aunt Susie's fried chicken, white gravy, and dewberry pie, the devil got me. Sneaking out the back way, I knocked a big wasp nest off the eave of the barn, got my fishing pole and can of worms, then circled through the cedars towards the millrace — headed for Blue Hole. On past the molasses mill, where a young cypress grew in the deepest part of the race channel, I had to stop to try my luck. The worm hadn't hit the water good till he took it — a big goggle-eye. Didn't try for seconds.

At Miss Minnie's little foot-bridge across the race, I staked the goggle-eye, caught a big grasshopper off a skunk bush, and made my way to the lilypad-covered pond above the dam.

Using no sinker, I flung the grasshopper into an opening among the lilypads. When he started kicking, two spotted Kentucky bass, a great big one and a little one, came up to take a look. The big one just sat there and let the little one beat him to the grasshopper. One bass was enough. I'd started out to go perch fishing and I was going to do it on that big cypress log sticking out in Blue Hole, and I wasn't going to be wasting any more of my time.

Fish were biting. Everytime the white wasp grub sank down past the side of the log, a perch would grab it. Not many pumpkin seeds to throw back either, and my stringer got longer and heavier in a hurry.

There wasn't a soul around. I had Blue Hole to myself. I ran the last part of the way. Out on the old log there was enough room to sit down good, close to the water, with my stringer hanging on the upper side and not bother my fishing on the other.

Then it happened. Cars and a truck and some wagons and buggies started coming down the hill and stopped in the flat over by the big cypress tree on the other side. People got out and started gathering around down at the crossing. Some had hymn books and started singing "Shall We Gather at the River" and the preacher waded out into the water with his clothes on. He stopped when the water got up to his belt and turned around and other people started wading out towards him, two or three at a time. And now I knew what it was: a baptizing. But everybody was busy singing and looking at the preacher and them that was getting baptized, so I went on fishing 'cause nobody would be taking any notice of me.

Next thing I knew, some boys with knee-breeches and stockings and shoes on and wearing caps on their heads were standing on the bank right across the creek, looking at me. Not for long. A lady come up then and shooed 'em right back down the creek like a bunch of chickens—after she'd give me a look like she was seeing one of the devil's imps setting there on that log.

Now the fat was really in the fire. I layed my pole down easy-like and pulled my knees up under my chin and just sat there wishing my straw hat would swaller me.

After a while, something started dragging my pole off and I had to grab it. When that hook set, I was in for it. Round and round we went. Even when I got him up to the top and saw that it was a great big sucker, he kept running circles and making the line sing through the water. On top of that, he made an awful lot of splashing and started all the rest of the fish to raising Cain when I put him on the stringer.

Down the creek all faces were looking in my direction.

The baptizing was over and the people were beginning to leave. So I put a big gob of earthworms on the hook, let it sink to the bottom, and waited. I'd done had my day in at Blue Hole, and it was about time to start figuring on what would be the best thing to do next.

About that time, a good split-tailed, speckled channel cat hit that gob of worms. You always know when a speckled blue hits.

He don't fool around.

When I got in, my girl cousins said the devil was going to get me for fishing on Sunday. But that didn't stop them from eating my fish when Aunt Susie cooked them on Monday.

From *The Wimberley Mill*
October 1975

Childhood Christmas

It was an inexpensive toy. It was a little tin monkey with gaudy clothes painted on in bright colors. But he would never climb up and down the cord as intended. By accident, the strange mechanism which caused him to gyrate had been broken within as he was being removed from the tree; yet, this was the most cherished Christmas gift I ever received.

Any attempt to recall my early childhood spent in the hills of Wimberley and Wayside is immersed in nostalgic events of that era: the New Year's they fired the anvil at Grandpa Adare's shop and the echo boomed like thunderclaps from the bluffs along the Blanco; the sound of Harvey Cowan's cowboy yell ranging across the hills to where you stood in the frosty night; the comfort of Grandpa Lawrence's arm and his words after a panther had screamed in the night ("Hit's just a big cat passing through — he won't harm anyone"); and now it was the Christmas season, the first time I attended a Christmas tree held at the old Wimberley schoolhouse.

My parents had been living in San Marcos for only a short time when they decided to return to Wimberley to see old friends

147

and kin at the school Christmas tree. For forgotten last-minute reasons, Mother stayed at home, leaving Dad and me to make the trip alone and late.

The old Stoddard-Dayton was our mode of transportation. Equipped with isinglass curtains and a canvas-covered bow-top, this horseless vehicle was of closer kin to the spring wagon than the horseless carriage. And the slip stream of cold air coming in about those curtains caused more discomfort than experienced by any means of horse-drawn transportation. Wearing a hand-me-down overcoat that might fit me two years hence and a knit cap pulled down over my ears, I was wrapped in an old quilt and great expectations as Dad drove through the chilled darkness in methodical silence.

Well out upon the open prairie of the old Wren Ranch, we had a blowout. While Dad in wordless labor replaced the ruined tire with one of the numerous spares carried for such occasions, I listened to the coyotes' feisty chatter coming from the breaks along Sink Hollow to the south. For mechanical reasons or from force of habit formed by long years of handling teams, I know not which, we stopped again after fording the Blanco at the Townsend crossing. The Blanco had not lost all its summer heat to the chill of winter, and the river bottom held a damp warmness for us.

At the schoolhouse there were many buggies, wagons, and saddle horses tied to trees and several automobiles were parked. For a time, Dad led me by the hand as he talked and shook hands in a crowded room that was all trouser legs and coat bottoms to my height. Soon, however, I was sitting on a hard bench with my feet sticking straight before me — alone and lost. The too-big coat and knit cap hid the most miserable drip-nose, chap-cheek, lost-in-the-crowd, lonesome kid known to these parts.

Then it happened. Someone had taken a toy from the tree and was calling my name, and the little tin monkey was shoved into my hands. It was mine. I belonged. Grasping the monkey, I was a part of the gaiety. And Grandpa Lawrence came through the crowd to sit beside me. Joy was complete. Grandpa had come to take me home with him.

Holding the toy monkey with both hands, I sat beside Grandpa Lawrence in the hack as the horses, Mox and Bill, jogged across Cypress Creek on towards Wayside. Near the mill, a group of galloping horsemen passed on either side of the hack and, yelling like Indians, they fired their pistols in the air as they clattered off towards Blanco City. Grandpa Lawrence cautioned: "Young hellions

148

will get themselves in a heap of trouble with those six-shooters — if they don't take care."

Other horsemen spoke as they passed, and then it was quiet. Grandpa talked to Mox and Bill as the old hack rocked and rolled along the way. I went to sleep with the warm smell of clean horses in my nostrils and the toy monkey clasped to my bosom with both hands. This was my Christmas to be remembered.

From *The Wimberley Mill*
December 1967

Brummet's Studebaker Wagon

Nowadays, a pickup truck can be a sight to see: two-tone paint job an' lots of chrome; a deluxe cab, radio, heater, air-conditioned, a speed stick with four forwards an' twin reverse, wide-vue rearview mirrors on either side; fancy bumpers with double trailer hitches. When it comes to making people sit up and take notice, Detroit hasn't come up with one yet that would hold a light to what a dandy good team and a brand spanking new wagon could do for a family when they pulled on to the Wimberley Square come Saturday evening back in the good ole days.

Back in them times, the Brummets had a little place on the Blanco down in Little Arkansas just below the mouth of Lone Man Creek. Down there this ole man and his lady done a little farming, raised some livestock and a whole bunch of kids. Like everybody else around here they had their ups and downs, but managed to get along pretty fair. Then, along comes one of those good years when it rains a lot an' at the right times.

That fall Mr. Brummet had six or eight bales of cotton to sell, about a dozen good yearlings to go, and a bunch of hogs that growed fat on the range. With all that money on hand, Mr. Brummet snook off down about Kyle and bought a new wagon — the best money could buy.

The following Saturday, the Brummets were "up an' at 'em" early; for that day they was headed for Wimberley. The trail upstream from Little Arkansas — with three back river crossings — made it a mean trip, even on horseback. But that didn't faze the Brummets one bit.

By 10:00 they had done pulled out of the Blanco at the crossing above the old Wren Ranch. After a short snack, the old man set about grooming the horses — from stocking-footed fetlock to bay ear tips—and brought luster back to the double-breeching harness. Meanwhile, the ole lady and kids fell onto the wagon with buckets of water and rags and a broom they had brought along for the job. And soon they had the wagon as spick and span as it had been the day it had rolled from the factory.

The Brummets had about everything in apple-pie order when up rode Crock Harris and John Wren on their horses. Though Crock and John had spent most of their lives in the saddle, they were friends and neighbors to the Brummets. (Here I'll have to stop and let you in on something. You see, Western movies and color TV hadn't yet come along and started the range wars between the ranchers and the dirt farmers. Each one had his opinion of the other, which he kept to himself. With no disrespect intended by either, the cowman figured that, any way you looked at it, farming was a heck of a poor way of making a living; while the farmer felt that a man would have to climb down off his horse and stand on his own two feet in order to do a decent day's work.)

Even before the "howdies" were finished, John Wren started with his questions—and he could ast more danged fool questions than any man aliving. He didn't wait for answers; some he answered himself. But a fellow would have trouble getting a word in edgewise while he was around. Crock Harris just set in the saddle a-grinnin'.

"Say now, did you ever see such a pretty sight in your life? Ain't that some humdinger of a waggin? Never owned one in my life—that is a new one. Where did you get it? How'd you come by it?"

Swelled with pride, old man Brummet injected, "If'n you want something bad enough an' long enough an' try a little bit—well, hit's bound to come your way bye and bye."

Crock's grin got bigger, but John just kept on with his questions. After a while, when it looked like his clock had about run down and his horse was chomping at the bits, he ast: "Say, ah, wot's the capacity of that vehicle?"

Right off, Ole Man Brummet spewed like a green prickly pear leaf that had been layin' in hot coals for a long while.

"Kaypacity, the devil," he said. "Why, I wouldn't let one of them come on my place for free—let alone pay good money for it. Wot's the matter with you? Can't you read writin'? Right there before your eyes an' as plain as day it says 'STUDEBAKER.' That's the kind of waggin it is—best make made." Turning his back, he

150

said, "Come on Maw, get them younguns and plunder into this here Studebaker. We're off to Wimberley. They's no call for us to be standing around here an' jawing with ignorance."

From The Wimberley Mill
March 1966

Bobcats and Doodlebugs

If your granpappy wasn't here to help chase the Indians out of this neck of the woods and your folks didn't get around to moving in here till about the time the government sent men through this country buying up horses for Teddy Roosevelt's Rough Riders — well then, there's just not much hope of your ever being thought of as a real native citizen of Wimberley, Texas. Nope, not by a long shot they ain't. Best thing an outsider like you can do is learn to tell a good yarn about the Blackwell boys, an' use it now and then to impress some city slicker a-seein' the sights. Now, I've got one here that might just do the trick for you, but don't you go trying it out on any of the old-timers hereabouts — for they have all got their own way of telling it.

Back in the coal-burning days, Joe Blackwell had taken a wagon-load of charcoal to Dailey's General Store down on the courthouse square at San Marcos. While there, he told about finding a bobcat's den with little ones still in it. Right off, Ole Man Basil Dailey offered Joe four bits apiece for these here bob kittens, cash on delivery.

On the way back to Wimberley, Joe figured it out that a sack full of them cats would bring more'n a sack of charcoal. So's the next day, Joe and his brother Felix took a tow sack apiece and with their potlickers (hounds) afollowin' 'em, set out up the Blanco towards Moon Peak and the cat's den.

When they got to the bluff up by Moon Rocks and Joe stuck his head in the little cave what was the bobcat's den, the little cats was at home and their mama too. But not for long. She just squirted out of there, over Joe's head, and waltzed through them hounds a-handin' each one a face full of claws, then took off down the Blanco just a-hittin' the ground in high places. Trying harder for loud than they was for speed, the hounds went hollerin' after her on out of hearin'.

While all this was a-goin' on, them little cats had left the cave

151

an' was now in the top of a big ellum tree forty feet high, a-hangin' on to the uppermost limbs like popcorn balls on a Christmas tree.

Joe just stood there a-lookin' up at them cats, and Felix stood there a-lookin' at his feet. Right by his big toe there was this great big doodlebug hole. A cut ant was a-tryin' to get out and the doodlebug was kicking up sand a-tryin' to keep him in.

After awhile Joe throwed his tow sack on the ground and says: "You stay here while I shinney up there and get them cats. When I ketch one, you hold your sack open so's I kin drop him in."

Felix don't say nothin' because the doodlebug's a-kickin' up sand like mad on account of the ant's about to get out of the hole. The ant gets out and stands there a-wavin' his whiskers in the air a minute and takes off. But he runs around in a little crazy circle, which ends up right back in the doodlebug's hole — clear to the bottom.

About this time, the top of that ole ellum tree exploded in the durndest bunch of hissin' an' spittin' an' growlin' you ever heard the likes of, and Joe's hat comes a-sailin' down with a shower of leaves and little pieces of bark.

But the doodlebug kept Felix's eyes. He's got the ant by the leg, a-shakin' him. He's a goner. As the ant goes out of sight in the sand, the leaves are still fallin' and there's some little pieces of Joe's shirt along with 'em now.

Still looking at where the ant was, Felix hollers up: "Hea . . . Joe . . . need any hep ketchin' them cats?"

An' down from the ellum: "Nope . . . reckon not . . . been a-tryin' to turn this'n a-loose again ever since I first got up here."

From *The Wimberley Mill*
April 1966

Confederate Grandpas

To err may be human, but anybody that had done much time sitting around the old general store at Wimberley would have known it would never do to send a mere boy in to break up the fray when a couple of those old-timers got busy at refighting The War. Spectators always kept a safe, respectful distance while they gave the Yankees hell, for Confederate victories were the only battles refought in these hills and the fur did fly.

If you happen to be among the last batch of younguns raised around here — when boys wore knee-length breeches and stockings

153

on Sundays until they were sixteen or seventeen years old—well, you probably were twenty or more before some normal-schoolteacher let the cat out of the bag for you and you heard for the first time that the South had actually lost The War.

Up until that time, you had heard your history to run about like this: Sometime in '65 they called a recess in The War so Lee could catch up on his school teaching and the boys came home to make a crop or two while they waited; before they got around to having another go at it, the Spaniards sank the Battleship *Maine* and it was a whole new ballgame with Teddy Roosevelt at the helm and everybody pitched in to give him a hand; then, there was that European skirmish to save democracy for a bunch of people that didn't know a thing about it and by the time Kaiser Bill had been put to chopping wood in his Holland exile, the old-timers were still ready and chomping at the bit to get back to their war, The War, and they let her rip—though now confined to battle stations in the ole rocking chair. And a little boy sitting quietly in the corner seldom missed any of the action.

One time Great-grandpa Lawrence came over from Alabama to visit Great-grandpa Adare on Pin Oak Creek above Wimberley. After breakfast next morning, they manned rocking chairs before the fireplace and, with the opening guns, the ladies beat a retreat to the kitchen while three later generations of men and boys sought neutral grounds elsewhere.

The Yankee debacle at Fredericksburg, Pennsylvania, was Grandpa Lawrence's long suit, while Grandpa Adare never seemed to tire of swamping the Yankee's major offensive towards Texas in the cane brakes at Mansfield. With both battles going strong, the tempo slowed to sporadic action only during the delay for the noonday meal.

Along towards the middle of the evening, while Grandpa Lawrence was busy singeing General Burnside's renowned sideburn whiskers and Grandpa Adare was bogging General Banks deeper into the Louisiana mud, the backlog in the fireplace burned in-two, sending a huge chunk of red coals rolling across the hearth onto Grandma's throw rug.

Smoke from the burning rug failed to hinder operations in either battle; however, after a long delay, it did bring Grandma from the kitchen to the smoke-filled room. After opening all the windows and doors, she formed a bucket brigade of grandkids reaching from the well to the house with a couple of spares to work the pump handle.

After considerable confusion, the fire was put out. But Grandma's rug was a complete loss. A big hole had been burned in the floor, and yet, there had been no respite for the Yankee generals in either battle. Finally, Grandpa Lawrence leaned back in his chair to sneeze and caught Grandma's old black tomcat's tail under the rocker. Tom let out a blood-curdling squawl that brought Grandpa Adare to his feet like a banty rooster.

"Lawrence," he says, "a noise like that might get by for the Rebel Yell over on your side of the Mississippi River, but west of that creek and clear onto the Rio Grande, it went like this —," and spradling his legs, he throwed back his head and let out a howl that sawed up and down through the scales for a bar or two then climbed to double high C, which he held till vibrations sent Grandma's snuff bottles jigging across the mantel towards the clock, which lost two and a half minutes that day. Three loose shingles came down off the roof, and a bunch of wild hogs broke through the yard fence to rally about the front porch steps. And across the Blanco, Uncle Willie Schneider was about to turn his wagon off the Blanco City Road at the foot of the Devil's Backbone when the echoes from this racket spooked his gentle old workteam, causing them to run away, hub a gatepost, tear up the gate, and pull bobwire a-loose from ten line posts in both directions.

Uncle Willie felt like he had not been done right when Grandpa didn't show up to help fix any of the damage he had caused; that is, until he learned how busy Grandpa was over at his own place with tightening loose shingles on his roof and, at the same time, trying to run off forty strange hogs which had started hanging around his house.

And I swear every blasted word of this is factual history.

From *The Wimberley Mill*
November 1, 1970

Lifestyles and Loners

Back when most people around here farmed for a living and everyone lived close to the soil, these hills produced some real and unusual characters. While everybody about the place had to pitch in to help make the living, everyone seemed to develop a character all his own — even the chickens that roosted in the big live oak behind the barn. To be cock-of-the-walk about the horse lots then, the rooster had to have the biggest comb, the longest tail, the oddest color combination, and crow loud enough to be heard a mile or more downwind. The hen looked like a cross between a parrot and a roadrunner and laid about a dozen eggs between settings. To survive, she had to be able to fly like a buzzard, to whip twice her weight in wildcats, to outrun the dog, and to steal feed from the horse's trough or from an old chicken-eating sow's pen without getting her head snapped off in the act. And in them good ole days, man's problems of survival were pretty rugged too.

After The War, Santa Anna Cruze returned to his home on Lone Man Creek, but he continued to be a Rebel bugler so long as he lived. At his place, the day began with a Confederate reveille and the day's activities were determined by bugle calls. There was a call to work in the fields, a dinner call, and the bugle was also used while working with cattle. All hands had better be on deck ready to help and the gates open when Santa Anna's bugle announced that he was bringing some wild ones out of the cedar brakes to be penned. And when he hunted, a bugle call would bring him a kid on a horse to carry the deer home.

Old men are soon forgotten and their accomplishments turn to dust in the attics of faded memories. S. P. Bozarth was the pioneer horticulturist of this area and an inventive genius, of sorts. Nearly all the old home places hereabouts had some fruit trees in the orchards and flowers in the yard grown from his nursery stock. Today's gnarled old pear tree stands alone in an abandoned field near the Twin Sister Peaks where Mr. Bozarth's lush orchards once grew. Near Curlo Morris's house, honeysuckle continues to grow along the remains of the millrace. And over on Cypress Creek, he can show you a hybrid grapevine which looks like a mustang yet bears sweet fruit. These plants are the last survivors of the Bozarth nursery. In the local cemeteries, you can still find some moss-grown headstones made of Mr. Bozarth's gypsum cement. Fame and fortune might have been his — if he had given the gypsum rock a heat treatment before having it ground into powder on the Wimberley grist mill. Though it was never mechanically perfected, his working model of a reciprocating engine fueled with gunpowder would forever remain a mechanical marvel worthy of a place in any museum.

The old loners belonged to these hills like the cedars and cypress belong, except that they are gone and the trees remain eternal. Kim Tinney was the loner for whom most old-timers hereabouts have fond memories: the little song-and-dance act he gave when met on the road, the shoulder-length hair, the cut-off breeches worn at half mast, and his own brand of homemade sandals. Everyone had his own tale to tell about Kim.

Kim could hang his hat on a hollow log by the creek and it was home sweet home as long as the fish were biting and the hunting was good. Skunk hides and coon furs brought in Kim's winter spending money and, during the warm season, he was often seen carrying a tow sack filled with buzzing, writhing rattlesnakes thrown across his shoulder — a-making his summer pocket change.

Once in awhile, a job that would suit him might catch up with Kim. For a time, he drove the mail hack for Uncle Billy Henson. Uncle Eli Hill's little house was one of the places where Kim was a squatter tenant from time to time. But when the going got too rough, Kim could always find a place at the table set by Aunt Mattie Gay Harris. During a stay at the Crock Harris home, Kim, by his own choice, had his pallet in the crib at the horse lots where he slept using an empty gallon-size stone jug for a pillow.

For many years, Aunt Mattie Gay would often return home from a visit to find that all the cooked food in her kitchen had been eaten and a crock of sweetmilk had been drained. She knew Kim had been by, for he always washed the dishes and usually left a shirt or two that needed patching. Only a mighty good woman could tend her own brood and care for the strays, but that was Aunt Mattie Gay Harris for you.

When the "chicken ranch and white Leghorn" fever first struck this part of the woods, a promoter from San Marcos set up shop over on the big hill close to the Blanco City fork of the road. This fellow was a better hand at talking than at country living for, on the promise of a share in the profits in the business, a shack to live in, nights off to roam the woods, and a small salary to boot, Kim found himself to be the chamber maid to several hundred white Leghorn pullets.

Things looked good to Kim for a while, until he took stock and found that a batch of chickens were missing. Without any telltale varmint sign about, the few who talked with him assured Kim that the hoot owls were on the prowl. Nights later, two men carrying a lantern rattled the shack door, then headed for the henhouse. Before they could open the door, Kim peeped down from the roof above and shoved the business end of a double-barreled shotgun in their faces, then made his longest speech:

"Hold on jest a minit — been a-layin' up here nights a-tryin' to figger out jest wot kind of two-legged chicken-eatin' hooty owl would take the footwipin' sack off my step everytime to carry off my chickens in. Now I see."

Soon after this event, Kim decided that taking care of a bunch of chickens that didn't have enough sense to roost in a tree and take care of themselves like a chicken ought to . . . well, it was just too confining. Kim was off to Little Arkansas to catch a bait of catfish and chop some cedar — maybe.

From *The Wimberley Mill*
November 1966

Law West of the Cypress

Before federal spending got Washington's finger into about everything everywhere, the old-timers living in these caliche hills had their own ideas of delegating governmental powers. They figured Washington to: coin the hard cash of the realm, issue paper money backed by silver or gold, run the post office, take care of the Indians, and the Texas Rangers could take care of outlaw elements while the state legislature kept its eye on the railroads. But real interest lay in the county courthouse, only a good horseback ride away, where they could keep a close watch on its operation. For it was there they filed the deeds to their land, allowed the sheriff to handle horse thieves, let the judge preside over murder trials, and gave the commissioners power to round up all householders for three days' labor each quarter to maintain county roads. The constable and J.P. could deal with other minor affairs, but the final authority rested with local public opinion — of the people.

In 1891, after a bitter and heated contest, the voters of Blanco County elected to move the county seat from Blanco City to Johnson City. Blanco City is now known as Blanco. And in that city square, the old courthouse still stands as an edifice of little use except to air the embers of an old issue which refuses to die in some quarters. Believe me, I know!

Adolph Wolf — justice of the peace, real estate agent, merchandiser of sorts, and barber — used to hold shop on the west side of the Blanco square. I was in this shop a few years ago when, to escape Wolf's efforts to sell me a quart of honey and a pair of Mexican boots along with his haircut, I asked him if there was a bank

158

in Blanco. Before Wolf could answer, a bearded old-timer sitting in a corner jumped to the floor, waving his cane, and declared:

"Of course Blanco's got a bank — why, Blanco's got everything," and pointing his cane towards the old courthouse, "See that patch of grass out there? That's where they drove down a wagon spoke for the first stake an' built Texas around it. Why, son, Blanco's the hub an' all Texas turns around it."

On the spur of the moment, I then committed a regrettable blunder and said, "Must a-been a little off-center or how come they moved the county seat to Johnson City?"

The old man's beard fluffed up like a mad housecat's tail and fire was in his eye as he lunged towards me with his cane raised high. Stopping short with the cane held menacingly over my head, he demanded: "Where you from, boy?"

Meekly, I told him that I was from down the river apiece.

"Don't believe a word of it . . . people down Wimberley way got more sense 'un to put their noses in other folks affairs!" And he stalked out in a huff, leaving me without a well-deserved knot on the head.

Circa 1900, Hez Williams created another political furor when he laid out the township of Hays City in the geographical center of this county, made tentative arrangements for railroad connections, and offered to build an $80,000 courthouse there if the voters would elect to move the county seat from San Marcos to Hays City. The issue split the county into two long-lasting political factions: the Hill Country vote versus a coalition of San Marcos city dwellers and blackland farmers. A Hill Country woman named her baby "Hez," and a blackland farmer accused Williams of promoting self-interest in this issue. Our old-timers remember Hez's rebuttal verbatim:

"Show me a man who does not work for self-interest and I'll show you a dam fool." (Hill folks amended this to read: "The best interest of this county and my interest are the same in this case.")

After two heated elections, San Marcos held the county seat with a majority vote, which some Hill Country people contend was made possible by chicanery in qualifying voters with questionable titles to vacant lots in the Westover Addition and to wood-cutting tracts in No Man's Land on Purgatory Creek. (With each building let in the original townsite of San Marcos, the early citizens received an additional wooded tract in No Man's Land to provide

159

them with a source of firewood.) And to some degree, this old political division within the county still exists.

At that time, the fact that there was a precinct-level courthouse in Wimberley helped placate the issue here. This two-story wooden building used to stand on the northwest corner of the square. There, a deputy sheriff, a constable, a justice of the peace, and the commissioner lawed in offices on the first floor and the Masons and Woodmen of the World held sway in the hall on the second floor, which was accessible by an outside stairway. This building was abandoned and razed in 1927, but now that the area is regaining its lost population, the need for such a building to serve similar purposes is again being felt.

Joe Cruze used to tell an old tale exemplifying the judicial powers which local public opinion once held in this area.

Back in my Grandpa Zack's time, any old range cow was a milk cow if cottonseed and top fodder made her give as much as a teacup full of bluejohn once a day without starving the calf, and she was a good 'un, too, if you could extract it without getting your teeth kicked out or having a horn hung in the seat of your breeches everytime you tried. Under these ground rules, it took a dozen or more cows to furnish milk for Grandpa's family, so he was not very excited when one of his milk cows came up missing. He just shook the bushes a bit, then put out word at the mill that one of his cows was lost.

Santa Anna Cruze could track like an Indian; always knew pretty well what went on in the woods, and was a good friend of Grandpa's. In a few days he showed up at the mill to tell Grandpa where his cow was: she had been stolen and he offered his services in recovering her.

Led by Santa Anna, Grandpa and several mounted men left the mill that evening and made their way down to a nester's place on Lone Man Creek. Arriving at dusk, they tied their horses in the cedars and closed in on the place from all sides, on foot. In the lot, they found the fresh hide where the cow had been butchered and the carcass hung in the smokehouse. After forcing their way into the house, they found a poor scared woman, a bunch of half-starved kids, and poverty. Milch cow meat stewed in a pan on the stove beside a pot of re-boiled coffee grounds, and the pantry held a few dried-up potatoes, a small batch of moldy meal — nothing.

Wishing they were someplace else, the men stood in an uneasy silence till Santa Anna spoke:

160

"We're not goin' to flush your man out of them cedars where he's hiding. But when he comes in, we want you to tell him and tell him good — there's no sense in a man starvin' his family in this neighborhood. People here will help anybody needin' it — if you jest let 'em know. Now, if he's too proud to ast an' thinks it's easier to steal or is too triflin' to try, he'd better not plant a crop here 'cause he won't be around long enough to gather it — that's for shore."

Men didn't carry much money with them in those days, but there were several coins left on the table after they had gone. And for several days thereafter, some old-timers with a sack of goods tied to the saddle were seen heading towards Lone Man. In the local idiom of the day: "They didn't say what they were driving at."

From *The Wimberley Mill*
January 1967

Model T Days

If you have not driven a Model T Ford, you have never driven an automobile. Today, Detroit's dated models of planned obsolescence were designed merely as prestige markers and make no further demands of their owners, except to meet time-payment plans, accept periodic garage bills, and carry the ball for the insurance companies.

Henry's tin Lizzie was designed as a means of transportation and each vehicle had a distinct personality, all its own. Like buying a halter-broke colt, it was up to you to train and adjust Lizzie to her new environment. Factory adjustments were void after the maiden trip home. Thereafter, her response on the road reflected your skill as an owner and operator of a Model T.

First on the agenda were the tools. To the spark plug and knuckle-buster wrenches stored beneath the rear seat cushion, you added an adequate supply of stillson, monkey, and open-end wrenches; a box of cold or hot patches, boots, and numerous pieces of old spring leaves that served in tire changes; along with a jack that would lift instead of sink into the mud, and more. When the space beneath the seat became crowded, you resorted to installing a tool box or rack on the left running board. (Added weight on this side assisted in overcoming a lean-to-the-right caused by the hog-backed roads.) And Sears Roebuck sold a decorative, useful set of emergency canteenlike containers — white for water, red for gasoline, and green for lubricating oil — that looked right snazzy attached to the running board. One of our erstwhile bootleggers delivered enough hooch in these containers to pay off the Federal Land Bank for the loan on his place.

The ignition system was next to come under scrutiny. Spark plugs were removed and the gap set to the thickness of a new dime or a worn Liberty head nickel. There were several schools of thought in tuning the vibrators on the coils. I have seen a T run smoothly with the vibrators rendering a discordant version of "Chop Sticks," but I remain a firm believer in the theorem of the first three notes of "Taps" with a repeat on the third note by the fourth coil.

Before the self-starter loused up the noble sport, a man could test his mechanical skill on the field of honor each time he went to crank his Model T. Approaches differed with individuals. There were the strong-armed, spin-till-she-starts disciples; the by-the-count choke-her-slowly on the down stroke, three times, and jerk her off quick on an up stroke; and various combinations of the two.

Most of these methods usually worked. But if ole Lizzie was in a balk mood, nothing would. Until this mood passed, no amount of mechanical pampering could change matters. Readjust the gas lever, if you willed. Advance the spark lever to the kick zone, change plugs, fiddle with the coils, clean the timer, hold a torch under the carburetor until the gasoline boiled in the manifold, and crank your fool head off without results. Balked. Now, amble off down towards the creek whistling; then, circle back quietly on her blind side. Be durned, if she didn't kick off on the first twist, nuzzled forward against your leg like a race horse at the starting gate. And again, I have come in with ole Lizzie hot and she refuses to stop when switched off. Had to head her against a big oak to choke her down. In defiance she coughed, backfired, and sputtered in reverse order about forty revolutions before she finally gave up the ghost.

With 30 × 3's on the front, you could dodge chug holes and rocks on the county roads like a good cutting horse on rodeo grounds. You could go from low to high or high to low anytime and use reverse for brakes without inviting mechanical disaster. Against a high norther, you would have to find low on all the hills, but with a tail wind you could climb the big hill in high or coast gas-free miles from the top to Ada Leath's place.

The Model T was a durable old lady. And a flood of accessories offered by mail-order catalogs could update her through the years. To nudge the T from the road, it took Ford's own Model A and a host of other old brand names which have long since been absorbed by General Motors and Chrysler Corporation.

When no longer considered the family car, Model T's had little chance of retiring to the junk yard while there were mechanically inclined youngsters like Wayne Lewis about. In fact, they gave Lizzie a new day in the sun. Without fanfare, these youngsters put the T through paces which, decades later, another vehicle duplicated before an amazed public to become the renowned Jeep.

With a strip of bacon rind scraped thin from the fatty side, Wayne could remedy a leaking front main and a dose of oatmeal would cure a leaky radiator. An overdose of the latter would cause Lizzie to burp like a baby and bring odors from the engine room that smelled like fire in the mess hall. Nevertheless, this did not deter passengers from a young generation who traveled more often on shank's mare than on wheels.

Wayne could convert a T to burn kerosene. The only hitch was you had to start her on gas and let her idle awhile on gas before allowing her to die, or there would be the devil to pay before you could crank her up again.

One night Wayne and I were hunting bullfrogs on York's Creek when we found a bootlegger's cache of home brew in the weeds. After loading our illicit booty in the T, we decided to sample some. Instead of the expected exhilaration in spirits, we suffered considerable gastric disturbance before turning green about the gills.

With the fate of our loot a burden to be determined at a later date, we started home. Well on the way, fickle fate struck again — the oatmeal had loosened in the radiator, causing Lizzie to steam for water. Unwilling to risk returning to the scene of our first debacle for water, we created another crisis by filling the radiator with the available liquid — bottles of home brew.

Lizzie chugged docilely while her radiator was being filled, only to revolt when Wayne started to replace the cap. Following a throaty rumble, brew geysered into the night air, soaking us and the T with a malt liquid that smelled to the high heavens. Throwing caution to the winds, I sat on the fender bottle-feeding the burping Lizzie while Wayne drove the back roads to a low water bridge on the Blanco. There we laundered ourselves and Lizzie good, for our parents did spare the rod because they had found the razor strop to be a more effective tool.

During the early '50s, I was looking at a cedar brake on Riley Mountain when I found a muffler that some cedar hauler had lost off his Model T truck while the timber was being worked in the summer of 1923. After being exposed to the elements for some thirty years, the muffler had remained sound.

Like I been tryin' to say all along, they don't make 'em like the Model T anymore. An' this guy Nader keeps barkin' treed at the wrong end of a trail forty years long.

From *The Wimberley Mill*
April 1969

Chicken Snakes

Chicken snakes used to steal my Grannie's eggs and, sometimes, even swallow little baby chicks alive, which made them about the meanest creatures to come on to my Grandpa Lawrence's place. This was my considered opinion at the not-so-tender age of six. I know, rattlers were more dangerous and a polecat could stink up the whole place. But a rattlesnake usually rattled and, even though I seldom managed to leave well enough be, more than one polecat had asked to be left alone by bushing up his tail and patting his front feet at me before the trouble started. Nothing good can be said about a dirty sneaking chicken snake that came at night to crawl under a poor old setting Dominique biddy and swallow her eggs — especially after you had held those eggs to your ear and listened to the little chicks talk inside them that very evening before it happened.

Excepting her yard about the house, where Grannie raised all kinds of pretty flowers for people to look at, and the big garden spot, where she raised all sorts of nice things for us to eat, chickens had the run of the place. They roosted in big oak trees behind the horse lots and the hens laid in the barn or under the cribs and around the haystacks or by the rail and rock fences and nearly everywheres. With all kinds of places for them to hide, sure made it hard to find a durned old chicken snake.

Grandpa had some eggs made of chalk and four white doorknobs he used for nest eggs. Once in awhile, Berkley and I would find one of these nest eggs in the brush thickets along Pin Oak Creek where the snake that swallowed it had come to die.

Berkley was my Mama's little brother, but I didn't call him Uncle because he wasn't much older than me. He had two dogs, Tip and Chum, who would help us hunt snakes. When they found one, Chum would grab him by the middle and shake the life out of him, or Tip might grab one end and then they would pull him in two. Afterwards, they would always roll and slide in the grass to get the stink off themselves before they would hunt anymore.

One day we had a big chicken snake treed in a thicket at the end of the field. The dogs were barking and trying to get at it, and we were trying to chunk it out with rocks when our Uncle Tom Adare — great-uncle to me — walked up.

"Hold on, boys. Let me give you a hand," he said, as he walked to the brush, snatched the snake by its tail, and stepped back twirling it above his head like a lariat. At the edge of the cotton rows, he swung it across his shoulder and snapped it just like he was popping a whip. The snake's head sailed out into the cottonstalks and Uncle threw the writhing carcass on the turn row as he walked away, wiping his hands with green cotton leaves.

Guess I should have been considering the fact that I stood little more than belt-high to this six-foot mass of brawn and bone I proudly called Uncle. Instead, I stood marveling at this new and very proper way of disposing of a dirty old chicken snake. Berkley was busy too. He was watching the snake's twisting body to see which way it would lay when the tail stopped wiggling. Belly-up meant it was going to rain in a few days; belly-down was a sure sign of dry weather ahead. Now and then he tried to help a little with his big toe, but the body would turn until the back was up again. Finally, we stretched it out tight and left it belly-up in the sun, with the tail still wiggling and flat rocks on each end and in the middle to hold it in place. Knew we had cheated some but didn't feel a bit sorry about it for, back then, everybody was glad to see it rain in the summertime — unless it was on the Fourth of July, or new hay was on the ground drying, or it was the middle of cotton picking.

About two weeks later, I was down behind the barn by myself when it happened: sure enough, I saw a chicken snake's tail dangling from the side of a stack of fodder. Remembering Uncle Tom's act, and feeling my heart thumping in my throat, I eased over, grabbed that tail with my right hand, and pulled hard. Nothing happened. Using both hands, I had pulled till I was about to have some other ideas about matters when things loosened up and everything happened at once. The snake's head came gliding down his back to see who had him by his handle, and was he a big one!

Running backwards to straighten him out, I dragged him clear out into the cowpen, where there was plenty of room. Sure had a heap of trouble getting started swinging him in the air and, after I

had got all the speed I could, he twirled just like a sorry wct rope
— kept kinking his back in places and reaching for me with his
head. Things went worse when I tried to pop him. Instead of the
head following the tail end over my right shoulder like it ought to
have done, most of him came over the left shoulder. With a sicken-
ing wallop, he wrapped around my neck and came to a stop with
some two feet of him hanging down my front like a long black tie.

Still holding onto the tail, I stood waiting for the world to quit
turning round and round and watched as the head slowly arced
up to look me in the face with baleful eyes then, with mouth askew,
burp a vile concoction of rotten eggs that dribbled down between
the bib of my overalls and shirt.

That done it. Sans honor, the contest had turned into a dirty
fight and to heck with Tom Adare and his smart aleck ways of
killing a snake. Shedding the snake in a hurry, I found a good stick
and took care of him the right way and, still in a hurry, headed for
the swimming hole on Pin Oak to wash up. On the way I decided
to tell Grannie I fell in the creek when she saw my wet clothes and
not say one word about snakes. Her scoldings were not too bad.
She always left you feeling good inside, and wanted.

From *The Wimberley Mill*
August 1969

A Danged Good Hundred Years

1874 to 1974 — a danged good hundred years. Though some
people seem to think the world has done been turned upside down,
here in this place we all call Wimberley — Wimberley is still Wimberley. And that's just how it ought to be.

Gone are the yoked oxen, the cotton sack, and the old gray
mare no longer pulls the double-shovel plow. The ladies no longer
go down the river to do their family wash in the shade of the trees,
and the old secret swimming hole on the creek — where all the
boys used to go in nakid — is now very private property. With elec-
tric lights, the telephone, city water, paved roads, and the automobile, progress has done brought easy country living to these hills of
Wimberley.

But, if you'll just stop and look around a bit, all these changes
have not been such an all-fired, earth-changing shock. The hills are
still dominated by the small landholders. Most folks do a little gardening of sorts, and there is still some stem-winding interest in horses

and dogs and such. Relics of the past are being polished up to be put in the house or, in some cases, put back to use. Though the post office is under its own roof and the general store is represented by a dozen business houses, the people still come to town to get their mail and trade and look around. And Wimberley is still a community of churches and schools.

In 1874, when Great-grandpa Pleas bought the Mill tract, the Wimberley Mills stood at its apex as a frontier pioneer industrial complex. Even with the energy crisis upon us, it is difficult today for us to comprehend the fact that, at that time, a small turbine water wheel delivering only twenty-two horsepower of mechanical energy could be the very heart throb of the community's economical and social life. Elbow grease supplemented this meager source of power to get the job done — lots of it.

The turbine powered the saws and turned the wheels, but oxen dragged the logs; men muscled them into place and carried the lumber or shingles away. The turbine turned the stones and bolt, but man toted the wheat up the stairs and poured it into the hopper; gravity delivered it down the bolt where man sacked the flour, shorts, and bran. Man also shelled the corn, poured it into the gristmill's hopper, and sacked his meal. Cotton was fed into the gin by hand, the seeds scooped away; the lint was carried to the press and trampled tight under his feet, then pressed into a bale by a horsepowered screw.

And the mill yard was the town's wagon yard where men gathered to rest and loaf, to swap lies and horse trade, to learn the news and tend business in general as they waited their turn at the mill.

The rock ledge across the mill yard was worn smooth by the seats of their breeches each summer and, through the winter months, the millhouse often afforded standing room only on many a Saturday evening.

It took years for the Industrial Revolution of 1850 to truly affect the livelihood in these raw hills of Texas; yet, by 1934, this old millsite had become a vacant, unused acreage.

Was this the end — the finis? Not by a long shot. It was merely the completion of a cycle. Come 1974 and the Wimberley Bank and the old millsite beside Cypress Creek began on another cycle as a vital organ in the economic and social life of the community. And, like I said, Wimberley is still Wimberley — if you'll just take that look.

Let everybody toot his own horn and sing his own verse.

From The Wimberley Mill
May 1974

Quit Kickin' My Dog Around

Every time I go to town;
  Boys keep kickin' my dog around.
Makes no difference if he is a hound;
  Boys better quit kickin' my dog around.

Back when my Daddy was one of the barefoot boys around ole Wimberley town, this plaintive little ditty was a popular tune hereabouts. It was also a ballad of sorts for, in those rugged days, you might get by with slapping another feller's kid or, maybe, talking about his wife, but never kick his dog in public unless you really craved to have a no-holds-barred fight on your hands.

Times do change and so has the power structure of the family. Nowadays, if you are on the prod and aching for a fight, I figure you had better jump the old man first. Otherwise, after getting whipped by his kid, then by his wife, and being bit by his dog, you might not have just one helluva lot of fight left in you.

So much for levity and back to the dogs. In them good ole days there was always a dog or two about each household, sometimes a half-dozen or more. Feist, curs, and hounds were the most popular breeds. And these dogs served a useful purpose in the lives of those people.

Often more brave than smart, the feist was an intelligent little creature about the size of a fox terrier and came in assorted color combinations with an alley cat type of pedigree. About the old home places of that era, his lack of size was compensated by boundless energies, raw courage, and devotion to his master.

Aunt Fannie Wimberley, widow of Little Pleas, had a little black-and-tan feist by the name of Bruno. He was her house dog and her place was Bruno's very private domain. Children and neighbors transgressed without notice, but strangers were held at bay at the gate until Aunt Fannie told Bruno to hush. Any chicken impudent enough to venture into this yard paid for its visit with a mouthful of tail feathers. No matter how ornery a bull or kicking a cow might be, they soon learned to keep their distance from this yard fence for, after the initial fray, they were always in a hurry to points yonder, with Bruno nipping at their heels or, sometimes, hanging on their tail. How he kept from getting his head kicked off or a horn hung in his rear is beyond me. And when Aunt Fannie made a trip to the wood pile for an armload of stove wood, Bruno always brought in his stick — carrying it in his mouth.

Pluto was a white bob-tailed feist with a pale yellow spot on his left shoulder and another covering his right ear, and he afforded me the chance to blow about the dogs I once owned.

Though he had trouble working out a trail and usually fell behind in the race, Pluto did love to hunt. Shep treed squirrels in the ratio of about ten to fifteen to Pluto's one. While night hunting with a pack, Pluto spent most of his time following at my heels. But he was a star in his own right.

A big boar coon riled is a pretty tough customer for any dog or pack, anytime or anyplace. And when one has had his fill of running, backs up to a stump, stands snarling and pawing the air, a pack of any wisdom will usually circle him — barking, parrying, and building up their courage for that opportune moment. Not ole Pluto. Dashing unchecked as he reaches the scene, Pluto wastes no time with the yowling circle but wades right in, latches onto Mr. Coon head-on, and the fur begins to fly.

About the time you figure you are going to have to risk some of your own hide to keep ole Pluto from being plumb et up by the coon, the little cuss would break loose from the fray, run out to where you stood, look up at you, wag his stub of a tail, then dash right back into the waiting arms of the coon. I believe he would have treated a grizzly bear with the same disrespect. Probably cost him his life, but I'll bet ole Pluto would have died with a grin on his puss and a mouth full of grizzly hair, for he never saw a booger nor did he ever learn to tuck-tail and run. Being more brave than smart did have its handicaps. Shep would reluctantly bay a skunk — well out of range. But skunk or no skunk, no varmint shook his tail at Pluto without paying his price, and Pluto would have to sleep about the barn until he was again presentable — odorwise.

The cur was the workhorse of the dogs about the old homesteads. With little care in training, they could be taught to do about any sort of a chore about the place, except milking the cows or changing the baby's diaper.

169

Charger, Grandpa Lawrence's dog, had been snake-bit during his younger days and, of his own accord, made it his business to see that the children about the place did not get close to a rattlesnake. Anytime a snake was found, Charger would get between the snake and the children and herd them away. Then he would set about deviling the snake for an opportune moment when he would grab it by its middle and shake it to death.

It would be safe to say that the cur dog put more squirrels on the dinner platter, caused more coons to get their hides stretched on the barn door, and drove more cows in from the pasture than any other breed. Of course, there were some dumbheads among the canine family, but, most often, they merely reflect the interest level given them by their masters and/or a true measure of their masters' I.Q. — just as a biting dog reveals a mean streak in its owner.

The nondescript, flea-bitten, half-starved-looking old hound lying on the old-timer's front porch could be the most deceptive of the lot. Lying there whipping the floor with his tail, watching you across his shoulder — too lazy to get up and too meek to bark worth a dam — he don't look like much. But to hear one of those old coon hounds warm up on a trail deep down in the creek bottoms on a cold wintry night, it'll stir you sort of like listening to Charles Laughton read the Bible.

And there was also the hound music of the wolf chase when the pack ran fast and true, coming your way, nearer and nearer. Crossing a long glade, you can see them running in the dew-laden moonlight, running hot on the scent with heads held high, running in a pack so tight you could have spread a blanket to cover them one and all. Then they are gone and as the chorus fades into the night, you realize how any man could be a hounddog man. That is, if your wife would only learn to like them too.

Now that this column has done gone to the dogs, another word about the feist. Back in the days when everybody and his dog went to town on Saturdays to fill the square with horses and wagons and buggies, and there were throngs of people with dogs milling about, the feist was a busy-body and the number one troublemaker. He had not been in town five minutes before he spied the storekeeper's cat; chased it through the store to tree it among the canned goods on the uppermost shelf; spooked one or two nervous horses; and, for the evening's finale, started a fierce fight among all dogs present. And, from a safe distance in all innocence, he watched angry men try vainly to quell the snapping, snarling melee among their danged fool dogs.

From *The Wimberley Mill*
August 1976

Old-time Squirrel Hunting

Hardtimes and pore people, that's the way Wimberley was when I was a kid. Of course, folks were too busy making a living then and too proud to realize that they were the unhappy impoverished, so they hadn't got around to looking to Washington for handouts — yet. Then too, in them days, there was a sort of neighborliness among these hills, which made the little things in life seem a lot more worthwhile. The old-timers who first rode these hills and farmed the little creek bottom patches for their living were a friendly lot. Their holdings were open range to the hunter and fisherman, and nobody would have the audacity to begrudge a fellow the right to sit on any creek bank he might choose to cook his catch — fish or fowl or any fair game.

Tuna may be the chicken of the sea today and fried chicken is everywhere, but back in those days the fox squirrel was the chicken of the hills and a bounty of the land hereabouts.

Around here a squirrel could be cooked more ways than anybody's chicken, and it was better eating too. Only legal excuse for having chicken on the table was when you were showing off for the new preacher with his first Sunday dinner at your house. And he'd been the first to ask for second helpings if the fare had been squirrel and dumplings, with oodles and oodles of good ole dumplings.

To conjure up the fond memories of those ole days, it takes the crispness of autumn's first norther, the odor of fresh fallen cypress and pecan leaves in the creek, the smell of the campfire, crows arguing among the pecan limbs in the evening sun, the bullfrog's groaning last tune before hibernation, owls hooting in the shadows as the moon rises, the distant bark of a house dog declaring himself as guardian of his home grounds, the splash as a fish breaks water, and the rare, far-off scream of a panther. We are there and it is good.

A man can find his soul while sitting about the campfire. There is a feeling of accomplishment in having taken your game clean, of having the campsite in order and the lines all set. And friendship's finest hours can be found beside the campfire, when old cronies

Little Arkansas on the Blanco River near Wimberley

unexpectedly break the brush to join you at the fireside. It could be Harvey Cowan, Uncle Emmett, Gay Harris, Johnny Howell, Lee Hill, an Adare or one of the Schneider boys who broke the quiet night air to ask, "Is the coffee ready?"

One and all were welcomed. Skillet bread was broken, squirrels or fish or both were fried in the iron pot. Clay Gay was the only fellow I ever knew who could drink a cup of boiling hot coffee straight from the fire without burning his tongue. And these fellows might stay up the whole night and return home to do a hard day's work come the morrow — without a wink of sleep. They don't produce the breed anymore.

One night Dad and I were camped at Dripping Springs crossing on Cypress Creek. The Hughes boys brought up their Walker hounds, and we combined some hound music with fishing while the Walkers chased a fox around Joe Wimberley Hill. During the chase a bluetick bitch joined the race. The next morning she refused to leave, and we learned by experience that she was a crackerjack squirrel dog too. About 3:00 that evening Duncan Dobie rode up to camp. "Rufus," he says right off, "why didn't you send my dog home? She's got a batch of pups she needs to be with."

"I know," says Dad. "But I didn't know whose dog she was and I'd like to see anyone run her off. I tried to but she does love to hunt."

"I understand," says Duncan. Taking the dog in the saddle before him, they sit and talk old times for hours before parting.

Ole Spot, a black-spotted pointer, was the best squirrel dog in Wimberley during those days. Spot gained his name from a black patch which covered most of the right side of his head. Sub Pyland gave Spot to Uncle John Will Pyland, and paradoxically he became the best squirrel dog in these parts. I say paradoxically, for Uncle John Will was no hunter. He and Aunt Susie with their all-girl family lived in the rock house on the hill. He ran the mill and gin and farmed some with a span of little black mules. Went to church on Sunday and that was it.

About every hunter in Wimberley, at one time or another, hunted squirrels with ole Spot. When he got a day off, Dad would drive the ole Stoddard-Dayton up and we would make a hunt with Spot. Sometimes we would be behind the Saunder's store and hunt up Cypress Creek past the Twin Sisters, then cut across country to the Wilson Branch, down it to the Blanco, and back to Wimberley. By the time we had completed this hunt, we would have thirty or forty squirrels. Often as not, we would have given a dozen or more to old neighbors and friends met along the way.

Other times we would hunt up the Blanco from Wimberley to the Schneiders' crossing and back. The squirrels bagged would be about the same in either hunt. The friendly meetings along the way would be the only difference.

With me doing the holding, the squirrel-skinning would take place beside the old millrace. Dad could shuck a squirrel without getting any hair on the carcass better than any person I ever knew. Also, he removed the musk sacs from each leg of the animal. Squirrels were a delicacy when Dad cleaned them, and Aunt Susie was quite a cook.

One thing more: once in a while, when the squirrel was close to the ground on the tree, ole Spot would revert to his breeding and point without barking. And he was known to point quail on occasion.

More as an aftermath of the old days, Red Dailey, Prunes Conner, Pottie Leffingwell, Mitt Murry, my brother Pot, and I used to walk up from San Marcos to camp at the springs in Little Arkansas. Here we would often be joined by Johnnie Howell, Lawrence Howell, John E. Harris, Gib Gay, and a sprinkling of the Saunders tribe for some good ole times.

Them days are gone and fellowship seems a bit harder to come by today. Maybe I'm not trying hard enough, these days.

From *The Wimberley Mill*
November 1975

* * *

Editor's note: Here it is fitting to add a story written by John Tom Dailey for his book *The Pioneer Heritage: Yesterday–Today–Tomorrow* (Arlington, Virginia: Allington Corporation, 1981). The story is about a group of boys growing up during the twenties in San Marcos, Texas, when growing up was quite different from the way it is today. C. W. Wimberley plays a prominent part in the story as "Weldon" and "Hoss."

Please meet:

The River Rats

In my early teens I started hanging around with a bunch called "The River Rats" because they frequented the head of the San Marcos River. We fished, trapped, and hunted according to season and our clubhouse was originally the kitchen of Weldon Wimberley's home on Saturday nights while his parents were off to a dance in the country. We would drink coffee and listen to the Grand Ole Opry until it was time to go hunting or to run our trotlines. Later we built our own clubhouse up the hollow a couple of hundred yards.

The clubhouse was about twelve by sixteen feet and was dug into the side of the hill. It also had a cave dug under and behind it. The roof had a foot or so of earth on it and the area around it was landscaped with all sort of exotic transplants such as Spanish Dagger, Century plant and the like. Nearly fifty years later, after the clubhouse burned, the hole is still there and the plants have spread all over the entire hollow. We once had a party there when I was about fifteen and brought our girlfriends to it. We managed to raise one dollar, and with this Weldon's father Rufus Wimberley bought

174

a goat and barbequed it for us. Together with a few trimmings we scrounged from home, we made a mighty fine feast. After eating, we hiked over to the old Fern Bluff and killed a five-foot rattlesnake that one of the girls nearly stepped on. We also had fine ice cream treats from time to time. We could get eggs and sugar from home and then catch an old cow in the pasture to obtain a supply of milk. The nearby ice plant had a night watchman who would let us have scraps of ice to put in our hand freezer. As I remember, it was real fine ice cream and I would eat a quart of it at a sitting.

Weldon and I and the other River Rats had a lot of good times and adventures together at the old clubhouse. One night, in the middle of a poker game, Weldon's old dog Shep treed a big skunk up the hollow apiece. We adjourned the game and ran up to where Shep was baying at the skunk on the ground. In the confusion there was a momentary breakdown in coordination. Just as Weldon was behind the skunk hitting it with a club, I dropped a large rock on top of it. It has taken the better part of fifty years for Weldon to forgive my lapse. Upon another occasion Weldon and I were hunting possums up Sink Springs Creek with fantastic luck. We were hunting them with a spotlight and could see the reflection of their eyes for a hundred yards. Nearly every tree had a possum in it, and we soon had thirteen possums and a small coon. When we stopped to skin the varmints we found that we had a serious problem on our hands. It had been an unusually warm season and the furs were crawling with fleas. They were so bad that it was impossible to skin and scratch simultaneously; so we had to team up where one would skin while the other one would keep him scratched.

The River Rats ran their traplines in the winter and their trotlines in the summer and hunted squirrels and fished for bass in between. They were also mighty good at catching bullfrogs, crawfish, wheybelly perch, and finding bee trees.

Of course, they all had nicknames. There was "Hoss" (C. W.) Wimberley, "Pot" (Stanley) Wimberley, "Wheybelly" (John-Red) Dailey, "Prunes" (R. S.) Conner, "Israel" (Logan) Roberts, "Peleg" (Wayne) Lewis, "Mitt" (Talmadge) Murry, and "Censored" (Jack) Neal.

Back in those days, the country was pretty well open and nobody had a car so they all walked. They'd walk out ten miles and back for almost any reason at all. A twenty-mile trapline was nothing to them or even a thirty-mile coon hunt.

One day "Hoss" Wimberley said his Pa had told him about the "Big Spring" in "Little Arkansas" eight miles down the Blanco River from the town of Wimberley so they decided to try to find it. This wasn't very easy since there was no road to it. Finally, "Hoss" talked his Pa into taking him and "Pot" Wimberley out to the Blanco River bridge so they could walk up the river to the Big Spring.

The first day of walking got them as far as the old Nance Mill, where they camped after exploring the big sink hole cave that runs under the river.

After walking most of the next day they came to some signs of inhabited country and soon there was the Big Spring. This spring gushes out of the bluff about twenty feet above the river and has built up a broad level shelf with pools of water, large trees, and then a twenty-foot waterfall. It was a paradise for camping.

Near the spring was a man and an eight-year-old boy building a rustic fence and gate. It was John Howell, the patriarch of the Howell clan of racehorse fame and his young nephew Lawrence. Lawrence is now a well-known trainer of racehorses in Chicago.

Old John had a lame leg where he had been shot and couldn't walk very well. So he was the one to stay at the ranch and raise the horses (and goats) while the rest of the clan raced the horses on the Chicago racetrack circuit. Gib Gay was an eighteen-year-old jockey then who had gotten too big to ride. He became part of the Little Arkansas bunch who were joined by the San Marcos River Rats. Gib is now a prominent breeder and trainer of racehorses in Kentucky.

Old John made the boys from San Marcos welcome and they started spending as much time in Little Arkansas as they could. They would have stayed there most of the time in the summer except for the matter of food. Back in those days, money was mighty scarce so it was pretty hard to get enough supplies together to go camping.

About all they could do was maybe get fifty cents apiece and pool it to buy a few .22 shells, a little tobacco, coffee, lard, and some corn meal. Each of the boys would have one blanket, a bucket, and a tin plate.

The boys would head north from College Hill and in three hours would walk the twelve miles over the hills to the Big Spring. This was after they finally learned the easy way to get there. They'd be terribly thirsty when they got there and the cool spring water sure tasted fine. There was only one windmill on the way and no-body ever had a canteen.

The food was pretty good most of the time. They had fish, squirrel, and cornbread for beakfast; cornbread, fish, and squirrel for dinner and what was left over for supper. Once in awhile old John would let the boys go get a bucket of eggs laid by the game chickens he raised.

These game chickens weren't particular where they laid their eggs, and the hens weren't too particular how long the eggs had been laid. The eggs were broken into the frying pan and once in a while one got thrown back out of the pan.

Once in awhile, there would be wild honey to add to the menu, but not too often since the local boys usually got to the bee trees first. High in the bluff by the river was a large bee cave that had been there as long as anyone remembers.

One day "Hoss" took a notion to go rob that bee cave even if people said nobody ever had. He cut down a thirty-foot sapling and trimmed it up, leaving stubs for his feet. He climbed up the sapling to the bee cave and smoked it up some. A bee or two got under his bee veil but all he could do was cuss, seeing he was on top of a thirty-foot pole!

While he poked into the cave and raked out the comb and honey, the other boys held a tub thirty feet below and caught the honey as it fell like a small waterfall.

Soon they had a wash tub nearly full of honey, combs, bees, grubs, dirt and what not, but straining it took care of that. Every-body in Little Arkansas ate honey for weeks afterward.

One time before the low-water bridge opened up Little Arkansas, Hoss figured out that a car could get there if it went out to the end of the Lime Kiln Road to the river and then three miles up the wagon road on the other side.

He convinced his Daddy of this and one day several of the River Rats and Rufus Wimberley took off for Little Arkansas in an old Essex. Everything went fine except where the body of the Essex became separated from the chassis and it came to a lurching halt. Hoss finally figured it out and fixed the body back by tying it down with some barbed wire. That's how a car got to Little Arkansas one time.

And during that trip Rufus and the boys were sitting around the camp fire at the Big Spring when a big coon squalled near by. Hoss wounded him with a shotgun blast and then chased him down the cliff to the water and then finished him off. Rufus baked him with some sweet potatoes in a Dutch oven. It sure was a feast for a bunch of hungry River Rats.

The boys of Little Arkansas were pretty tough boys but never got in any real trouble. Their feet were so tough that they could and did go barefoot most of the time and nothing could stop them when they had a mind to do something.

One night Gib Gay was in bed with a high fever (later claimed he had double pneumonia) when some boys came by to get him to go coon hunting. He got up and went along. After treeing a couple of coons he felt pretty good even though it was below freezing.

He was doing just fine until his prize hound got a coon in the water and the coon climbed up on the dog's head and was about to drown him. Gib jumped into the water and saved the hound. Gib said it took him some time to get dried out by a fire he built but he was feeling fine the next day.

It wasn't long before a low-water bridge was built and the Howells could drive to Wimberley for supplies instead of having to go on horseback.

Today Little Arkansas is practically a suburb of Houston. Rich folks fly their private planes there to spend the weekend at their fine estates.

Little remains from the old days except the memories that still are fresh to "Hoss" and "Wheybelly" and a few others.

J. Frank Dobie's Snakes

On June 4, 1963, J. Frank Dobie wrote the following letter to C. W. Wimberley:

Dear Mr. Wimberley:

I'm always looking for more tales and facts about rattlesnakes. As a matter of fact, I have material now for a book of rattlesnake lore. Whether it's ever going to be put together or not, I don't know. Sometimes I think that readers of my columns might get a little tired of the rattlesnakes that crawl into them. Just the same, some more are crawling, and you are apt to see your own snakes in it some day.

With appreciation and good wishes, I remain

Sincerely yours,

J. Frank Dobie

The letter came from 702 Park Place, Austin, Texas, his home on Waller Creek. Soon thereafter, Frank Dobie used C. W.'s snake stories in his syndicated column in the *Austin American-Statesman* and he called it:

Snakes Worth Remembering

I met C. W. Wimberley of Wimberley, Texas, for the first time in a new book to which he contributed *Wimberley's Legacy* published by the Naylor Company, San Antonio. He had met me as a narrator of rattlesnake stories. Now in two letters he has introduced some of the snakes out of his personal recollections:

About three months after the Buchanan Lake had filled for the first time, Allie Hughes and I were boating on it when, more than a mile from the nearest land, we discovered a rattlesnake floating on the water. Drifting about with the breeze, the snake floated high in a tight coil with head and tail in the center. The tail was a raw nub where the rattles had been, and the snake's skin had faded like a piece of sunburned rubber — evidence of a long time adrift. When we touched the snake with a paddle it uncoiled, crawled across the water, much as a snake moves on land, and tried to get into the boat. It was then that I put my paddle to a more serious use. With the first blow the rattler deflated itself with a hiss and put up a swimming fight that was soon over.

This experience confirmed a theory of mine that rattlers inflate themselves before entering water. Years earlier I had sat on a creek bank and watched a rattler sally forth from the other bank with head and tail held high, floating as lightly as an innertube. The creature was not so large around after I blasted its head off with a shotgun.

Brown rattlers I found on the Pat Welder ranch on the Gulf Coast below Bloomington reacted differently. Several times I have gotten after one of them with a green switch and seen it take to the water like a moccasin or climb through the rose hedges like a chicken snake.

Jess Carter lived alone in a three-room house on the west bank of the Little Llano River. He used the shed room as a kitchen, slept in the north room during the winter and on the porch through the summer. The south room held cottonseed for which the ginner had failed to meet Jess's asking price back in 1917.

Though he failed to get along with most of his neighbors, Jess and I used to spend a lot of time sitting and talking in a way

179

that did not burn up words. We were on his porch late one summer evening when I called his attention to the movement of mice among grapevines growing on chicken wire nailed along the edge of his roof. "Yeah, I been thinking about that," Jess replied. "A rattler has moved in with me. Rats move to the ceiling every time one does that. Sack of flour been on the floor in the kitchen a week now and nothing's bothered it. Guess I'll have to take off a day and scratch through my plunder and find him."

About two weeks later Jess greeted me from his porch with: "Whimp, I told you I had a boarder. Got a four-foot rattler out of the kitchen and a big chicken snake was working the seed room. Next day had to put my flour in a lard can — rats had already cut a hole in the sack."

Back when my Uncle John Will Pyland ran the old mill in Wimberley and lived in the rock house on the hill, a big rattlesnake spent several winters under it. On a mild day he might remind you of his presence with a rattle in response to a sudden noise that jarred the floor. Often he would sing for a good while after an armload of wood had been dropped hard upon the floor near the fireplace. There was no way to get him except by cutting a hole in the floor. After several holes had been cut it was decided that the snake was there to stay.

One summer Dad helped Uncle John Will replace the wooden floor of the front porch to his old rock house with a concrete slab. That fall while Dad and I were skinning squirrels out back of the house, one of the girls alarmed us with a gesture. We rushed to the front of the house, and there stretched out on the new concrete floor along the wall on the porch was one of the biggest rattlers either of us had ever seen. Ignoring us completely, the rattler moved ever so slowly along the wall as he probed the new concrete with his nose in search of a hole that no longer existed. It was the time of year when rattlesnakes hole up for the winter. I went for the shotgun. When I returned the rattler lay on the porch in a loose coil. He never rattled. His earthly career ended with the dual blast of the shotgun. Two blue streaks where the shot splattered on the concrete remained for years to mark the spot.

The next year, 1964, Frank Dobie was gone. He died in his sleep on Friday, September 18. His grave is in the Texas State Cemetery.

Back to Model T's and Horses

They's jest nothin' else to it. We are goin' back to Model T Fords and saddle horses. What's more, I can prove it to you. The president done said that this here slaughter on the highways is got to stop, and he nearly always gets what he asks for. And then, this here Nader feller has done gone and sicked the hounds of Congress on to the automobile industry, all of which makes this thing a pretty hot political issue. From there on, it don't take no lotta logic to figger jest how this problem is goin' to be worked out.

Everybody knows that gasoline and alcohol won't mix, and anybody can tell you that when you put a nut behind the steering wheel of a fast automobile it's jest a matter of time till somebody gets hurt or kilt. Then consider this new voting rights law where any nut has his poll tax for nothin'. Now, jest what kind of a politician is goin' to tell his registered voter how to drive or not drive his own car? Nary a one, that's for shore. The only political out is to find a safe means of travel for nutty drivers.

A team of mules hitched to a wagon ain't the answer, for I once heard of a feller that was a-sittin' on top of a load of cotton goin' to the gin when he leaned back too far takin' a swig from his jug an' fell off to where a back wheel run right over his head. He left his widder a cracked jug and a sharecropper's interest in six bales of cotton to raise ten younguns on. Anybody knows that won't do.

The Model T Ford is one answer, for it was a safe car. I know because when I lived back in the cedar brakes on the other side of this LBJ ranch country, I had a neighbor who would of got kilt right off if they was any danger in driving a Model T Ford car. All through the week, he was a danged good neighbor but, come Saturday, he'd crank up his Model T and go hellin' it for the county seat, where he'd spend all day an' half the night a-tryin' to have a drink with every one of his friends because after the first snort, everybody was a friend of his. Soaked to the gills, he'd drive home away in the middle of the night. This went on for years and he never had no bad accident. Oh, once in awhile, he'd miss the concrete slab-crossing and come Sunday mornin' we'd have to go pull him and his Model T out of the creek. Other times, he'd take a wrong fork of the road and drive around in them cedar brakes till daylight come before he could find his way home. Only accident he ever had was when he run broadsided into a big Bremmer bull a-standin' in the road. The bull lost a patch of his hair about the size of a Stetson hat, but what that mad Bremmer done to that Model T more'n evened the score, for he had done growed new hair all over that bald spot before my neighbor got his Model T back in runnin' order again.

The saddle horse is a better answer to the problem, for a good horse will, if given half a chance, take care of about any kind of a rider. My mother-in-law said that when she was a girl, there was a man livin' over towards the Colorado River who was a lot like my neighbor. This feller always rode a big dappled grey gelding and, lucky for him, that horse was a real good 'un, too. Most Saturdays, he'd ride through our community on his way to the saloons over at the county seat. About the middle of the evenin', he'd be back and pull up in front of the general store where he'd spur his horse until both front feet was on the bottom step and its head was stickin' through the doorway, clear inside the store. Then, leanin' over in the saddle, he'd low-rate our community and her people for a spell a-fore goin' on home.

Now, them people didn't exactly like that sort of treatment comin' from an outsider. And they was a stock of people that wouldn't skin their knuckles up a-tryin' to knock some sense into any thick skull. But they did love a good horse above everything else — even pride — so they didn't take any outside chance of hurting that pretty dappled grey gelding or of makin' him gun shy just to get to shoot a durn fool from the saddle. And that blamed feller never did know why he lived so long.

Now after all, you can see for yourself, goin' back to saddle horses won't be so bad because a good horse is good in more ways than one. Besides, people might learn a lot from horses, once they quit hurrying to get to some place they ain't got no business being at in the first place.

From *The Wimberley Mill*
July 1966

The Unreconstructed Rebel

By the time I was five or six years old I was sure of one thing: Gen. Robert E. Lee and my Great-grandpa Bill Adare were going to heaven. Today, I figure Lee might be called upon to explain why he kept wasting blood in a cause that had become hopeless long before Appomattox, but I remain quite certain of Grandpa's fate. If for no other reason, there's simply not enough room in all Hades for him and all them dam Yankee soldiers.

Though Grandma was able to make him hang up his sword and put away his six-shooters, this old warrior kept re-fighting the Civil War, that's THE WAR, and gave them Yankees hell for the remainder of his days. I loved him for it. He had fought under the Bonnie Blue Flag in the services of state's rights and, maybe, just for the hell of it. Slavery had no place in his life.

Grandpa did dearly love to camp out. While a young man, he spent so much time alone in the wilds that he was often accused of being an Indian. During his old age his neighbors told it for gospel that he would sometimes camp out on the road close enough to draw water for his morning coffee from his well. I arrived upon the scene too late to confirm or deny the matter but I do know Grandpa was never known to hitch up a team without his bedroll and chuck box being in the back and, on the trip from Wayside to Wimberley, he would stop at Wilson Branch to boil a pot of coffee and have a snack. After all, it did take an old man and an old horse awhile to make a five-mile trip in a gig.

Gathered from Grannie Lawrence's tales of traveling to and from San Marcos with Pap while she was a child (she always referred to her father as Pap), Grandpa must have been quite a woodsman. Their trips were made by way of the Devil's Backbone via Hugo and the Old Blanco City Road, now Purgatory Road. Together they saw the Wimberley area while it still wore some of its pristine glory. The cedars stood in brakes and had only begun their invasion of the hills and grasslands. From the heights of the Devil's Backbone, there were few intervenient trees to obstruct a detailed view of the valley below where the cypress-lined Blanco snaked its way around bluffs, across glades, and through canyon walls. The oak-motted open range of Crawford's Prairie extended from the present-day Fulton Ranch southwestward to the vicinity of KLRN-TV tower and the cedar ridges above Gruene's store.

Sitting on the high wagon seat beside Pap, she watched the land slowly roll by as the team plodded along. Out upon Crawford's Prairie, the deer were hidden by tall grasses until they stood up. With only their heads exposed, the smaller deer peeking through the grasses presented an amusing sight for the little girl's pleasure.

183

Sometimes the great lobo wolf or a sneaky little coyote might be seen on a distant knoll as it paused briefly to stare about before restlessly moving on. Those fleeting shadows which darted across the road ahead and dogged the wagon's trail at dusk just happened to be a pair of curious foxes doing a little looking for themselves. And as one by one the darkening sky revealed the many marvels of its stars and the hoot owls began to talk in the distance, she fell asleep on the small pallet spread beside the dying embers of Grandpa's campfire.

At San Marcos, rainy weather would turn the streets about the courthouse square into a quagmire where horses waded belly deep to pull wagons down deep ruts with axles dragging on mud between the wheels. Always observant to the beauty of any flowering plant, she said that at that time there was an unusual red-blossomed native flower growing in profusion during wet seasons in the vicinity of the square. According to her account, those plants disappeared from the scene long before she had reached adulthood. Another vanished species?

While returning home on another trip, Grannie and her sister Mamie were with Grandpa when a blizzard caught them on the road. Weather forced Grandpa to pitch camp on the slopes of the Devil's Backbone. The two little girls slept snug and warm in his camp while Grandpa kept the fire going as a sleet and snow storm swirled through the hills, turning them into a fairyland of ice. The next morning was clear and cold. While they ate a good camp breakfast by the fire, the little girls could look down across the Blanco to where their home stood beside Pin Oak Creek. It was a memorable experience related to me during her ninetieth year.

By 1907 or 1908 my Uncle Chandos, Grannie Lawrence's second eldest son, was a boy big enough to go along with Grandpa on his trips in the old hack to Gruene's Store for supplies. Grandpa's sons and sons-in-law — my great-uncles Charlie and Tom Adare, Grandfather Lawrence, great-uncles Willie Schneider and Lee Hill — lived on their small places scattered along the Blanco and Pin Oak Creek. Periodically they would make their list of needed supplies which Grandpa would take to Gruene's to be filled. Sometimes he would camp at the wagon yard at Gruene's Store and sometimes he would camp on Crawford's Prairie. This was the scene for one wild experience for Uncle Chandos and Grandpa, especially little Uncle.

William Branch Adare, The Unreconstructed Rebel, and Mary V. O'Banion Adare

They were on their way to Gruene's and had just topped the steep hill when the horses became increasingly nervous in the harness, fought the bits and snorted the air. Below, a bedlam of bellowing, lowing cattle created quite a stir on Crawford's prairie. As Grandpa urged his horses on under tight rein, the source of the trouble was soon to be seen beyond the creek. Followed by a herd of bewildered cattle, two panthers were dragging a calf across the prairie toward the fences. The pair had dragged the dead calf through the fence and lay crouched in the grass clinging to the carcass, watchful as the hack approached. Beyond the fence the cattle milled and lowed and the horses shied and twisted in their harnesses. Grandpa prodded them past the scene under tight rein. Only after a considerable portion of the prairie had been put between them and the panthers did the horses quiet down in the harness. Any false move along the way by Grandpa and those horses would have peddled that hack and its contents across the land in small pieces.

In his younger years, Grandpa had done some hard hunting in these hills to kill the big cats and a few bear, but he had found peace with the world about him during his later years. Only them dam Yankees continued to suffer the ire of his verbal battles. To burn any powder in one of his skirmishes you had to have worn the gray uniform with honor. Small-fry kinsmen were allowed to listen quietly at a safe distance.

May 12, 1923, we buried him on a little knoll beside Pin Oak Creek: William Branch Adare, Trooper, 32nd Texas Cavalry, C.S.A. And Wayside can no longer be found on any map. The passing years leave few to remember.

From *The Hays County Citizen*
January 22, 1976

The Last Battle

Contrary to what you might find in history books, the last shots of the Civil War were fired right here in Wimberley some forty years after Appomattox. Witnessed by a group of schoolage youngsters, the exact date should be easily ascertained. This military action took place when old Bill Adare, late of the 32nd Texas Cavalry, C.S.A., discovered a platoon of Yankees in the big cypress tree and hidden in the bushes at the mouth of Wilson Creek, singlehandedly opened fire, and sent them fleeing to the north.

To validate this claim and to give you a proper perspective of this matter can best be accomplished by further examination of characters involved and reviewing preceding events that were culminated here at Wilson Creek on the River Road in Wimberley.

Among the first to join the "Civil War," my great-grandfather, William Branch Adare, was on hand to disarm Federal troops stationed at the forts along the Texas frontier, leaving them with only the food and transport necessary to make their long trek back to Union territory. Throughout the conflict, he gloriously busted his breeches with the cavalry across Texas, only to be on foot when severely wounded during the Yankee debacle at Mansfield, Louisiana. Unable to march into Texas, the Yankees came by sea — after the surrender in the East and Grandpa had been mustered out of the service at Houston.

Undefeated and unconquered by war, he settled in the hills above Wimberley, where he remained unreconstructed — that's for shore. He did entertain some benevolent feelings for Teddy Roosevelt and might have, with some reservations, rejoined the union during the Harry Truman administration, had he lived that long.

At his little place on Pin Oak Creek in Wayside community, he refought The War, farmed some, raised a big family, hunted,

186

tinkered in his shop, studied the Bible, and refought The War. At that time, Walter Estes lived on what is now known as the Harvey Cowan place. One morning after breakfast, old man Estes told his wife that he was going up to Bill Adare's shop to have his ax sharpened and would be back right away. The morning passed and he failed to show up for dinner. Towards the shank of the evening, Mrs. Estes, distraught with all sorts of imaginary fates suffered by her faithful husband, lit out up the trail leading to the Adares. She found him and Bill pondering over an elaborate field map drawn in the dust before the shop where the tides of history were being reversed; that is, until Mrs. Estes routed the home forces.

With the infirmities of old age, Grandpa's legs played out on him, so he retired to his shop to build a gig-like affair with a chuck box attached beneath the seat to get about in. He became pretty much of a loner and with this unusual vehicle made frequent forays out into the countryside. In emulation of the days of old, when he had been a woodsman and hunter of some esteem, he developed the peculiarity of often stoppping along the trail to build a fire, boil a pot of coffee, and have a snack while his horse grazed.

On this particular day, he was on his way from Wayside to Wimberley, a distance of about five miles, when the notion struck him to stop and pitch camp at the confluence of Wilson Creek and the Blanco River. Old Jim was peacefully grazing on the lush grass growing along the creek bank as Grandpa stood with cup in hand waiting, watching for the coffee pot to come to a boil. Suddenly, intuitively alerted, the old warrior dropped the cup lightly to the ground, raised his walking stick, and took careful aim into the heights of the tall cypress beside the creek.

"Bang! Bang! Danged pesky Yankees," and swinging his weapon about, he went volley after volley at random into the brush growing along the ridge; then, holding it above his head in a victory salute, yelled: "Yeah, that's right — run — run, you blasted Bluebellies. That's all you were ever any good at."

Lowering his walking stick, he returned to his coffee. The pot was boiling. Undetected by the old one, a small group of young boys on the hillside stood in silent perplexed amusement at what they had seen.

The big cypress growing beside the Wilson Creek bridge on the River Road is the proper location to place the Historical Marker.

From *The Wimberley Mill*
May 1970

Early-Day Doctoring

They say that change is the mark of progress, so Wimberley must be a progressive place. Used to be when a family drove to town on Saturdays, the horses were up front a-pulling the wagon, the man drove with his woman and younguns huddled about him on the spring-board seat, and the dogs trotted along in the shade beneath the vehicle. Nowadays when the horse comes into town, he is pulled behind the station wagon in his custom-built trailer, the dog sits beside the woman driver, the kids are fighting on the back seat, and the old man stayed home to mow the lawn and do the dishes.

But if you were not around here when the old men used to carry a buckeye seed in the back-seat pockets for the rumatiz and the kids wore a pouch of asafetida hung from a string about their necks to ward off the flu — they's been more changes hereabouts than meets your eye.

Now say if your Junior was to fall out of a tree and break a limb or was a-standing in the driveway when the wife backed out the car — what would you do? Most of the time, the preacher here would be the only one you could call on for any help. But you are in luck should it happen between the hours of 9:20 A.M. and 3:30 P.M., sharp, on a Monday, Tuesday, or Friday — that are not bankers' holidays — for then you could load Junior into the car and drive forty miles to the nearest clinic and find it open. After presenting your Blue Cross and Blue Shield badge, four valid courtesy cards, and assuring the nurse receptionist that you were agin' socialized medicine, then your boy could join the long line waiting to see your family doctor — a man you had never seen before.

But if it's the colic your registered Domino prized pedigreed whitefaced Hereford bull has got, you are in much better shape to face such troubles. The nearest telephone will put you in contact with the veterinarian's roving van and, while you receive verbal assurances and instructions via the air, this animal mercy wagon, traveling at a 70 MPH clip, will bring to your cow lots a laboratory containing operating table complete, an iron lung, x-ray machines, atomic isotopes, the latest in wonder drugs, and a space-age computer which will figure your bill into the most favorable rate of E-Z monthly, tax-deductible payments.

Back when my Grandpa Lawrence raised bumble-bee cotton and children on his little place up on Pin Oak Creek, close by the

188

Wayside schoolhouse, then things were a shade different. His family doctor lived in Wimberley and Grandpa thought enough of him to name one of his sons "Berkley" after this doctor.

One night there was an owl in the chicken roost. Grandpa left the house with his shotgun and come back with his middle toe shot off his right foot. While Grannie bathed the foot in kerosene and stanched the blood with camphor-soaked sugar, one of the boys went to fetch Doctor Berkley. The good doctor came as fast as his buggy would carry him and spent the remainder of the night probing for bird shot and sewing. After breakfast the next morning, he was off to deliver a set of twins, but he visited Grandpa regularly until he was up and about and always dropped in when he was up Wayside way.

In them days, you done your own horse doctoring—usually by doubling the dose of medicine used on a man. When things sort of got out of hand, you could call upon the faith doctor, Aunt Emma Justice, for she could read certain passages from the "Good Book" and stop the flow of blood in a bleeding wound or cure a case of screwworms without touching the infected animal.

Once, while Lon Tanner lived with him, Wyatt Brooks had an old range cow with a bad case of screwworms and she was a wild old huzzy. After about a week's chase through the cedar brakes, Wyatt and Lon had their horses worn down, tore up their clothes, lost a hat, and skinned themselves up pretty good without getting close enough to lay a rope on this cow—much less pen her. Next morning, Wyatt was having a little trouble a-sittin' down at the breakfast table when he said: "I'm just gonna write Aunt Emma a post card and have her faith doctor that old cow—'at's the only way to handle it."

"Well," says Wyatt to Lon, "We been calling that cow every name we could think of for over a week now, and there ain't one of 'em we dast put on a post card because the postal inspectors would have us in jail before dark if we did, so I'll jest have to bring Aunt Emma over here."

"They's just one thing," says Lon. "I'm shore not goin' to be around while she's here. If she can do anything to that cow by just lookin' at her, I'm not goin' to be looked at too."

From *The Wimberley Mill*
June 1966

189

Barnyard Nostalgia

From where I sit, it shore looks like our country scene has done gone and lost an awful lot of its character. How long has it been since you have seen or heard an old bull beller, paw up the dirt, and tear up the cedar bushes—just to let everybody know he was the baddest, meanest bull in this neck of the woods? And how long has it been since you have heard night talk among the cattle—the comforting soft moo of an old mother cow answered by the bleating bawl of her calf in the distance, or the frantic lowing bawl of a cow as she runs all over the pasture trying to find her offspring who's out of pocket, or awakened during the night to hear the sad lowing of a brood herd of cows standing about the pens from which their calves had been shipped a day or two ago, or the clang of the ole boss milkcow's bell as she goes about the business of leading her share of the herd? Today's beef herd may produce more and better meat, but they have no more character than a wilted head of soured cabbage.

By the same token, caged hen's eggs and brainless battery-raised fryers may fill the order at the supermarket, but they sure don't do much for a man's soul like the ole barnyard chicken did in the past. For the sheer joy of it, have you stood in the quiet predawn light to listen to the roosters across the neighborhood announce the birth of a new day? Each crowed in his own way to tell the world he was the cock-of-the-walk at his home place.

My old rooster—part fighting game for moxie, part Cornish game for bone, and part brown Leghorn by accident—had a cock-a-doodle-doooo that left no doubt things would soon be stirring around the barn. Over towards Slick Farris's place, the old rooster fared not so well. Three perky banty roosters tried to outdo him by crowing a half dozen times to his every effort. Riley's Wyondott roosted under the shed of the barn, so his clarion call was muffled somewhat. With the right atmosperic conditions, you could go on and on pinpointing home places by their roosters. But best of all, from way back over the hills, Turkey Johnson might make the day for you with one of his cowboy yells. He and Tom Allen were the only old-timers of Harvey Cowan's class when it came to calling cows or just letting go with a good cowboy yell. With the bluffs along the Blanco to give all those added echoes, Harvey was a hard man to beat.

Now, back to the henhouse.

Back in those hard times of the Great Depression, laying mash was sold in gingham sacks of many patterns. Two matching sacks would make my wife a good dress and one, a good apron. When the choice in sacks failed to meet the wife's taste, or money ran short, I'd blow off a batch of laying mash of my own making. The recipe went something like this: take the headlight and .22 and kill about a dozen jackrabbits; shuck them and remove the entrails; using cedar ax, chop carcasses into a fine bone mealburger; place in washpot; add two gallons corn meal or cracked wheat, one cup of chili petines; cover with water and boil till tender; serve on shallow tin trough once a week with other grain when needed. I guarantee this mix to make an old hen's comb red and put her to laying in mid-January; also eliminates the need for worming pills of oyster shells. An old doe would do just as well in this stew. The deer carcass would necessitate more chopping with ax but would also save in the number of .22 shells used and afford two good hams and backstraps for dinner table use.

One day, during these times, I was on my way home from town when I spied a brand new nailkeg lying beside the road. Now, there's just nothing better than a nailkeg for a good hen's nest. So, I stopped and picked it up. On the way home, I figured it would be a good idea to nail this nailkeg onto the side of the barn right next to the door. With it there all I'd have to do after I got through milking the cows each morning was to go by this nailkeg and pick me up a handful of eggs to take to the house for my breakfast. This way, I'd always be sure of having fresh eggs for my breakfast, and the rest of them gathered elsewheres, I'd trade in on my account at the grocery store. But my best ideas always seem to have a way of going sour.

We had an old pet Dominique hen by the name of Biddy. Ole Biddy must have been ten years old. She hadn't laid an egg or hatched a setting of eggs in over four years, and the rooster had done quit flirting with her. But no sooner than I'd nailed the nailkeg to the barn, made a fine nest in it out of oat straw, put a new chalk nestegg in it and—what do you know? Ole Biddy declared this nailkeg to be her very own private personal property and ran off every hen who even tried to look at it. She even roosted in it.

Every time I went about the barn, Biddy would come flying out of that nailkeg, either cackling like she had just laid an egg or clucking like she was about to hatch that danged chalk nest egg.

Of course, she didn't fool me one bit, or the rooster either, for that matter.

In time I sort of got used to it and kind of liked having ole Biddy around. In fact, I'd usually throw her some feed when she come flying out of that nailkeg.

But this story does have an awfully sad ending. One night we heard ole Biddy squalling for her life out at the barn. Before me and the dogs could get there, a rogue coon had done kilt poor ole Biddy. Afterwards, I took the nailkeg off the barn and burned it in the fireplace. I just couldn't stand the sight of it without ole Biddy around. Yet if you will just wait long enough, the clouds will regain their silver linings. You may have to help things a little bit, though.

One of these days, I'm going to move back to the country and the first thing I'm going to do is to get me some barnyard chickens that roost in trees. Then, I'm going to take our $479.95 TV set and nail it onto the side of the barn for a hen nest.

Yeah, I know I'll be missing the next ninety-six re-runs of the "I Love Lucy Show" and won't get to see Marlin Perkins hogging the show from the animals on "Wild Kingdom" anymore. But one thing's for shore: never again will I have to set before that boobtube to hear our president make a speech, then have my intellect insulted by a bunch of media experts jumping up and telling me what the man just got through saying. Hell, I could see the man when he said it, and if he'd needed any help in making his speech to the American public, those media experts should have been standing with him at the podium.

Maybe, then, the barnyard hens will lay some better eggs in the $479.95 TV set than it has been used to having laid in its tube in the past. Not bigger, just better.

From The Wimberley Mill
March 1975

Uncle Hick Wimberley

Editor's note: Calvin Hickman Wimberley, my father, was known for his humor and interesting tales of his boyhood in Wimberley. C. W. Wimberley's father, Rufus, and my father were brothers. C. W. writes of my father: "Uncle Hick was my touchstone while writing for *The Wimberley Mill*. Born in 1882 in the shadows of the old millhouse and learned to swim in the millrace, he was there. The good old days of the Wimberley past were his. Well into his eighties it took some talking and a smile from Aunt Mabel to get him to record some of his memories in his own hand." One of his memories is presented here, in his own words.

In the good old days at Wimberley, back around 1892, after crops were laid by, the men folks would get together and build a big brush arbor, and all the available preachers would have their round with the devil under this arbor. They cut forked cedar posts, setting them on about four foot center, then covered these with cedar boughs making a dense shade. As well as I can remember, they were about seven and a half feet high and fifty feet square, with a row of long benches down each side and an aisle down the center, and up front there was a platform with an organ and the pulpit; then in front was the mourners benches arranged in a square. After the arbor was built, then would follow in their regular order: Methodists, Baptists, and Christians. The Methodists usually had from two to four preachers and sometime their meeting would last two weeks, depending on how the mourners responded. Sometimes, the big boys would have to go to the mourners bench on alternate nights to keep the meeting going.

I remember the meeting in 1892 better than any as this was the year I was "saved," but I will explain this later. During the Methodist meeting, one of my cousins and I put a good supply of throwing rocks upon the roof of the shed room of Grandfather's smokehouse which was in throwing distance of the road to the camp ground, and we were busy throwing at passersby. We made one bad mistake by throwing at Parson Bridges. In just a little while, a big strong hand gripped me by the leg and hauled me down to earth and began applying a wicked mulberry limb. I still remember the sound of that limb.

After two weeks of meeting, the Methodists closed with numerous additions to the church, and lots of babies were "sprinkled." Then the Baptist meeting began. That ran only one week, but took in lots of members with only three preachers. Then the baptizing was on a Sunday afternoon in the old millrace just above the bridge on Cypress Creek below the square. The old-timers will remember what a perfect place this was for baptizing. As a boy I was always in some way or other making myself conspicuous and usually got a good licking when I got home. On the lower end of the bridge, there was a sort of fence to keep cattle out of the garden. There was a long pole making the top rail on this fence, so of course, I sat way out on the end of this pole so that I could see over the crowd assembled for the baptizing. They had eight or ten to be baptized. While I was busy watching, Clay Gay loosened the wire that held the pole and down I went into the water and surfaced in the midst of the group to be baptized. Brother John Mitchell, Sr., a grand old man, gave me the right hand of fellowship and then and there, I was "saved" all unexpectedly. I guess I should thank Clay. Clay was a good boy and a good man and everybody liked him.

Then the Christian preacher took over and preached good sermons and baptized lots of new members and the annual series of meeting was over.

The campers returned home, and then the winter dances came on and the preaching all had to be done over the next summer.

* * *

Back around the early 1880s, Cell Riley and a crew of men were camped down on the Blanco cutting shingle timber for the Wimberley Mill. Mr. Riley was cook and was extra good. Mr. Spence Townsend had the habit of raiding Mr. Riley's kitchen in the afternoon while all the crew was at work, so Mr. Riley cooked up a big house cat with all the fixin's . . . leaving it in the skillet where Mr. Spence found it and ate very hearty of the wonderful stew and stayed in camp as was his custom until the men came in from work.

Mr. Riley examined his skillet and began raving about someone eating the cat he had cooked for his rheumatism. Mr. Spence thought he was joking about it being a cat, but after being shown the hide, feet and head, his stomach began to rebel and the cat came back! Mr. Spence didn't.

From The Wimberley Mill
April 1967

Pets and Wildlife Parable

At the crest of the hill all pleasantries of the drive through the countryside abruptly drained away. Jamming the brakes to a dead stop, we sat in a state of disquieted relief as a small herd of frightened deer dashed from the timbers to run helter-skelter around the pickup as they crossed the road wide-eyed, with ears layed back, taunted necks reaching for distance and white flags at half mast — theirs was a flight of panic.

Three fine old does bound across in front of the pickup, swerved broadside to collide, and fell to the pavement in a mad scramble of legs. On regaining their feet they dashed on.

Bringing up the rear, two yearling does labored frantically not to be left behind. Both mouths were opened wide with tongues lolling, fighting for breath. At the ditch they faltered but moved on.

Hot on their heels a beagle stopped in the road, turned to await reinforcement. They came in short order.

It was not a hunter's pack that spilled from the trees. It was a sorry sight. It was a loose running hoard of unattended, neglected pedigreed dogs representing many fine breeds from many elite homes scattered along the creeks and country sides of New Suburbia among the hills.

Driven by a newly found lust for blood, this disorganized mob swept across the road on a broad front — hell bent on destruction.

The site of the kill could not be far distant. Within a few brief moments, this crazed pack would overtake the two little does, surge about them as they turned to make their fatal stand. There would be no respite. In a snarling melee of snapping, tearing jaws, the two little does would soon be reduced to a gory mass of mutilated flesh, left for the buzzards as the beagle beckoned on with the chase.

The real shame of this matter lies in the fact that this was not an isolated incident. Packs of dogs, large and small, and old rogues spasmodically lay waste to wildlife and livestock somewhere in the countryside most every day or night.

To fully appreciate this scene, you only need one look at your old pet goat with her nose gnawed away and an ear pulled from her head for trying to defend her kid, or the sight of a promising colt that had been chased through a barbed wire fence during the night.

Don't waste your time looking for the owner of any of these naughty dogs. They are phantoms.

Hell, you don't know what you're talking about. Ole Ring was raised around goats and sheep. Besides, he never leaves this place. All I got to do is whistle and here he is — anytime, day or night.

One Sunday morning Ole Ring died of lead poisoning. He was chewing at the throat of an old ewe at the time of his demise.

Somebody musta come and stole Ole Ring. He never left the house.

Now, I'm not going to bore you with all the good dogs I've owned during my day, or the time old Lassie was struck twice about the head before my boy realized the danger he was in and ran to the house to tell his mother how they had found a big rattlesnake in the barn and, "Lassie just stood right in front of me looking at him."

Somewhere betwixt and betwine there's bound to be an answer.

In the year 3001, two learned scholars sat digging through the rubbled heap of beer cans, throw-away bottles, TV tubes, and automobile parts which carpeted netherland Americana.

"I say," says one of these worthies, "the most unusual facet of this extinct twentieth-century culture of homo sapiens can only be that, with all their scientific expertise, they deliberately chose to destroy their water supply by dumping raw sewage and industrial waste into it. Novel way to go, Egad!"

"Nope," says the other, "can't compare to the riddle found in their exodus from the cities to the countryside. Why did they take an abundance of canines and felines of many breeds with them? Was it the manifestation of their primeval ethics to allow these animals to wantonly destroy the last vestige of all native wildlife in the new area? Or could it be that these animals defecating in and about the immediate premises of their abodes fulfilled some mystic taboo?"

From *The Hays County Citizen*

Wimberley's First Waterworks

The water system, as it existed at the turn of the century, hardly merited the reference to the Panama Canal as Uncle Joe Wimberley mentioned it in his speech. Uncle Joe's civic pride got the better of him for his generation had been used to "drinking water" coming from a bucket toted from the spring and the "house water" being brought from the creek in the same manner or from a barrel on a sled, dragged behind a yoke of oxen. This newfangled means of having running water was a magnificent mark of progress — shore nuff.

John Henry Saunders's waterworks consisted of a hydraulic ram which pumped Cypress Creek water into an elevated tank from which a system of pipes carried the water to taps at the back doors of the following: Billy Henson, Dr. J. W. Pyland, J. C. Ragsdale, the Saunderses, and S. J. Pyland. When John Will Pyland lived in the Old Pleasant Wimberley home on the hill he had a hydraulic ram installed at the old mill which pumped water to the house, but that too was a late development.

Having a name for each water hole along the streams and for each spring would indicate the importance of surface water to the early settler. To the country traveler, the name of a water hole would locate a rural home as readily as a street address would a suburban dwelling. Available water determined the home site for the country home.

Carrying water was an endless chore which plagued children for generations. Hanging on the gallery, the old cedar bucket (made of cedar stays hooped with brass bands) kept the water cool and fresh. The old gourd dipper was the object watched by the children. While it floated level with the bucket rim, all was well. But it was time to be scarce when an elder had to dip the dipper deep into the bucket to get a fill, for when there was a child handy the remaining water in the bucket usually went to a potted plant. Borrowed from the Dutch, the water yoke with its two suspended buckets cut the trips in half, doubling the burden carried each way. The old rain barrel at the corner of the house did not alleviate the chore. Rain water was for milady's hair and the finer part of the family wash. The laundry job with its wash pot, tub, and rub board was done in the shade of some creekside arbor.

Some people living on high bluffs or steep hillsides had a novel method of getting their water from the stream below their home: the old "water-trolley." The trolley line was a heavy wire, stretching from the house to the river bed and anchored at each end. A pulley with a bucket and long line attached to it rolled down this wire with a gravity pull. A weight on the rim of the bucket tipped it to fill with water. A windlass was used to rewind the line and retrieve the filled bucket. Willis Ferguson had one of these contraptions at his home on Cypress Creek near Jacob's Well. My great-uncle Tom Adare had one at his place on the Blanco above Bendigo Crossing. The bucket on his trolley developed considerable speed and whistled as it sailed down to the river. Once while the bucket was on its way to the river it met a flight of ducks going up the river. The blast of a double-barreled shotgun sent two loads of number four chill shot through the bucket and dropped not one feather from the ducks. Standing and viewing his riddled bucket, Uncle Tom's mounting fury exploded into a boisterous horse-laugh when a red-faced neighbor approached and offered three prices for the riddled bucket if there would be no public mention of the incident.

Wimberley Square, 1890

On the home place of my great-grandfather, Bill Adare, there are three of the old dug wells. These were dug with short-handled pick and shovel. The windlass and bucket system, used to remove the loose dirt from these wells as they were being dug, was the same method used to get the water from them. Shallow wells were lined with rock walls to keep the earthen wall from caving in. One of these wells was a spring well; during rainy seasons the water level raised till the well flowed. Grandpa was one of the early-day water witches. With his forked branch cut fresh from a peach tree, he was called upon to locate water for the new wells to be dug in the Wayside community. By the time age had bent him into a withered old man and he had reduced his voluminous Civil War tales to three Bangs ("Bang" went Wall Street, "Bang" went Stonewall Jackson, and "Bang" went Bill Adare and down came a Yankee soldier), he had become the grand wizard of the water witches from Pin Oak Creek. Surreptitious doubts may have been entertained, but he was always called upon before the location of a new well was made final.

Grandpa Zack Wimberley had one of the early drilled wells of Wimberley village. It was located near the back door for the utmost convenience. This was an unseen error which was soon revealed by the constant screech of the pulley wheel as neighbors, by day and all hours of the night, pulled up the well bucket. Tired of having her sleep disturbed, little Minta Wimberley once threw several hands full of crushed garlic into the well. The pulley wheel remained silent until her father cleaned the well good.

Mrs. S. J. Pyland was not a satisfied customer of the Saunders "creek water" system. Used to more potable water of her father Zack's work, she prevailed upon her husband to have a well drilled at their new home. Foster Massey was the first water witch to locate water. This location was confirmed by Frank Holt, who had learned the art from his father John. But Mrs. Pyland was not satisfied until Ole man Bill Adare had passed judgment on the site. After a careful peach limb survey of the area in question, he came to report a startling discovery. The property was crossed by a shallow vein of water, not over two feet deep. Perplexed and adamant with his findings, he demanded tools to dig with and prove his theory. A two-foot hole revealed the main pipeline of the Saunders water system.

Grandpa Adare lived to learn the wonders of early plumbing, but he never gave his stamp of approval for all the facilities of the modern bathroom to be installed under the same roof of the living quarters of his home.

Granddad Lawrence had a drilled well with a deep well cylinder installed and pumped water with a long cedar pole handle. The cypress lumber windmills were rare in the area, and until the prosperous war years the metal windmills were few and far apart. It took FDR and the REA to put Wimberley uptown water-wise.

From *The Wimberley Mill*
May 1972

199

Spare the Rabbit, Spoil the Child

They will stay out all night chasing after a pack of potlickers in any kind of weather just to hear some hound music, when they could have been at home with mama and the kids all the time. Then they will spend the next three days scouring the woods looking for a bunch of fine hunting hounds that can't find their way home. Although I have never met one I didn't like, the more you are around them the less you know about what is and what ain't with a hounddog man.

While James Fowler lived up about Rotan, his pack of hounds were the best catch dogs on the Double Mountain Fork of the Brazos River. They had to be good for they ate what they caught. Everything went into a big black pot in which their chow was prepared. The day I was by, James was blowing off a batch of coyote-bobcat stew thickened with corn meal, seasoned with a lump of tallow, and spiced with a few pods of chili peppers. The chilies controlled stomach worms and avoiding the pods kept the dogs from gobbling their food too fast. The pack was in fine shape, glossy-haired, and each carried enough hard lean flesh to run like the devil.

My fence-building friend and houndman, Worthy McLamore, lives near Buda. He has built some of the best barbed wire fences in these parts, and I will take his word on hounds any day. We were talking dogs one time — I was listening and he was doing the talking — when he asked if I knew the best way of breaking a dog from chasing rabbits.

"Well," I says, "in a case like that, I'd be like Corrie Smith. Deny the charge and claim that any hound you just might have seen chasing a rabbit must belong to somebody else. Maybe Alvin Day or Roy Acrey?"

"That's the easy way," says Mac. "But if you really want to break one of the habit, you catch him in the act, hold him up by the tail, and beat him across the posterior with a dead rabbit until your arms are tired. One dose usually cures."

Not much of a houndman myself, but if these modern parents would try this cure on their hip younguns, I believe it would close the so-called generation gap quicker than rain settles dust.

From *The Wimberley Mill*
September 1969

200

The Colony

They were the people — and their descendants are the people — of the Colony. Slaves freed by the Civil War were the people who came to found this community in the hills of Blanco County, Texas, and today their heirs are the people who perpetuate the Colony's name in the area. This is their story as told by the old ones who still live upon the land.

Following the Civil War, freedmen who aspired to make a life of their own came to build their cabins on pre-empted 160-acre tracts or small plots of land they bought near the eastern edge of Blanco County. Based upon the pioneer economy of that era, the community grew to encompass some 5,000 acres and supported a school, church, general store, and post office named "Payton" after the community's founder, Payton Roberts.

During this pioneer period, Eli Crownover built his home with slab cypress lumber hauled from Cypress Mills and had the distinction of owning the first board house in the community. Interestingly enough, when the post office was moved from its original location to a place hear Eli's home, its name was changed to Boardhouse Post Office.

Prior to World War I, the Colony celebrated Juneteenth in a manner which rivaled anything neighboring towns or villages did for the Fourth of July. The Colony people would barbecue forty goats, three beeves, and invite neighboring white folks and friends over to dinner on the grounds and revelry lasting into the night.

But the changing economy was to take its toll from the Colony, and this celebration was the first to go. The young left the land for city life and many of the small places have been sold to large landowners. They are gone — the school, general store, and post office. Like many of the early rural communities, the Colony is now a rural route number and a memory of the old ones.

Aunt Mandy (Mrs. John Jackson Coffee) is eighty-seven years old and the Colony is home to her. According to her, the Coffee family came from Bastrop. Bony Coffee and Jack Birch joined Payton Roberts there to search for high ground, leaving behind the oft-flooded Colorado bottom lands "where the river always ran muddy and the trees wore whiskers (Spanish moss)."

Little Bony broke horses on the ranches around Wimberley, but Aunt Mandy cannot recall whether or not one of the Coffee men worked at the old leather house located at the mouth of Lone Man Creek (circa 1880).

London City, freighter, mail carrier, cowboy and farmer, is the Colony's patriarch. Ninety-one years old, he can recall the days of the open range, when he had to ride to the Pedernales or the Guadalupe to bring back cattle that strayed from the home range, and when Jack Stubbs used to cut the tall grasses on the meadow below Timber Top Hill for prairie hay to be used at his livery stable in Blanco City. Their former owners, the Rawls family of St. Landry Parish, Louisiana, brought London City's grandparents from Opelousas to the Colony and helped them get established there.

Other early settlers or family names of the Colony as recalled by London City are Payton Roberts, the Jacksons, the Hines, Sam Parch, Anderson McConico, Susie Brigham, Jasper Birch, Alex Upshaw, and Dick Morgan (who built the lime kiln in 1874 or 1875). London City was one of the youngsters who went to this kiln to get a bucket of lime which his folks used to patch the chimney or to daub the cracks between the logs in their cabin. Jasper Birch and Alex Upshaw freighted with ox wagons from old Indianola and Bastrop before the railroad came to Central Texas.

Many members of the Colony were freighters. In an era when the light farm wagon pulled by willow-tailed ponies was the usual fare, the Colony's heavy freight wagons pulled by matched spans of big Missouri mules were the Cadillacs of the trade.

My father, Rufus, was impressed by these teams. He remembers when, periodically, two of these big wagons loaded with sacks of corn to be ground into meal would pull into the mill yard at Wimberley. Each of the seamless sacks held two and one-half bushels of corn belonging to a family in the Colony. My dad was too small to empty these big sacks into the mill hopper and had to get John or one of the other members of the family to help him. I asked London City why they chose to come to mill at Wimberley when there were other mills closer.

"The Wimberley's big water mill was faster," he said. "The toll was lighter and the sack was fuller, for old man Zack Wimberley treated everybody alike. He was a good man."

Childless at the age of sixty-five, Thad Upshaw, another resident, is justly proud of his heritage and his nephews: Eugene, who plays with the Oakland Raiders; and Marvin, who plays with the Cleveland Browns. One of these nephews will inherit his place because Thad wants the land to remain Upshaw after he is gone.

It took modern roads and the automobile to break the Colony's hold on the freighting business in this area. About 1890, a man tried to do it with a steam tractor. After hooking onto eight floats at Blanco City, he made it to San Marcos on his maiden and only trip.

From *Frontier Times Magazine*
June–July 1971

Legend of Lone Man

The late Joe Cruze belonged to the hills of Wimberley and he belonged to a way of life that is soon to become another era of the past. He was a man of saddle, he always rode a good horse, and he was a person worthy of J. Frank Dobie's label "a Texian of the old order." He was an artful talker schooled by the soil, a fine storyteller, and he left his family a legacy of folklore rich in hither-to-fore unwritten facets of local history which, I feel, should be perpetuated as a part of our heritage. By combining his memoirs with those passed down verbally from his father, Santa Anna Cruze, and his grandfather, Bill Cruze, Joe's tales span the local history from the present back through the days of the early Republic. Though not mentioned by name by either, the authoritative published memoirs of Noah Smithwick and John Holland Jenkins corroborate the tone, time element, and factual evidence presented in Joe's tales. And interestingly enough, Santa Anna and Jenkins were among the Confederate troops led by R.I.P. Ford in the battle of Palmito Ranch on May 13, 1865.

To eulogize this old friend of mine is not the true purpose of this article, nor is it merely a vehicle for retelling a tale of his, but it is an effort to bring into focus the Wimberley area's most colorful legend, as Joe told it, and to give a proper perspective to the historic significance of Wimberley's last Indian fight.

To gain this perspective, and to eliminate any conflicting hypothesis, we dismiss from this text the ancient redman and the splinter tribes of Indians whose artifacts can still be found on the slopes of these caliche hills and in earthen mounds built along the Blanco and her tributaries. These people I leave for further study by the archaeologist, the anthropologist, the amateur collector, and the tired history professors who need to see their names in print — for these Indians had little or no enduring effect in shaping the course of history of our present society. The ancient redman had gone

Blanco River at Fischer Road.
— Photo by Anita Miller, staff photographer
San Marcos Daily Record.

before the white explorers reached this area and, though the splinter tribes did extract some toll in blood, they never seriously deterred the pioneer's march into the area. Like the small black bear and large cats that once inhabited this area, those who failed to move ahead of the frontier paid with their lives for the delay.

The next subject creating a conflicting hypothesis that needs to be eliminated concerns the Indians of the depredations period, an era beginning with the Civil War era and ending in the late seventies. James Foster Massey probably encountered the last war party to invade this area when, back in the early seventies, he rode up to the springs in the Blanco on the Will Burnett place and looked up to see five mounted braves, in war paint and carrying spears, standing on the opposite bank. In all haste Mr. Massey retreated downstream spreading the alarm, while the braves fled up the Blanco. This is an incident of local interest but, like all marauding Indian invasions into Texas during the period, it was of little historical consequence because the die had been cast for these Oklahoma reservation-based, part-time refugees of the Indian Wars. While on a tour of inspection of Indian affairs for President Grant, General Sherman's stage stopped on the road to Ft. Richardson (Jacksboro) at the scene of a massacre — the wagon was burning, the bodies of the crew lay in the dust, and the Indian sign was fresh, much too fresh for Sherman. His report to Grant and the subsequent action taken on the reservations brought an end to that era. Satank shot to death on the trek to face trial by Texas courts, Santana's suicidal leap from a Huntsville prison window as he sang his death song, and Big Tree's escape to the north brought the finale to Indian raids on Texas soil.

It was the Plains Indian, the Horse Indian, the Comanche who molded the history of this area — determined that it would be of Anglo heritage rather than Spanish, that gave Wimberley the legend of Lone Man and Lone Woman peaks and fought the last skirmish of the Battle of Plum Creek which marked the ebb tide of Comanche power.

When the Comanche clambered aboard the horse brought to the New World by the Spaniard, he became the world's finest horseman, fiercest warrior, best huntsman, boldest thief, and developed a savage way of life so appealing to the baser human instincts that young captives, regardless of their race, nationality or sex, grew to become true Comanches of the tribe. Astride the horse, he was not the redman who cowered before Coronado nor was he the one to do peon labor necessary for the expanding Spanish culture. The *padres'* religion concerned him naught, and he found less than no reason to fear the Spanish soldier.

The Comanches were The People of the Great Plains (aided and abetted by the Kiowas in the north and, to some extent, the Apaches of the southwest). And they established their own frontier boundary beyond the outer perimeter of the Great Plains and held Spanish expansion into the area at bay for more than two centuries.

205

When the *padres* attempted to establish the San Saba Mission on Menard Creek, the Comanches massacred them, fired the mission, and on canyon walls near Paint Rock painted in pictograph an exaggerated accout of the deed. And from their Plains sanctuary, war parties invaded Spanish territory as far distant as Monterrey, where they exacted women slaves and horses in tribute without battle. While Texas was a Mexican state, Comanches sat boldly on the streets of San Antonio locating horses to be stolen, for they were the Comanches, and the Mexicans had rather lose horses than suffer reprisals.

With these facts in mind, it should come as no surprise to discover in the summer of 1840, a Comanche foray a thousand strong invading the Texian's land. Bypassing San Antonio, they sacked Victoria and moved on to pillage and destroy Linnville. With their savage lust for blood satiated, their war ponies jaded, surfeited with stolen horses and mules, and burdened with a mountain of assorted looted plunder, their minds filled with visions of savage rituals pending on their homecoming. They formed a noisy, bold caravan and headed across the coastal prairies toward the upper reaches of the Colorado. Three days out, they were ambushed by Burleson's Texans and Tonkawa forces and lost in the ensuing fray eighty-six braves killed, two thousand horses, and much of their stolen plunder before they could scatter and fade into the woods. And there was the huge warrior wearing a stovepipe hat, a frock-tailed coat on backwards, gloves, and carrying an open parasol. White men call the ambush "The Battle of Plum Creek," but Burleson did not pursue the enemy; instead, they retired from the field that evening to divide among themselves the recovered stolen horses.

The Tonkawa foot soldiers gained mounts during the fray and, afterwards, feasted on the flesh of the fallen Comanches, hoping in this way to gain the bravery of this fearful foe. At Plum Creek, the Comanches' long and bloody losing struggle began and ended when Quanah Parker led the remnants of the tribe onto government reservations. In November of 1840, they first felt the conqueror's heel when the Texans raided their villages near where Colorado City now stands, and at Bandera Pass, six-shooters of Capt. Jack Hays's Rangers proved to the Comanche that skill and bravo must bow to superior weapons on the battlefield.

The Cruze Prairie (Hays City area) was a far piece from Burleson's headquarters at Bastrop, and while Burleson was at Plum Creek, a body of men from this general area led by Captain Kyle met an element of Comanches below Kyle and engaged them in a running battle which ended at Indian Mott on the old Duncan Dobie Ranch. It was said then that a chief and his squaw were killed there. After the settlers retired, the Comanches buried the fallen chief and his squaw atop the two most prominent peaks in the area to avoid mutilation of their bodies, because the Comanches believed that a dismembered body could not enter the Happy Hunting Grounds. And according to Joe, his Grandfather Bill Cruze and one of the Blackwells named these peaks Lone Man Mountain and Lone Woman Mountain.

From *The Wimberley Mill*
July 1966

About the Author

C. W. "Cedar Whacker" Wimberley was born March 14, 1913, at his grandfather Lawrence's place in the bygone community of Wayside near Wimberley, Texas.

A Depression dropout of old Southwest Texas Teachers College, he served a hitch in the army before marrying Iolene Rogers and moving to the cedar brakes near Lone Grove, Texas (Llano County). It was their home for thirty years before moving back to San Marcos, Texas, his boyhood home.

Through talks with the old ones — the sore-necked dirt farmer, landed rancher, hounddog man, and cedarcutter — he received eyewitness accounts of how it was fifty years before his time. In the true vernacular of the period, he presents these experiences in *Cedar Whacker*.

Wimberley was a regular columnist for *The Highlander* (Marble Falls, Texas), *The Wimberley Mill* (Wimberley, Texas), and *The Hays County Citizen* (San Marcos, Texas). His writings have appeared in *The San Marcos Daily Record* and in *True West, Frontier Times, Relics, Old West,* and publications of the Texas Folklore Society.

He has contributed to numerous publications and is the author of two books: *Stone Milling and Whole Grain Cooking* and *Wimberley Hills — A Pioneer Heritage.*

About the Editor and Illustrator

Dorothy Wimberley Kerbow and C. W. Wimberley, great-grandchildren of Pleasant and Amanda Wimberley, are cousins who grew up together in the Central Texas area of San Marcos, New Braunfels, and Wimberley. Their fathers, Hick and Rufus Wimberley, children of Zachary and Mary Elizabeth Wimberley, were brothers. Dorothy lives in Wimberley and is a columnist for the *San Marcos Daily Record*. Her column entitled "The View From Persimmon Hill" covers the life, ways, and opinions of the Hill Country. She authored the portion of the history of Wimberley and Purgatory Springs for the book *Clear Springs and Limestone Ledges, A History of San Marcos and Hays County*, published by the Hays County Historical Commission for the 1986 Sesquicentennial anniversary of Texas independence.

Illustrations for the book are by Bernice Brown of Houston and Wimberley. Bernice is a renowned artist who has been painting since early childhood. Primarily a realist-impressionist, she is accomplished in a variety of media and subject matter. She excels in the painting of children's portraits and nature paintings of the Texas Hill Country. She teaches art in Houston and in the summer at the Western Colorado School of Art. She lectures and conducts art workshops across the state, including the Hill Country Arts Foundation at Ingram, Texas. Her paintings have been displayed by invitation at The Cowboy Artists of America Museum in Kerrville, Texas. She is a member of Texas Fine Arts Association, Houston Civic Arts, Water Color Art Society Houston, Pastel Society of the Southwest, and Texas Artisan.

209

Index

214